cat.

THE VENGEFUL SEA

THE VENGEFUL SEA

BY EDWARD ROWE SNOW

Illustrated

DODD, MEAD & COMPANY

NEW YORK

1957

Published September, 1956
Second Printing October, 1956
Third Printing January, 1957

Library of Congress Catalog Card Number: 56-10918

Printed in the United States of America
by The Cornwall Press, Inc., Cornwall, N. Y.

INTRODUCTION

Almost nothing else in the world has so inspired writers down through the centuries as the sea. It affects each of us differently. To most people it is a vast sheet of usually smooth water, with a thin horizon line far in the distance. To some unhappy voyagers it is often a necessary but brutal interference with the usual joys of travel.

To many deep-water sailors it is only the vicissitudes of the ocean which make living really worth while. To manufacturers and business men all over the world, the sea stands merely for the cheapest method of shipping the goods in which they are interested from one part of the world to another.

The progress of man on the sea goes back to the dawn of history. Our neolithic ancestors were more or less familiar with the ocean, and while every early civilization was at first anchored to the land, each in turn became slowly interested in the sea.

The Phoenicians were the earliest sailors with whom we are familiar. Pharaoh Necho, who killed Judah's king Josiah in 608 B.C., was also noted because of his expedition of Phoenician sailors which actually circumnavigated Africa almost two thousand years before Vasco da Gama reached the Cape of Good Hope.

It is not generally known that the Greek explorer Pythias reached Iceland and the Arctic Circle four centuries before the birth of Christ, and when the Scandinavians arrived in Iceland early in the tenth century they found that the Irish had already been there. And so the sea was used by various races and nations for exploration and settlement early in this world's history.

I first began writing about the sea and the surrounding shore line and islands in 1935, and in twenty-four of my books the sea plays a prominent part. Scores of shipwreck stories have appeared in these volumes, and there are eight still in print which include storms and shipwrecks. They are *Mysteries and Adventures along the Atlantic Coast, Strange Tales from Nova Scotia to Cape Hatteras, Secrets of the North Atlantic Islands, The Story of Minot's Light, Great Gales and Dire Disasters, New England Sea Drama, Amazing Sea Stories Never Told Before,* and *Famous Lighthouses of America.* However, I have saved for this volume the most outstanding stories of the sea's vengeful attributes.

Not one of this collection of true stories about hurricanes, floods, shipwrecks, storms at sea, disasters, strandings, ships in trouble in the arctic and the antarctic, and many other calamitous occurrences is now elsewhere in print!

Only after the most exacting research into ancient and modern newspapers, documents and records and through personal interviews, has it been possible to give you this book of true stories of the sea, each of which has been chosen from hundreds of others because of some unusual feature of the sea's vengeance. There were many who gave me important information and I list them at this time: Grace Bixby, Alton Hall Blackington, Mary E. Brown, Walter Chapman, Myron R. Currier, Kenneth C. Dalton, Mrs. John E. Donlin, Capt.

Frederick R. Eldridge, Robert M. Evans, Gerald Flynn, Eleanor Gannon, Lt. Comdr. Henry Livingstone Geer, Don Guy, Margaret Hackett, John R. Herbert, Katherine Kuechle, Sarah R. Livermore, Dr. Paul F. McBride, Helen J. McClintock, Ruth Merrill, George E. Moore, Marjorie Phillips Murray, Ann O'Neil, Parker Phillips, Ronald Poole, John M. Richardson, Lawrence Rideout, Mrs. John P. Rogers, George C. Shields, Irwin Smith, A. E. Sweetland, Alice Rowe Snow, Sally Snow, Winthrop J. Snow, Winthrop J. Snow, Jr., Sarah H. Wollaston and Charles Wood.

I also thank the following institutions: Bostonian Society, Harvard College Library, Boston Athenaeum, American Antiquarian Society and the Associated Press.

My wife, Anna-Myrle, should receive special acknowledgment at this time. Although she gave outstanding help in all my other books, never before has she done so much to see that a volume was finished in time for publication.

In reference to the book's title, I cannot claim that the sea has arisen in vengeance to send to the bottom every shipwreck in history. In fact, I was once told that the sea should not be blamed at all, for it is the air and the wind which should be held to account. But winds would not form most of the time if the areas over the ocean were not breeding grounds for them.

Of course, I feel that the sea *should* be blamed, or I would not have written this book. Nevertheless, I welcome letters on this general subject.

Many of my readers may have only a single, vicarious contact with the sea, that contact being the fact that one or more of their ancestors were mariners. The reader himself may never have gone out on the ocean at all. If that is so, I trust that in these pages he may get some understanding, some insight into the problems and dangers facing the mariners who through the centuries have gone down to the sea in ships.

From my Marshfield study I look out at the mouth of the famous North River, whence over a thousand vessels were launched. Almost all shipping from Boston, Portland and many other marine centers passes off our home going to and from the Cape Cod Canal. In the summer months the Provincetown boat slides by twice a day. Occasional white sails, tugs and barges, lobster fishermen, draggers and trawlers are seen to make our location an ideal one from which to write this book.˙ I trust that you find its pages of interest.

For those of you who look in vain in this volume for the story of the sinking of the *Andrea Doria*, it will be in my coming book concerning man's many triumphs over the sea.

EDWARD ROWE SNOW

September 4, 1956
Marshfield, Massachusetts

CONTENTS

ILLUSTRATIONS

(Photographic supplement follows page 52)

TO MY MOTHER

ALICE ROWE SNOW

WHO SPENT MOST OF HER EARLY LIFE

AT SEA

CHAPTER ↕ ONE

THE SEA

> *Upon the watery plain*
> *The wrecks are all thy deed.*

INTEREST IN THE SEA is almost universal. From earliest times it has been both the inspiration and terror of man, and this is expressed in music, art and literature. In the Bible we have many references to the sea, and the quotation below reflects the inborn fear of it felt by the ancient Greeks.*

Ναυηγοῦ τάφος εἰμί· σὺ δὲ πλέε· καὶ γὰρ ὅθ᾿ ἡμεῖς
ὠλόμεθ᾿, αἱ λοιπαὶ νῆες ἐπ οντοπόρουν

Actually, the great hurricanes and storms which sweep in out of the ocean are confined mostly to those areas of the world unknown to the ancients, but the treacherous depths of the sea itself have been written of and sung about in all ages and climes. The dangerous voyage which Saint Paul made to Rome is familiar all over the world, and Jonah's experience with the whale is also a classic. Homer tells us of the remark-

---

* I am the grave of a shipwrecked person, but you must sail, for even though we lost our lives, the other ships sailed on over the sea.

able adventures of Ulysses at sea, while Vergil's poems concerning the perils of Aeneas afloat are known wherever books are read.

In ancient times the mariner was exposed to far greater peril from the vengeful sea than he is today, but in addition to the actual dangers, the sailor's imagination created scores of beliefs and traditions to disconcert him. For example, Horace in his Third Ode laments the departure of Vergil for Athens and paints a terrifying picture of fantastic monsters and giant waves to be encountered.

Many of the ancients looked upon sea voyages as sacrilegious. Several tribes feared the deep as a sort of taboo, and some castes of Hindus even today continue this attitude. Much of the background of myths connected with the ocean comes from these groups.

Even after the days of antiquity the imaginary terrors of the sea did not disappear. The early charts had large numbers of great monsters of various types, dragons, giants, serpents and fish, usually placed on the edge of unknown areas of the ocean. Sailors of all times have believed in legendary fancies concerning wind, waves and the sea in general. At Gibraltar, according to Edrisi of Arabia for example, there was a stone pillar one hundred cubits high with a brass statue on it indicating to mariners the limit of navigation. A noble Persian named Sataspes allegedly was unable to circumnavigate Africa, claiming that his ships were stopped by the mud in the shallow ocean. Pytheas of Massilia declared that around Thule one could neither walk nor sail because of a sea-cloud mixture of mud and air resembling jelly fish, while a giant was reported to stand at the Canary Islands threatening all who ventured farther westward.

Down through the years Chinese and English mendicants were reputed to have done a good business in selling fair winds, with George and Eppie Foreman the last Britishers known to have carried on this unusual business. If a mariner wished a quick voyage with favorable winds, the mendicants would brew it up for him.

Many curious legends have been told concerning those who have drowned in the sea. Sailors have often refused to attempt rescuing others in fear that the rescuer himself would later drown. Mariners have explained the belief by saying that the water spirit, foiled in his efforts to drown his victim, bears a grudge against the rescuer which is only satisfied by his death. In Scotland many persons refused to reclaim a body from the sea, believing that if they did they would meet death by drowning.

Some Chinese who concur in this attitude say that the soul of a drowned person is in a strange sort of purgatory whence it is released only by finding someone to take its place. There were Hindus who not only would refuse to rescue anyone, but would even assist in a drowning.

Around the year 1630 English people had such a fear of drowning that rings made of coffin nails were worn to prevent a swimmer from getting a cramp. Often they were blessed by the English sovereign, and many wills of the period included bequests of favorite "cramp rings."

The case of Mr. and Mrs. Bailey is a classic example of the prevailing fear of drowning. In 1635, Mr. Bailey on his voyage from England to America survived the shipwreck of the *Angel Gabriel* at Pemaquid Point in Maine. He was so frightened at his narrow escape from death that he wrote back to his wife a particularly vivid description of the shipwreck in which he nearly drowned. After she read the letter Mrs. Bailey made up her mind not to cross the ocean. Since her husband was too afraid of a sea voyage to return to her, they passed the remainder of their lives apart, he in America and she in England.

Shakespeare knew well the might of the sea. His *Tempest,*

for example, begins "on a ship at sea," with a storm of "thunder and lightning," and he gives to Ariel the immortal lines:

> Full fathom five thy father lies;
>   Of his bones are coral made;
>   Those are pearls that were his eyes.
>   Nothing of him that doth fade,
>   But doth suffer a sea-change
>   Into something rich and strange.
>   Sea nymphs hourly ring his knell:
>   Hark! now I hear them,—Ding-dong, bell.

Longfellow, Wordsworth and Tennyson made notable contributions to the literature of the sea, and Lord Byron reflected his love for it in his poetry.

In America, the literature of the sea began with James Fenimore Cooper and has been perpetuated by such writers as Dana, Melville, Robertson and London.

After World Wars I and II with millions of troops crossing the ocean the sea took on a new importance in the United States. A new school of readers, numbering in the millions, have become familiar with it by reading the works of such writers as Rachel Carson and Anne Lindbergh, and the tide of authors and readers devoted to this subject is just starting to rise. Books on yachting, treasure hunting, skin diving, underwater photography and oceanography are finding their way to the libraries of those interested in the sea along with tales of ships, pirates, solitary voyagers, storms and shipwrecks.

But it would not be fair to blame the sea entirely for all the tragedies which have been enacted on its bosom. For years, according to the records, much of the loss of life could be attributed at least in part to many of the shipowners of the world. Greedy and irresponsible, their craft insured to the hilt, these wealthy but conscienceless men loaded rich cargo on vessels which under the laws of humanity should have been broken up for junk. Then these unscrupulous merchants sent their craft abroad on the treacherous deep.

The owners would make good profits whether the ship was lost or not. What mattered if a few human beings were sacrificed, for they were the cheapest commodity of all! In spite of the many honest shipowners, the scheming merchants and investors tipped the scales the other way.

It was not until the days of Mr. Samuel Plimsoll * that the sea's greatest rival, man's greed, was in any way challenged. Plimsoll as a young man had the audacity to shake his fist in the face of the great Disraeli when the speaker disagreed at first with Plimsoll's plans for proper shipping inspection rules. Eventually Plimsoll won out, and later he apologized to Disraeli. Stressing the inability of the government to control crafty shipowners, Plimsoll went on record explaining what confronted the sailors of that day.

"You may build a ship in any way you please, you may use timber utterly unfit, you may use it in quantity utterly inadequate, but no one has any authority to interfere with you. You may even buy an old ship two hundred and fifty tons burden by auction for fifty pounds, sold to be broken up, because extremely old and rotten.

"She had a narrow escape on her last voyage, and had suffered so severely that she was quite unfit to go to sea again without more being spent in repairs upon her than she would be worth when done.

"Instead of breaking up this old ship, bought for four shillings per ton (the cost of a new ship being from ten to fourteen pounds per ton), as was expected, you may give her a coat of paint—she is too rotten for caulking,—and to the dis-

---

* He was born in Bristol, England, in 1824. While I was in Bristol in 1943 I made a special visit to the site of his home.

may of her late owners, you may prepare to send her to sea. . . .

"You may engage men in another port, and then, having signed articles without seeing the ship, you may send them to the port where the ship lies in the custody of a mariner. You may then . . . , if you have managed to insure her heavily, load her until the main deck is within two feet of the water amidships, and send her to sea. Nobody can prevent you. Nay, more, if the men become riotous, you may arrest them without a magistrate's warrant, and take them to prison, and the magistrates who have no choice (they have not to make, but only to administer the law), will commit them to prison for twelve weeks with hard labor; or better still for you, you may send a policeman on board to overawe the mutineers, and induce them to do their duty!

"And then, if the ship is lost with all hands, you will gain a large sum of money and you will be asked no questions, as no inquiry will ever be held over these unfortunate men."

A typical example of such terrible conditions is the *Dryad* which left Liverpool September 7, 1839. An old rotten craft loaded with worthless goods and heavily insured, the *Dryad* was purposely wrecked by her captain, Edmund Loose, in the West Indies on November 10, 1839. At the trial which followed she attracted great interest all over England as a "coffin ship."

Because of Plimsoll's agitation, laws for proper shipping inspection and operation were passed and put into effect so that such inhumane conditions became a thing of the past.*

In addition to the greed which occasioned Plimsoll's comments above, there were other ways in which men seemed to conspire with the vengeful sea. Many of the early vessels

---

* The Plimsoll line, now known all over the world, is a mark placed on a ship's side designating various points to which cargoes of different commodities may in safety be loaded.

were sent out without satisfactory charts, and even if charts were supplied, they were often so out of date that proper markings of shoals and rocks were absent.

The greatest loss of ships in polar regions has been among those on ill-advised whaling or sealing voyages rather than on exploring expeditions. One of the strangest stories of all times concerning craft doomed in these areas was that of the *Rufus*, whose sailors have been eulogized in verse. A whaling vessel in 1774 came across the *Rufus* which had evidently been abandoned. Going aboard, the men found a death ship with the frozen members of the crew scattered around in the postures assumed when they succumbed to the cold in 1762, twelve years before their remains were discovered!

There are many other reasons for disasters at sea such as storms, pamperos, typhoons, hurricanes, lightning, waterspouts, tidal waves and icebergs. A boiler explosion may send a vessel to the bottom. Even a leak in the ship will suffice when the angry sea makes it worse by tossing the vessel around and wrenching her joints with its violence. But the most dreaded of all marine calamities is fire at sea on a steamer or sailing vessel.

In battle cannon shot or torpedo will doom the man-of-war and cargo ship alike. Again, if a vessel ventures too far into the polar region, she may be trapped and crushed to a pulp by the pressure of the ice. Human agencies may scuttle a craft for the insurance money.

A sailing vessel may capsize because of a sudden change of wind. If the captain has misjudged the position of his ship a rocky ledge or sandy shore may prove her final resting place.

Nevertheless, in spite of all these allies which the vengeful sea has, the sea itself is responsible alone for more disasters than all other forces combined.

Several people who have seen my stories of shipwrecks have told me that they have been so frightened by the events about which they have read that they would not ever want to take a sea voyage again. Then they often step happily into an automobile, an invention which each year kills thousands of people more than are lost at sea!

But to reassure those who are contemplating an ocean voyage, let us consider the question of safety at sea. How much safer are we now than we were fifty or one hundred years ago? Today we have radio, fathometers, loran, direction finding stations and radar as well as weather ships, improved aids to navigation and air-sea rescue groups. There are organized unions, training schools for officers and rigid inspection of well constructed modern vessels and equipment.

Consequently, we are eminently safer afloat than we were a hundred or even fifty years ago. But it should never be forgotten that whenever the human element is involved, it is probable we will continue to have occasional accidents and sometimes death at sea.

While it is possible to discount most of the superstitions and legends of the deep, we cannot explain everything in connection with the vengeful sea. At times the ocean has been conquered by what some consider supernatural means.

Possibly the most unusual example of miraculous events of this type occurred in the year 1857 when the *Central America* foundered at sea with 423 persons going down with the ship. After the sinking, 149 survivors were still afloat. The brig *Marine* took aboard a hundred of them, but the other forty-nine adrift surely would have perished in the normal course of events. I quote directly from the statement of Captain Johnson of the bark *Ellen:*

"Just before six o'clock in the afternoon of September 12, I was standing on the quarter deck. Suddenly a bird flew around me, first grazing my right shoulder. It soon flew at my face, when I caught hold of it and made it a prisoner. The bird was unlike any bird I ever saw, nor do I know its name. As it strove to bite everybody, I had its head afterwards cut off, and the body thrown overboard. When the bird flew to the ship, the bark was going a little north of northeast. I regarded the appearance of the bird as an omen, and an indication to me that I must change my course.

"I accordingly headed to the eastward direct. I should not have deviated from my course, had not the bird visited the ship, and, had it not been for this change of course, I should not have fallen in with the forty-nine passengers, whom I fortunately saved from death."

A natural concern for the fate of their fellow creatures is implanted in the breasts of most of mankind, and our sympathies are invariably aroused by a tale of misfortune concerning helpless sailors or passengers on vessels at sea.

Individual heroism is often brought into prominence during a terrible shipwreck when some people apparently acquire superhuman strength and determination to help those who need them. On the other hand, many of those who are terrified by the prospect of death in the sea often act in such a manner that they sink to the lowest levels of humanity in their efforts to save themselves at the expense of their fellow beings.

For those who go down to the shore and gaze out on the ocean, the sea is indeed an impressive sight, whether they stand on a sandy beach, a rocky promontory or a high, overhanging cliff. They cannot help but wonder at the vast extent of the deep.

The sea is a force which attracts and appalls. Few things are less explicable than the irresistible lure which throughout the centuries has compelled apparently sound-thinking men to leave the security of the land and the comfort and love of their homes and families to challenge the intractable deep. Man has gone to sea to earn a living by fishing, whaling and carrying on commercial enterprise. He has used the ocean as a means of getting from one place to another, and he has sailed abroad for pure adventure.

The sea has countless moods, and when we view it on a calm day, with hardly a cloud in the sky overhead, it is difficult to visualize it at its worst. Nevertheless, the ocean, beautiful and serene, can within a short space of hours become terrifying.

The soft green of the water may change to a dark angry blue, accentuating the white spray which dashes against the rocky headland, and as the blast of a gale howls, the surf crashes against the outlying ledges. For the watcher on the beach, the ocean then appears to boil and foam.

It is no wonder that man's strength pales in contrast to such an exhibition of the elements in which his ships are scattered like chaff. As Byron said over a century ago, man's "control stops with the shore," and the sea remains ungovernable, for it is more powerful than man. "Those who go down to the sea in ships, and do business on the great waters" have always commanded our greatest admiration.

CHAPTER TWO

THE *Grosvenor*

Oh rest ye, brother mariners, we will not wander more.

ON THE MORNING of June 13, 1782, Captain Coxon sailed his beautiful East Indiaman *Grosvenor* from Trincomalee, Ceylon, on a homeward-bound voyage to England with passengers and cargo. All went well until August 2 when a strong wind arose. The gale continued without letup the following day.

Before dawn of the fourth, a Sunday, Seaman John Hynes was aloft with several others striking the fore topgallant mast when he looked out over the early morning gloom at what he thought were breakers. His companion, Lewis by name, agreed with him, and they went down the rigging at once to communicate with Third Mate Beal.

"You are wrong," answered Beal. "We are now one hundred leagues from the nearest land." Nevertheless, Lewis ran to the captain's cabin, and so impressed Coxon that he ordered the crew to wear ship. The helm was put hard-a-weather, the mizzen staysail hauled down, the fore topsail and jib let go and the after yards squared, by which means the great

Indiaman's head was brought nearly around, but it was too late. A moment later the *Grosvenor* struck heavily. All hands rushed on deck, horrified.

The captain's first move was to try to find out how much water the ship was taking in. When the pumps were sounded it was declared that no water was in the hold, but what they did not realize was that since the *Grosvenor's* stern was high on the rocks, all the water had run forward into the bow.

In a little while the wind began to shift and blew offshore. The captain ordered the gunner to fire distress signals. Then it was discovered the powder room was filled with water, making it impossible for the guns to be used. The captain now ordered first the mainmast and then the foremast cut away, but this apparently did no good. The ship was lying about 300 yards offshore, and Coxon decided that it was impossible to save her.

Three men now volunteered to swim to the distant beach with the deep sea line. Two of them reached shore in safety; the other perished. With the small line ashore, a larger hawser was attached to the sea end and sent in. On the beach several natives had appeared and some of them offered to help pull the heavy hawser ashore. A giant rock was chosen as the land anchor for the hawser, the other end of which was secured to the capstan on board the *Grosvenor*.

On the wreck a large raft was built, but when the crew launched it over the side, the hawser snapped. Three of the four men aboard the raft drowned and only one was able to reach shore.

It was thought best to use the hawser in trying to reach land. One by one eighteen men attempted to get ashore in this manner. All but three dropped to their death in the ocean.

The ship started to break apart just abaft the mainmast, with the bow veering around to come athwart the stern. As

the wind shifted and began to blow toward land again, the
survivors all crowded on the poop deck, for it was nearest
to the shore.

When the towering waves and the violent wind appeared
to unite their forces in breaking up the deck, everyone tried
to crowd onto the starboard quarter. Soon this section floated
away from the remainder of the wreck into shoal water, and
the survivors aboard it leaped joyfully off when they found
the surf was only waist deep. All on the starboard quarter
were eventually saved. Only the cook's mate, who had indulged in liquor to give himself courage to face the ordeal
of death, was afraid to risk the leap ashore, and he could not
be induced to leave the wreck.

It was now dusk. The natives who had gathered on the
beach to watch the shipwreck returned to their homes, leaving the dying embers of a fire which the survivors gladly
stirred up into a warm blaze for their own comfort. They also
were able to collect several hogs and a few chickens which
had washed ashore from the wreck, and a hearty meal was
enjoyed.

A group of survivors decided to search along the shore for
debris. They found a cask of beef, a barrel of flour and a
leaguer * of arrack, all of which was divided among themselves. Two sails were then discovered buried in the sand,
and they were quickly made into tents for the women and
children.

All went well during the first night, but with the coming
of morning scores of natives returned and began to plunder at
will, believing themselves safe from attack by the survivors.
Captain Coxon wisely decided not to interfere, and the natives
did not bother his people.

The following day a decision was made to attempt an over-

---

* Liquid measure equal to about 150 gallons.

land journey to the Cape of Good Hope, which Coxon estimated was about fifteen or sixteen days away. A minority
was in favor of building a small vessel from the planks of the
larger one and sailing along the coast, but this plan was abandoned. Only one man, the cook's mate who had finally come
ashore, refused to make the journey and stayed behind at the
scene of the wreck.

On August 7 the trip started. Chief Mate Logie, who had
been ill, was carried in a hammock slung on a pole. The natives followed at a distance, sometimes closing in to take
whatever they wished from the survivors.

A short time later they met thirty natives who were accompanied by a Dutchman named Trout, a murderer who had
fled civilization. He asked the captain about his plans, and
when Coxon told him he was intending to take his party to
the Cape of Good Hope, Trout told him not to go, for the
route was beset with danger from both wild beasts and men.
Coxon was greatly discouraged and offered Trout a substantial sum to be the expedition's guide, but Trout refused, not
wanting to fall into the hands of the Dutch.

After parting with Trout, the survivors started out again.
Four days later they reached a deep gully where Coxon was
threatened by three natives. Surrounding the captain, they
held their lances at his throat. Finally Coxon seized one of
the lances, broke it across his knee and kept the barb. The
three savages, realizing that the Englishman was not to be
trifled with, then beat a hasty retreat.

The next day the mariners skirted a native village where
they were attacked by a horde of 300 savages, all armed with
the same type of lance. The white men held the natives off
by putting their women and children in a circle to guard
them, and the assailants finally agreed to a compromise of
peace and received gifts in return from the sailors.

The following day the Dutchman again joined them. He

had been at the wreck and was carrying a great load of iron, pewter, lead and copper. After a short conversation in which he again refused to guide the survivors, he left them and started off through the jungle.

The party now was faced with the task of replenishing their supplies, and the sailors began to weary of being delayed by the women and children. Therefore it was agreed that the more than one hundred survivors should divide into two groups, with forty-five of the active men pushing on ahead.

Strangely enough the two groups met again while the first was waiting for an ebb tide, and they pushed on together again as before. In the next village they discovered Trout, who showed them his native wife and their children.

On the following morning the survivors went down to the seashore where a substantial number of oysters, mussels and limpets were found. At four o'clock a final separation was agreed upon. This time the two groups were never to meet again.

The second mate, chosen as the leader of the sailor's group, led his men on a route which brought them down to the shore again on the sixth day. While exploring the beach, one of the party discovered a giant whale. Not having any instruments to cut it up, they built a fire on the dead whale's back, after which they dug out the grilled sections with oyster shells.

Fortified with the whale meat, they considered striking inland, but again they started arguing, and finally this group broke up into two smaller bands. Twenty-five men went inland at once, while the others, about thirty in number, walked along the shore.

A week later the two smaller groups came together once more when the party heading inland struck out for the shore. Two days after their reunion they found another dead whale and again feasted on grilled meat. When all had eaten a sufficient amount, a number of choice steaks were severed from the carcass for a reserve supply. Refreshed by the food, they resumed their walk toward civilization, hiking along the beach for four days. One by one, however, stragglers dropped from the band, and most of those who stayed behind were never seen again.

A dead seal was discovered and sliced up, and several days afterward a bullock was exchanged by natives for the works of a watch and some buttons. Their greatest worry at this period was the care of a young boy whom the carpenter had looked after up to the time of his death.

Natives gave them a deer one day, and they ate it ravenously. Two weeks later they found still another whale. The boy fell ill shortly afterward and died within a few hours. Later another member of the party dropped dead after asking for and receiving a drink of water, and several others died during the following days.

The group now was reduced to three survivors, Hynes, Wormington and Evans. Wormington, the boatswain's mate, suggested that they draw lots to see which one should be killed so that the others could be kept alive by consuming his flesh and blood. When the other two refused, he left them, sitting down by himself as his companions walked away.

Late that afternoon the two men found four members of the steward's party, one of whom volunteered to go back to get Wormington. In three hours Wormington was found safe and in fair condition, and arrived back with the others by midnight.

As the new members had plenty of fresh water, the three thirsty survivors indulged as much as they dared, after which they exchanged accounts of their experiences.

The next morning the seven survivors began their day's journey again, but that night they were exhausted. The following day they had an early start, and around noon the group met two men with guns who proved to be members of a Dutch settlement searching for stray cattle. The survivors were taken to the residence of Mynheer Christopher Roostoff, who did everything in his power to keep them comfortable and well fed.

After recovering sufficiently, the seven survivors were taken by carts through various settlements until they arrived at Swellendam, one hundred miles from the Cape. Here they were detained, as Holland and England were then at war. Eventually all seven men reached the Cape and finally were able to sail home.

A long period of time went by, and it was eight years after the wreck before a party could be organized to search for other survivors. On August 24, 1790, an expedition set out from Kaffer Keyl's River in search of others from the *Grosvenor* shipwreck party who might still be alive. After many hardships of travel, on November 3 the expedition stumbled on three survivors from an ancient wreck who were living with the tribe of Hambonaas. Interviewing the white people, the Dutch found that they were three sisters who had been shipwrecked with others while children. All three girls had married the same chieftain and were now middle-aged women with the viewpoint of natives. While showing an interest in returning to civilization, they stated that they first had to gather their crops. The leaders of the expedition could not wait the several weeks required for the harvest, and so the three sisters were left behind. They never did leave their chieftain and the only way of life that was familiar to them.

In July, 1791, the party returned to civilization, having failed completely to find a single survivor of the *Grosvenor*. They discovered that the cook's mate had lived for about two years after the disaster in the vicinity of the shipwreck, but had then been taken ill with small pox and died.

The loss of the *Grosvenor* was a subject discussed for many years, and a commentator of the period, Captain Rion, expressed himself as follows:

> Had a chosen body of ten or twenty men marched a few days to the northward, they must have fallen in with Rio de la Goa, where it seldom happens there is not a single French or Portuguese slave trading ship . . .

For generations afterward it was often wondered whether any of the survivors of the *Grosvenor* had married natives and reared families as the three sisters who were found by the Dutch exploring party had done, but no news ever came out of Africa concerning them.

CHAPTER THREE

THE LOSS OF THE *Centaur*

Restore the dead, thou sea!

DURING THE REVOLUTION, after France had joined the Colonies in their fight for freedom, the British and the French maneuvered in the Atlantic in a test of their relative strength. On April 12, 1782, in the West Indies, the British fleet under Admiral Rodney administered a crushing blow to the French squadrons commanded by Count de Grasse. After emergency repairs were made to the British ships and their prizes, they set out for England. The entire fleet had been battered by a great hurricane during August, 1782, but nevertheless, early the next month the squadrons departed from Jamaica.

The man-of-war *Centaur*, even as she sailed from Jamaica, needed two pumps going to keep the water from gaining in the hold, and many other craft were likewise handicapped.

On September 16 a new storm developed. Aboard the *Centaur* the mainsail was reefed and set, the topgallant masts struck and the mizzen yard lowered. Toward evening the wind changed to gale force, and the water in the hold began to rise. All hands were now put in relays on the pumps, but the leak continued to gain.

Captain Inglefield now entertained thoughts of "trying the ship before the sea," but realized that it would be improper to leave the convoy except in the "last extremity," and so he decided to wait and hope that the weather might improve.

At 2:00 the following morning the wind lulled, and all aboard hoped that the storm was letting up. But the sea was merely postponing its dreadful work. Within the hour a thunderstorm hit with devastating effect and terrifying winds soon battered the *Centaur*. The mainsail "was hauled up," the ship now being under bare poles.

Then came a gust of wind exceeding in violence anything of which Captain Inglefield "could conceive," a blast that laid the ship on her beam ends. The waves poured in to a depth which reached the men's hammocks and "scuttled the ports inward" from the pressure of the ocean. The captain ordered the main and mizzen masts cut away, but when this was done the foremast and bowsprit went over of their own accord.

Then, with a great but steady motion, the man-of-war righted herself. Three guns broke loose on the main deck. When several midshipmen tried to secure them, they were terribly injured, but finally the difficult feat was accomplished. While all this was going on, the heavy shot had been thrown helter-skelter, smashing into and destroying everything in its way.

The officers, naked when leaving their bunks at the time of the disaster, were unable to find any clothing to put on, and their shipmates were not able to help them.

Captain Inglefield was now told that the tiller had "broke short in the rudderhead" and the rudder itself washed away. This was the final blow, for the ship, without masts and steering equipment, was completely at the mercy of the vengeful sea.

Nevertheless, Inglefield ordered the men back to the pumps, and they worked so hard with them that they actually reduced the level of water by several feet. When the storm went down on the morning of September 17, the captain began to feel more optimistic. But, as he was yet to learn, the sea was only delaying her awesome retaliation.

At daylight Captain Inglefield scanned the ocean with his telescope. Aided by his officers, he located seventeen vessels of the convoy, almost all of which appeared to be substantially damaged. By 7:00 that morning another warship, the *Ville de Paris*, was seen, apparently not suffering from the gale to any great extent.

Captain Inglefield ordered a signal gun fired and his ensign hoisted union down on the stump of the mizzen mast. Before it blew away he was gladdened to see that the *Ville de Paris* had changed her course and was evidently standing toward the *Centaur*. However, just as the *Paris* came within hailing distance, she changed her course and passed the injured vessel without offering assistance. Captain Inglefield now contacted a merchantman and told the captain to get help if he could and to notify Admiral Graves of the dangerous condition of his ship.

Meanwhile all the quarter deck guns were thrown overboard, and the *Centaur* now lay in the trough of the sea. One of the small anchors was got over with a boom, and a topgallant sail was set on the stump of the mizzen mast, but the ship could not be made maneuverable.

Toward evening the weather became hazy and strong squalls developed. All that night, whenever the wind blew hard the water increased in the hold, but when the gale stopped, the men at the pumps gained a temporary advantage. By morning, however, the worn-out sailors reported seven feet of water on the keelson, one of the winches broken and useless and the hand pumps choked.

The men labored to construct a jury foremast, which was almost finished by evening when the storm set in again. During that fearful night several more sea tragedies were enacted under the cover of darkness, for when morning dawned the ocean was littered with wreckage.

The nineteenth of September was passed in thrumming a sail under the bottom of the ship to retard the leaking, and Captain Inglefield thought that the sail had some effect, for by the morning of the next day the forehold was cleared of water.

The sun soon came out bright and cheerful on a relatively calm sea, and all hands were encouraged.

Inglefield now decided to bail out the water from the main hold and ordered scuttles cut through the decks for the passing of canvas buckets. For some reason, however, the water increased by late in the night of the twenty-second, and at 7:00 the following morning a fresh leak appeared in the fore hold.

The desperate captain ordered another sail to be thrummed over the forecastle's bottom, but before this could be done the great man-of-war began to settle by the head, and Inglefield realized the *Centaur* was doomed.

Soon the lower deck ports were even with the sea and by noon water was over the orlop deck.* At this moment the faithful carpenter reported that the "ship cannot swim long," and proposed that rafts be made from the available timbers.

The orlop deck had been pushed up by the water in the hold, and the cables floated to the gun deck. All attempt at bailing was over, the sailors resigning themselves to whatever fate the sea was ready to mete out to them.

With the coming of evening there was no apparent reason why the *Centaur* was staying afloat. Nevertheless, the captain had not authorized the building of rafts. The seas, calmer than during the gale, would not, in Inglefield's opinion, allow a raft to stay together for more than a few moments. He also

---

* The lowest deck on which cables were coiled.

believed that should the rafts be launched at the time the *Centaur* was sinking, the ship would "carry everything down with her in a vortex."

About 5:00 that afternoon the captain noticed a group around the pinnace. Since he had no desire to "remain and perish with the ship's company, to whom I could no longer be of any use," and because, as he explained it later, "the love of life prevailed," he ordered his officer, Mr. Rainy, to follow him. Inglefield descended at once into the boat at the after part of the chains and ordered a select number to join him there.

Finally the captain and his chosen few pushed away from the *Centaur*, which disappeared from view in the gathering darkness half an hour later.

A blanket was discovered and bent to one of the stretchers as a sail. Under this they scudded all night long, battered and almost swamped by the great waves around them. With the coming of dawn, the weather again moderated.

The captain had left his ship with Fayal bearing about 250 leagues southeasterly and figured that if the wind held northwest for five or six days the pinnace would reach one of the Western Isles. Unfortunately for his plans, the wind changed at once.

Digging into the larder, the men found a bag of bread, a single piece of pork, a small ham, two quarts of water and a few French cordials. It was agreed that the food should be used sparingly by the twelve aboard, and rations were set up at once.

The wind blew from the south for nine days, at the end of which time Inglefield expected to sight the island of Corvo,* as the pinnace had been able to retain an east northeasterly course most of the time.

---

* Northernmost island of the Azores.

There had been hardship because of the limited amount of food. On the fifth day they discovered that most of the bread had been ruined by the salt water, and so what remained was divided into twelve morsels for breakfast and again for dinner. A bottle was broken off carefully at the neck, and with the cork in served as a glass. Each glass, filled with water, was doled out to the twelve men for a day's ration. Luckily, several rain storms replenished the supply from time to time or all would have died of thirst. A pair of sheets discovered in the pinnace served to catch the water whenever it rained.

Because of the rain and the general wet condition aboard the pinnace the men became bothered with terrible body sores which, as the hours went by, grew more and more painful.

On the next day Quartermaster Thomas Matthews suddenly complained of having no strength to swallow food, and soon became delirious. He died a short time later. As the others had the same symptoms it was feared at the time that no one would survive the terrible ordeal.

The tiny portion of water had been doled out, but several of the men had also drunk of their own body fluids and the ocean, and were showing the effects of this dangerous practice.

Captain Inglefield had kept up the spirits of the others every night by having them sing songs and tell stories. Now that one of their number had died, there was no heart for entertainment. With the coming of darkness that night a calm fell over the water, and each man feared what the sea might offer.

At midnight a breeze sprang up from the westward, but no stars were out and Inglefield did not dare to plot a course by dead reckoning. When dawn arrived, he saw by the sun that the wind was then hitting from the southwest. Spreading the sail, the men were gratified to find that the pinnace was moving along at a speed of four knots.

Shortly after the meager breakfast had been consumed, Quartermaster John Gregory declared that he could see land ahead. The captain cautioned him, however, reminding all the others of the many times when they had thought they had seen land and it turned out to be either banks of fog or low clouds.

The wind freshened, and soon the pinnace was sliding through the water at six knots. Two hours later even the cautious captain had to admit that land was in sight. It was a joyous moment, for each man felt that he had cheated the sea. Sailing all that day, they were discouraged to find the land apparently getting no closer. It was ten o'clock at night before they approached near enough to hail a small fishing canoe and follow it into the great marine road of Fayal, which they reached at midnight.

The next morning Captain Inglefield was taken to the British consul, who made arrangements for the eleven survivors to be fed and cared for. All eventually reached England safely, but they were the only survivors ever heard from who had sailed on the man-of-war *Centaur* that relatively peaceful September day of 1782.

CHAPTER FOUR

LOSS OF THE PACKET *Antelope*

> *Nor yet, O sea, shalt thou be cursed,*
> *If at thy hands we gain the worst.*

EVER SINCE I was a small boy I have heard the story of how my grandfather, Captain Joshua N. Rowe, was shipwrecked while aboard the clipper ship *Crystal Palace* on the island of Mindanao in the Philippines. After repairing the damage and fighting with pirates who attacked them, grandfather and the others sailed to Macao. From here they put out again on August 30, 1859, and after a record voyage landed at Plymouth, England, on October 27, 1859.

About three-quarters of a century before, another vessel which had sailed from Macao had met disaster on a reef located some 500 miles to the east of the island where Grandfather Rowe was wrecked, and that is the story I now tell.

On Sunday, July 20, 1783, Captain Henry Wilson sailed his packet *Antelope* out of Macao bound for England. Stormy weather beset them until Friday, the eighth of August when it began to moderate, giving way to a relatively calm Saturday. Since it was then possible to throw open the ports of the ship and dry out the cabin, the spirits of those aboard rose and all looked forward to better sailing conditions.

Unfortunately, early Sunday morning a breeze began which brought heavy rain and a thunderstorm. Suddenly breakers were reported dead ahead, and before any orders could be given to prevent it, the *Antelope* struck heavily. All was soon in complete confusion. The ship bilged within the hour and filled with water to the lower deck hatchways.

With his air of confidence and decision Captain Wilson brought order out of chaos, and within a relatively short time had the gunpowder and small arms secured, the bread safe on deck and many of the other provisions protected from the water. He ordered the mizzenmast cut away to prevent excessive heeling, and then gave directions for the main topmast and fore topmast to be removed and the main and foreyards to be lowered. The boats were hoisted out and filled with provisions, and plans were made to abandon the wreck hurriedly if necessary. The wait for dawn began. Two glasses of wine and several biscuits were doled out to each person at this time. Everything possible was done to allay the fears of the anxious passengers.

At daybreak they discovered a small island about ten miles to the south and later made out several other islands to the east. Captain Wilson chose the smaller but nearest island to the south for their destination, and the boats soon left the ship with orders to proceed there.

Those who remained aboard the wreck began building a raft in case the *Antelope* should begin to break up. In the afternoon when the boats returned, the occupants explained that five men had been left with the stores on the island and that no natives had appeared. This good news caused the captain to order another glass of wine and more biscuit for all hands, but the loss of a man overboard at this time stopped the celebrating.

Finally the raft was finished. The men loaded it with a great number of stores after which they completely stocked the jolly boat and the pinnace.

The latter now started out towing the raft, with the jolly boat going on ahead. At times those on the pinnace could not even see the raft because of the giant waves, but eventually they reached the island and unloaded the cargoes.

The next few days the captain and several others spent attempting to free the ship. When a great wind blew up and it appeared that the packet would go to pieces, those at the wreck were able to return safely to the island.

Suddenly, at about 8:00 the next morning, two well-manned canoes were observed approaching the island. Tom Rose from the Malayan Peninsula was chosen to interview the natives in the canoes when they reached the shore, and as soon as they were within hailing distance Tom began verbal negotiations. The usual questions were asked concerning the presence of the white men on the island and satisfactory explanations were given. Finally Tom called to Captain Wilson, who strode down the beach and waded into the sea waist-deep to greet the strangers.

Among the eight natives were two princes, brothers of the king of their tribe on neighboring Ternate Island. The men explained that the masts of the *Antelope* had been seen by fellow islanders who were fishing from a canoe.

The whites, still very suspicious of the natives, tried to conceal their feelings, sitting down to breakfast with them shortly afterward. During the meal the men talked about the area where the *Antelope* was wrecked. The Palau, or Pelew, Islands, and especially Oroolong where they had been cast away, are situated about 500 miles due east of Mindanao Island in the Philippines, and were first called the Palos Islands by the Spaniards who believed the tall palm trees resembled masts of ships when seen from a distance.

The native men who sat with them around the breakfast table were copper-colored, admirably proportioned and quite naked. Their thighs were much blacker than the rest of their bodies because of tattooing. The chief or prince carried a small basket with him containing betel nuts and chinam, which is coral burned to lime. The natives would sprinkle the leaf of the betel nut with the lime powder, after which they would chew the leaves, forcing the red juice between their already blackened teeth until the discoloring gave them a weird appearance.

Finally the natives decided that their stay at the island should end and they requested Captain Wilson to appoint one of his number to return with them for a visit of respect to their own king. Wilson deliberated about this awkward predicament a few minutes and then chose his brother Matthias Wilson to represent them, telling him to ask for protection and also permission to build a vessel in which they could sail back to their own country. Captain Wilson sent a package of presents to the king, consisting of some blue broadcloth, a canister of tea, a jar of sugar candy and a bottle of rusk.

It was also agreed that the king's brother, Prince Raa Kook, and three other natives would remain with the white men and help them. The prince soon found a fine well of water on another part of the island for the survivors to use. Then he went down on the beach with his companions and the white men to say good-by to the natives in the two canoes as they started for the island where the king lived.

Meanwhile, other natives had been plundering the wreck, as Captain Wilson found out to his disappointment. He was especially concerned when he discovered that the medicine chest had been ransacked, the costly and vital fluids emptied and the bottles which contained them stolen. When the Captain told Prince Kook about it the prince was greatly enraged and promised with vehemence to kill any natives caught plundering the ship in the future.

There was a large store of choice wines and liquors on board the *Antelope,* and Captain Wilson knew the relative strength of such intoxicants on the empty stomachs of his men. Therefore he suggested to the other officers that they go aboard the packet and stave in every one of the scores of liquor casks. They agreed and the task was carried out at once, not one man taking even a farewell glass of "his beloved cordial."

On the morning of August 14 two canoes arrived with Arra Kooker, the king's other brother, and one of the king's sons. A third canoe, so the natives claimed, had been delayed by the wind, and aboard that craft was Matthias Wilson, which caused some of the white men to wonder whether he was being forcibly detained.

After introductions were over everyone who could went out to the wreck where they found twenty native canoes which Raa Kook dispersed at once.

Returning to the island Arra Kooker amused the others by telling of Matthias Wilson's concern while visiting the king, explaining by facetious mimicry the apprehension which Matthias had shown when he was the only white man in the center of hundreds of savages. Shortly afterward the canoe was sighted with Matthias aboard, and Captain Wilson heaved a sigh of relief.

As soon as he had been greeted by the other survivors Matthias told of his experiences while visiting the king. He had given the presents to the monarch in a respectful manner, and they were graciously accepted. Then Matthias had been allowed to mingle with the scores of people in the little enclosure where the king had received him. The natives crowded around the white man, believing that his clothing was part of him, for they all were completely naked and had never seen a clothed man before. When Matthias took off his hat, unbuttoned his waistcoat and removed his shoes, their wonderment knew no bounds. Here, indeed, was an extraordinary individual!

With the approach of evening, Matthias explained, he had been greatly concerned when two groups of natives lit large bonfires, one on each side of him, and he wondered if they were cannibals about to roast him alive. But the king, noticing the white man's apprehension, explained that the fires were to keep Matthias warm during the long tropical night, and Matthias shortly afterward fell asleep to be awakened by the bright sun shining in the east.

For breakfast he was given yams, coconuts and sweetmeats. A wind of great strength had come up, and the king decided that Matthias should await the following day and the possibility of a calmer wind before sending him back to Captain Wilson. The next morning two canoes were sent out ahead. A few hours later, in still calmer weather, a third canoe with a picked crew transported Matthias back to Oroolong, the island near which they had been wrecked.

Captain Wilson now felt highly pleased, as his brother's account made him confident that the natives were going to remain friendly. The king had shown no objections to the white men's building a craft in which to sail for home, and the captain at once started making plans for the construction of a vessel large enough to transport them all away from the island.

Meanwhile, certain formalities had to be observed. The king himself had promised Matthias that he would soon visit the white men's settlement, and when early the next morning a number of canoes were seen approaching, Arra excitedly told Wilson that the great king of the Pelew Islands was in one of the canoes.

Soon an impressive marine procession entered the little

harbor. The king's canoe was easily identified as it proceeded
with two other canoes on each side, making a dramatic spectacle with the five craft approaching the beach side by side.
Trained natives pulled their paddles high out of the water
with each flourish in perfect coordination. As the paddlers
neared the beach, four natives in each canoe brought forward
their conchs, and at a given signal blew the shells like trum-
pets to announce the arrival of His Majesty King Abba
Thulle.

Captain Wilson, instructed by Arra Kooker, then went
down to the low water mark on shore to welcome the king,
and was brought out into the shallow water to His Majesty,
who was seated on an impromptu throne built in the center
of the canoe. Stepping aboard, Captain Wilson and the king
embraced each other.

After the formalities had been taken care of, Captain Wilson repeated his request to build a new ship from the wreckage of the old, to which the monarch at once acceded. Wilson
next asked permission to have all his people with him as they
built the ship, and the king again agreed.

The monarch now stated that he was ready to go ashore.
Captain Wilson, as he was clothed, was then carried in to the
beach by the natives, but the naked king stepped out and
walked ashore himself. As he refused to enter any of the
tents which had been set up on the island, the white people
spread a sail for him on the ground and escorted him to the
center of it.

After Captain Wilson had introduced the other officers of
his crew, the king asked him to identify his badge of supremacy. At a loss for an answer, Captain Wilson was aided by
Chief Mate Benger, who surreptitiously slipped a beautiful
gold ring into Wilson's hand. Wilson, palming the ring,
stepped forward to the king, at the same time slipping it on
his own finger.

"Your Majesty," he began, "this is typical of my symbol of authority." He pulled the ring from his finger and gave it to the king, who tried it on his own finger, highly pleased at the token of leadership which Captain Wilson had shown him.

The captain now introduced his chief mate all over again, and the chief was called by the king "Kickary Rupack," which meant "Little Chief."

The native leader was greatly impressed with the ship's grindstone, which had been placed on a block on the shore. He took hold of the handle and turned it. Then his attention went to the muskets, and he asked questions about them. Captain Wilson promised that he would arrange a demonstration. In a short time the sailors conducted a drill on the low-tide beach, at the conclusion of which they aimed their guns at a saluting angle and fired three volleys. The king and his followers were overwhelmed at the exhibition.

To follow home his advantage, Captain Wilson asked the chief mate to put on a special demonstration of shooting. A fowl was released to strut along the beach. Benger took careful aim and fired, killing the bird, whereupon the natives rushed to the remains, examined them and were again dumbfounded.

That night the savages sang their customary songs which some of the white men misinterpreted as preliminaries to a massacre. A scuffle started which might have led to serious trouble, but the king and Captain Wilson soon quieted both sides. After a few English songs were sung, the remainder of the night was spent in sleep.

Then came the first efforts to build the ship. The natives were very anxious to watch the proceedings, but the English, not knowing how far to trust the savages, had concealed many of the tools and weapons from them. To the consternation of all, a native discovered one of the cutlasses, demanded it and finally stalked off in triumph as the white men let him have it. Seeing the man with the cutlass, Raa Kook angrily took it away and gave it back to Wilson. The incident caused not a little unpleasantness, for Captain Wilson had lost caste by giving the cutlass to an inferior member of the tribe. Native protocol dictated that royalty only should receive gifts of such importance.

A neighboring tribe at Artingall Island had bothered the king a short time before the arrival of the white men, and Abba Thulle thought a show of strength would be timely. It was arranged that five Englishmen armed with their magic guns would accompany the native warriors to the offenders' island. In the battle which followed the neighboring tribe was first terrorized and then overwhelmed by the firearms. On September 4 Captain Wilson gave permission for a second demonstration during which ten of his men were to fight on the side of Abba Thulle's warriors. This second battle with the king's enemies at Artingall Island also ended successfully, and the king returned to his own island well pleased with what had transpired.

Meanwhile the building of the vessel progressed. While the framework was being erected, Abba Thulle returned with the news that the chief minister at Artingall was suing for peace. Realizing the importance of the guns in obtaining the victory, the king requested that when Wilson completed his ship and sailed away ten muskets should be left behind for safety. Wilson tentatively compromised at five muskets, and there the matter ended for the time being.

The vessel was breamed by October 27, with the outside caulking completed, but as there was neither pitch nor tar to pay her with, they burned coral into lime, mixed it with grease and used it as a substitute.

On November 6 Captain Wilson sent the jolly boat across to Pelew, requesting the honor of the king's presence within a few days. It was also announced that Madan Blanchard, a seaman, was so impressed with native life that he was anxious to stay behind and become a native.

When the king arrived at Oroolong, Wilson told him that if Abba Thulle agreed Blanchard could stay behind and instruct the natives in firing their muskets and working the iron tools which Captain Wilson planned to leave with them. To this the king consented gladly.

On November 9, a Sunday, in the presence of the King of Pelew, the new vessel was launched and named the *Oroolong*. She appeared neat and trim as she lay at anchor in the cove.

After a happy breakfast the men began the task of carrying aboard all their possessions. Next, the ship was hauled into the basin, where there was about twenty feet of water, and the remainder of the cargo was loaded except for the heavy guns and other weighty objects.

A short time later Abba Thulle told Wilson that the local rupacks or princes had decided to make the captain an honorary prince of the first rank. Giving him a circular bone standing for the rank of prince, the king made a speech which the interpreter translated.

"You are now invested with our highest mark of honor, and this bone, the signal of it, you will carefully keep as bright as possible, rubbing it every day. This high mark of dignity must always be valiantly defended, nor suffered to be wrested from you but with your life."

Then came the great surprise. Abba Thulle informed Captain Wilson that he was sending his second son, Prince Lee Boo, whom he wished to get a thorough education, back with the new ship in the care of Captain Wilson so that he would eventually return with knowledge which he could impart to his countrymen. Overcome by the news, Captain Wilson accepted the information gladly and ordered quarters prepared on the *Oroolong* for the prince's convenience.

Among the ship's company was a huge Newfoundland dog which had delighted Arra Kooker. The prince was pleased beyond words when the captain gave him the prized pet for his very own. Arra Kooker planned to build a huge craft on the ship's ways which Captain Wilson left on the beach.

A final act was to hoist an English pennant on a tree near the cove and put up a copper plate on the trunk of the tree with the following inscription:

THE HONORABLE ENGLISH
EAST INDIA COMPANY'S SHIP THE ANTELOPE
HENRY WILSON, COMMANDER
WAS LOST UPON THE REEF NORTH OF THIS
ISLAND
IN THE NIGHT
BETWEEN THE 9TH AND 10TH OF AUGUST
WHO HERE BUILT A VESSEL
AND SAILED FROM HENCE
THE 12TH OF NOVEMBER, 1783

Now came an unpleasant discussion concerning firearms, for when Abba Thulle renewed his request for the ten muskets he met with opposition. Quick to resent this attitude, the king spoke out frankly.

"Why should you distrust me? I have never refused you my confidence. If my intentions had been hostile, you would have known it long ago, being entirely in my power, and yet, at the very last, you suspect me of bad designs!"

His straightforward manner brought blushes to the faces of the white men, and without further hesitation they gave the king five muskets, five cutlasses and almost a full barrel of gunpowder, with flint and ball in proportion. In this way peace and good will were restored, and Abba Thulle soon forgot their unkind suspicions.

During the evening Prince Lee Boo arrived from Pelew with his elder brother, and Abba Thulle presented him to all the officers. The night was spent ashore with the king giving advice to his son.

Early Wednesday morning a signal gun was sounded from the *Oroolong* and camp ashore was broken at once. All persons left the island, the white men not to return.

As soon as farewells were made the *Oroolong* hoisted sail and proceeded to a position outside the reef, where guns and other equipment were loaded aboard. Finally all was in readiness for the long trip back to civilization.

The king then directed that his canoe be brought alongside. Going aboard, he gave his son his farewell blessing, spoke briefly to the captain and prepared to leave the vessel. Great canoe loads of fruit and food of all kinds were now carried aboard from the native canoes, and then Captain Wilson ordered a package to be carried forward for the king. It contained a box, which the king opened to find a brace of pistols and a cartouch box of cartridges.

Now came the final moment. King Abba Thulle stepped forward and began to speak slowly. "You are happy because you are going, and I am happy because you are happy; but still, very unhappy to see you going away."

The captain, in this final moment, was so overcome that he was momentarily unable to answer, and the king was equally moved. Finally, pointing to his heart, Abba Thulle stepped over the side into his waiting canoe, which was the signal for a conch salute.

The *Oroolong* rapidly made progress out of the harbor, leaving the natives far behind within an hour. It was November 12 that the ship's company thus terminated their enforced stay at the island which began on August 10.

Aboard the *Oroolong* Prince Lee Boo was placed in the care of Mr. Sharp, the surgeon, who taught him the fundamentals of dress and behavior during the voyage to China. On November 25 the crew sighted the Bashee Islands. This greatly pleased the prince who was happy to see land once more. The next day Formosa was in sight, bearing northeast, and on the twenty-ninth the ship anchored near the high land called the Asses' Ears, arriving at Macao the next day. The Portuguese governor paid the captain a visit and told him that the war which had been going on was over, and peace now had been established in Europe. A message was instantly forwarded to Canton explaining what had happened to the *Antelope*.

Visiting the home of Mr. McIntyre, a friend of Captain Wilson's, Lee Boo was amazed when he saw his image in a large mirror, supposing it to be someone else looking at him. This and other wonders of civilization kept him at a constant pitch of excitement.

Arrangements were later made for Captain Wilson, Lee Boo and the officers to embark from Whampoa aboard the *Walpole*, leaving Chief Mate Benger to take over the *Oroolong* and sell her.

The crew was paid off with funds forwarded from Canton, and the next day the *Walpole* sailed away. On July 14, 1784, after an uneventful journey, the *Walpole* put into Portsmouth, England, her long trip at an end.

Back in the Pelew Islands, the king had been told on the day Captain Wilson departed that it would be at least thirty moons, and possibly six more, before his son returned. The king had then asked for a line of rope. He knotted thirty knots into the rope, left a little space, and then knotted six more.

Prince Lee Boo, however, never did return to his father, for about six months after he arrived in England, he caught the dread small pox disease and died. He is buried in Rotherheathe Cemetery where a magnificent tomb was erected to his memory by the East India Company.

The stone on the tomb reads as follows:

To the memory of

PRINCE LEE BOO

A native of the Pelew, or Palos Islands,
and Son to Abba Thulle, Rupack or King
of the Island Coorooraa:
Who departed this life on the 27th of December, 1784,
Aged 20 Years
This stone is inscribed
by the Honorable United East India Company
as a Testimony of esteem for the humane and kind
Treatment afforded by his Father to the crew of
their ship, the ANTELOPE, Captain Wilson,
which was wrecked off that Island
In the Night of the 9th of August, 1783.

Stop, Reader, stop — let NATURE claim a Tear —
A Prince of Mine, Lee Boo, lies bury'd here.

Back at the Pelew Islands a father waited in vain for his son's return. Many years after the time indicated on the rope of moons had elapsed word reached Abba Thulle of his son's death.

A nineteenth century poet, more than one hundred years ago, penned the following lines concerning this South Sea Island monarch:

I climb the highest cliff—I hear the sound
Of dashing waves—I gaze intent around.
But not a speck can my long straining eye—
A speck or shadow—o'er the rolling waves descry,
That I might weep tears of delight and say,
It is the bark that bore my child away.

Oft in my silent cave, when to its fire
From the night's rushing tempest I retire,
Methought the wild waves said amid their roar
At midnight, "Thou shalt see thy son no more."
Is he cast bleeding on some desert plain—
Upon his father does he call in vain?
Oh! I shall never, never hear his voice!
The spring time shall return, the isles rejoice;
But faint and weary I shall meet the morn,
And mid the cheering sunshine drop forlorn,
The joyous conch sounds in the high wood loud—
O'er all the beach, now stream the busy crowd;
And light canoes along the lucid tide,
With painted shells and sparkling paddles glide;
I linger on the desert rock alone,
Heartless, and cry for thee, my son, my son.

CHAPTER FIVE

THE *Halsewell* IN THE CAVERN

Should once the bottom strike the cruel shore,
The parting ship that instant is no more!

ON MONDAY, January 2, 1786, at three o'clock in the afternoon, the 758-ton East Indiaman *Halsewell* encountered a
stiff southern breeze while off the shores of England. It was
almost the very start of a long voyage from Great Britain to
India, for the vessel, under the command of Captain Richard
Pierce, had left the Downs on New Year's Day and was then
just offshore. The captain's two daughters were aboard with
him, and he looked forward to an enjoyable journey.

As the pilot was still on the ship, the *Halsewell* ran in close
to shore to land him, but suddenly the weather came on very
thick. A snowstorm soon developed, together with a freezing
rain, and all plans to drop the pilot were abandoned in the
face of the immediate danger of disaster.

By four in the afternoon of the following day a violent gale
was hitting from the northeast, and the *Halsewell* ran out to
sea. At that time they were off the coast of Dorset and were
able, with difficulty, to transfer the pilot to a passing brig.

Shortly afterward when the wind veered into the south, the captain ordered the sails to be reefed to meet the new onslaught. Unfortunately, the hawse plugs washed away, allowing much water to pour in on the gun deck. A few minutes later it was discovered that the *Halsewell* had sprung a leak. Every available pump was pressed into service, and soon it was thought that the pumps were holding their own. An hour later the leak became worse, and the water gained in spite of all the men at the pumps could do.

The next crisis came at 2:00 the following morning when the captain was unable to wear ship. He ordered the mizzenmast cut away, but the maneuver was unsuccessful. The now-desperate Pierce gave the command to cut away the mainmast also. Coxswain Moreton and four seamen were engaged in chopping away the mast when a terrific gust of wind struck the ship. Suddenly, with a loud crack, the mast snapped and fell overboard taking the five men with it to their death in the sea.

During the morning the wind went down, but a short time afterward the foremast showed signs of weakening. Creaking ominously as the waves smashed against the hull of the ship, the spar began to totter. Although the weather had calmed, there was just enough motion of the sea to weaken further the supports to the foremast. Then without warning, down it came in a tangled mass of rigging and spars, crashing over the side and into the ocean. The once-proud *Halsewell* was now little more than a floating hulk.

Another severe gale sprang up Thursday night, and in spite of everything the crew could do, the ship was slowly pushed toward her doom at St. Alban's Head, Dorsetshire. In the emergency, Captain Pierce called his chief mate into conference. Meriton suggested that all they could do was to prepare everyone for the disaster which seemed almost certain to follow when the dismasted vessel hit the Dorset rocks, now a short distance to leeward.

Less than ten minutes later their worst fears were realized. The *Halsewell* struck with great force on the rocks between Peveril's Point and St. Albans, and in almost no time began to go to pieces.

Chief Officer Meriton now ordered all survivors to remain on the larboard side of the vessel facing the rocks so that they could watch for a chance to get ashore as quickly as possible. The women, who had been placed in the roundhouse, were told to await dawn in order to leave the ship by daylight.

Unfortunately, when morning broke it revealed that the *Halsewell* had worked her way inside a gigantic cavern. All around the ship were great towering cliffs. It was one of the most fantastic shipwrecks in history.

Captain Pierce apparently lost his nerve, since he now turned the management of the ship over to Mate Meriton and retired into the roundhouse with his two daughters and the other women.

Meriton went out on deck to survey the desperate situation. Surmising that the *Halsewell* could not stay together much longer, he told those standing around that they might as well try to save their lives. Then he took time from his duties to visit the fifty women and the few men in the roundhouse and succeeded to some extent in allaying their fears. Obtaining a basket of oranges after he returned to the deck, he sent it back to the women who sat waiting their fate.

One by one the soldiers and sailors quit the wreck on Meriton's advice. The mate watched them with anxiety as they swam ashore into the gigantic cavern. While some perished in the sea, others managed to land on a slippery rock and make their way across to the cliff which they started to climb. Several reached a ledge forty or fifty feet high on the cavern walls before falling back into the turbulent ocean.

Some of the survivors were satisfied to stay just above the reach of the waves. Not one was able to escape from the cavern.

Suddenly, Meriton noticed that the deck was beginning to crack, and he went forward. There he found to his dismay that the ship had broken in two and that she could not be used much longer as a refuge. Now there must be no delay in attempting to save the lives of the women crowded into the roundhouse.

In looking for possible means of escape from the wreck, he discovered that a long spar had fallen across the deck reaching to the rocky ledge. Here was at least a slight chance for rescue. Meriton started crawling out slowly on the spar. He had just reached a point near the end when there was an ominous shifting of the *Halsewell's* timbers, and he found that the end of the spar no longer touched the opposite cliff.

Another wave smashed into the wreck with terrific force. Again the spar shifted. This time Meriton lost his hold, made a frantic clutch to regain his grasp and fell with a scream into the furious, boiling waters inside the cavern. Fortunately, he was able to swim to a projecting ledge and cling to it. A moment later another survivor, a soldier, helped him climb higher on the ledge, out of the reach of the sea.

Many of their comrades, however, were being dashed to death by the ferocity of the waves inside the cavern. Men would cling for a moment to a fragment of rock, only to lose their grip eventually and sink to their death in the cavern. Sometimes they were swept from the ship and smashed against the back of the cavern, after which their stunned and broken bodies would sink down out of sight.

Three of the more agile sailors decided to find a way out of the cavern. One was successful in climbing more than a hundred feet before he fell to his death, but the other two, a cook and Quartermaster James Thompson, reached the very top and escaped. They were the first to reach safety. Exhausted but triumphant, the two men rested a short time and then searched for help. They found the home of a quarryman nearby and told the astounded occupants about the tragedy of the *Halsewell*. The quarryman, whose name was Garland, aroused others in the vicinity and they all hastened to the top of the cliffs near the disaster with ropes and equipment to assist in the rescue of as many survivors as possible.

Back aboard the *Halsewell* no one knew that the two daring sailors had succeeded in climbing the cliffs and the women kept asking where the mate had gone. Finally, Third Mate Rogers called Captain Pierce aside and told him that Meriton had fallen into the sea. So that the women would not become too alarmed, they were informed that Meriton was up on deck making final arrangements to get them ashore.

Suddenly a gigantic breaker smashed into the *Halsewell*, and after it passed one of the women spoke up. "Poor Mr. Meriton," she sobbed, "if he had stayed with us he would have been safe. Now he has drowned."

But gradually many of the women still on the ship came to realize their terrifying position. Not only had they been shipwrecked on a rocky shore, but they were surrounded on all sides by the steep walls of a cavern, walls which in some cases reached a towering 200 feet above them!

The next to make plans to leave the ship were Rogers, Midshipman Manns and Mr. Shultz, a wealthy businessman. The three decided to combine their efforts, and they were joined at the last minute by Mr. Brimmer, a bridegroom of nine days. All four men seized a hencoop, and when the next wave came sweeping across the wreck they leaped into the ocean. Carried to a large rock which jutted out of the sea, they made a frantic grab and held fast. There were already twenty-three others there clinging desperately.

Meanwhile, Chief Officer Meriton, leaving his perch on the ledge, had started to climb the cliff, accompanied by the soldier. The first knowledge he had that the cook and quartermaster had scaled the cliff was when a long line dropped down by him. Meriton watched as the soldier grasped the line, almost falling into the sea as he did so. In his efforts the soldier dislodged the same stone to which Meriton was clinging, and had not another line come down at that very moment, the mate would have fallen off to his death. He clung to the second line tenaciously and was soon cheered by a shout from the top of the precipice.

"Tie the line around your waist and pull it up under your arms," came the directions from above. He did as ordered and then called to his rescuers to haul away. Two minutes later he was safe atop the cliff.

Back on the rock Rogers, Brimmer and the two others saw that it was then low tide and that the boulder they were on would soon be under water. They decided that before it was too late they should attempt to climb the steep, slippery sides of the cavern. Rogers and Brimmer succeeded in swimming from the rock to the side of the cave and came to a point within speaking distance of Meriton who was then about to be hauled to safety. The men could not reach each other as at least twenty other sailors were between them, all clinging desperately to the sides, and each man frantic with fear. Every once in a while a survivor would lose his strength, topple from the wall and crash to his death on the rocks below. The others remained clinging to the cold sides, enduring icy spray, nakedness, wind and the constant beating of the rain.

The quarrymen now attempted to rescue Lieutenant Brimmer. He and the three others had climbed the rocky cliff to a point fifty feet above the waves. When the rope came down to him he fastened it around his body and then signaled for the men to haul away. In his haste he had fastened the line improperly so that the moment he was swung out the knot slipped free. Brimmer, with an unearthly cry, fell to his death below.

Hardly had the unfortunate Lieutenant dropped from the ledge when Meriton and the others high on the cliff heard the terrifying shriek of a hundred anguished souls which echoed through the cavern even above the storm. Peering down over the precipice, the mate gazed in horror as the tragic scene unfolded before his eyes.

As if hypnotized, those who had been saved from a similar fate watched in grim silence when the last timbers of the *Halsewell* smashed to pieces and threw the occupants into the sea. The roundhouse where the hapless women had been huddling separated convulsively into a thousand pieces, and every human being aboard died almost instantly in that maelstrom of wreckage, cargo and waves. In the space of a few moments, all the women on the *Halsewell* had perished.

But there were still many men clinging for their lives to the inside walls of the gigantic cavern, and the quarrymen decided to try to reach them.

Although the rescuers could see only one or two of the survivors below, each time they would descend to the edge of the cavern and save a man, his place would be taken almost at once as another worked his way along the ledge. The distance from the top of the rock to the ledge was about 115 feet, most of which was a perpendicular drop.

Two daring quarrymen now arranged a rescue system. A strong iron bar was driven into the ground at the top of the cliff and a man secured by a rope to it so that he would not fall. He would then venture out over the edge of the cliff until he spotted a survivor below, after which he would lower another rope with a noose in it. Far below him the survivor would grasp the rope, slip it over his shoulders and under his arms and signal to be hoisted away. Thus, as was said at the time, the sailor exchanged the dangers of one element, the sea, for the dangers of another, the air.

But for those who escaped in this manner there were almost as many others who had failed to fasten the loop correctly. As they were swung off into space, they slipped out of their fastenings and were hurled to death on the ledges below.

Late in the afternoon a drummer boy was located. He had managed to get ashore but was suffering intensely from injuries sustained when he was dashed by a wave against the cavern walls. Nevertheless, he had clung tenaciously to the rock, and when discovered had given up all hope of being saved. His weakened body slid back into the sea, and the outgoing tide took him some distance from the rocky shore.

No one could save him, and although he kept afloat, for he had been a good swimmer, the tide carried him farther and farther away, until he was lost to sight in the swell of the sea, never to be seen again.

After all the other survivors had been taken from the top of the cliff and quartered temporarily in the spacious home of Mr. Garland, two of the quarrymen volunteered to return to the cavern and see if there might be a sign of the missing boy.

The two men again reached the scene of the disaster, and one was let down into the cavern. As he swung back and forth in the darkness of the cave, he thought that he heard a feeble cry, but try as he might, he could not get closer to the sound.

Returning to the top of the cliff, he and his friend arranged a longer line, and he again descended by rope into the mouth of the cavern. With the aid of the new line he went down to within a few feet of the sea itself.

Landing on a projecting ledge, he listened. There was not a sound except the roar of the waves in the cavern. Then he called out.

"Hallo! Hallo!"

"Hallo," came a faint answer.

Working his way over toward the voice, he soon discovered, in a tiny recess some distance from the place where the others had landed, a soldier named William Trenton. Yes, his mission had been a success. He had found someone still alive. It was then almost noon on the morning of Saturday, January 7, and the wreck had occurred early the preceding morning. How Trenton had been able to cling to the recess during two high tides he never could explain.

Trenton was hauled to safety, the seventy-fourth survivor of a craft which had started out on a trip to India with 243 persons aboard.

The survivors were all quartered in the vicinity for a few days, after which the officers of the India House visited them and presented each man half a crown, as was said at the time, "to help him on his way."

CHAPTER SIX

THE STRANGE STORY
OF THE *Guardian*

The burying waters close around their head—
They sink! for ever numbered with the dead.

IN SAINT PAUL'S CATHEDRAL, London, a monument was erected many years ago to Edward Riou, whose experiences aboard the warship *Guardian* are unusual enough for inclusion in this collection of tales concerning the sea. Captain Edward Riou sailed from the Cape of Good Hope as master of the man-of-war *Guardian* on December 11, 1789, bound for Australia. On board were a crew of ninety-six and one woman passenger as well as twenty-five convicts sentenced to transportation to Australia and three warders to guard them. This was actually the maiden trip of the vessel from England. She was acting more as a freighter than a warship, and because of this she was armed *en flute.**

Her large consignment of stores had been augmented at the Cape of Good Hope by a deckload consisting of a substantial

---

* Her guns, dismounted, were in the hold, and her gun carriages had been placed on the booms.

number of horses, sheep, cows, pigs and chickens together with great quantities of grain and hay.

The prevailing winds carried the *Guardian* into the "roaring forties," and on December 23, 1789, when some 1200 miles east southeast of Africa, an iceberg came into view.

Because of the great deckload of animals, which prompted many of the crew to call the ship Noah's Ark, the daily consumption of drinking water was much more than had been planned. Captain Riou, believing that the berg was from the Great Barrier and of fresh water, steered the ship toward the mountain of ice.

Running in very close, he shortened sail and sent his boats over to obtain a quantity of the ice. By 6:00 enough was chopped off, and ninety minutes later the boats were hoisted aboard. But a dangerous condition had developed in the meantime, for a fog bank had drifted in enveloping the entire area. The ship then hauled off to the northward to avoid the possibility of crashing into the berg. By 8:00 the *Guardian* tacked and resumed her original course.

She was then sailing at seven knots, when suddenly there came a warning cry from the lookouts on the forecastle that ice was dead ahead. Soon all on deck could see through the fog the outline of a gigantic iceberg. For a brief moment the berg appeared to be far enough off the ship's course for a collision to be avoided, but a few seconds later, before orders could be carried out, a submerged section of the monstrous mountain of ice caught the forefoot of the ship. The bow then swung around and slid free, but at the same instant the stern, drawing more water, lurched up on the hidden ledge. Unable to work free, the *Guardian* pounded there in the heavy sea until her rudder was wrenched away, the tiller smashed and the deck itself forced and splintered.

The vessel finally worked into the ice until she came to a dead halt with her stern balanced on the berg and her bow still afloat in the sea. Her position was one of spectacular danger. Towering twice the height of her masts, and threatening at any moment to drop gigantic pinnacles of ice weighing scores of tons down on the ship, the berg loomed as a constant threat to the terrified men.

Captain Riou ordered the sails trimmed, and the panic-stricken members of the crew were afraid to venture aloft. Only after constant urging and threatening did they climb into the rigging and carry out their orders. Riou had calculated correctly, for, with the sails trimmed, the *Guardian* slowly slid off the submerged shelf, and was soon free from the danger of being crushed down into the sea by the overhanging precipice of ice.

Unfortunately, at 8:15, the carpenter reported two feet of water in the hold with the sea still pouring in rapidly. The pumps were quickly set to work, and the captain ordered the ship lightened. All the deck load, including the pigs, sheep, cows and chickens, were thrown into the sea, together with the grain and hay. Then came the spare anchors and the gun carriages, after which supplies from the hold were brought up on deck and thrown overboard. Nevertheless, the height of water below steadily gained, and at 10:00 that evening five feet was reported.

A heavy sea continued to smash against the *Guardian*, and stormy weather and fog still prevailed. Dividing his crew equally, Riou had each group taking turns at the pumps. A ration of grog was administered to everyone, and the men worked with renewed efforts, but by midnight six feet of water was measured in the hold.

The storm increased to a gale, and the seas still battered the ship relentlessly. The captain ordered a sail thrummed,*

---

* Thrumming means threading short lengths of rope yarn through a canvas sail to form a thick mat, which is passed under a ship's bottom. The mat is sucked into the leak or opening and slows up the flow of water into the hold. Collision mats, used today, are made on the same principle.

The loss of the *Grosvenor* off the coast of South Africa, 1782. (*ch. 2*)

The wreck of the *Antelope* off Oroolong, Pelew Islands, 1783. (*ch. 4*)

Captain Wilson of the *Antelope* leaves the Pelew Islanders, 1783. (*ch. 4*)

Too late, a rescuer is lowered over the cliff to find the body of a victim from the *Halsewell*, wrecked off St. Alban's Head, England, 1786. *(ch. 5)*

The loss of the *Lady Hobart* on an island of ice, 1803. (*ch. 7*)

The wreck of the brig *Commerce* off the African Coast, 1815. (*ch. 9*)

The burning of the circus ship *Royal Tar* off Fox Island, Penobscot Bay, 1836. (*ch. 14*)

A contemporary sketch of the wreck of the *Mexico* off Hempstead Beach, Long Island, 1836.

(cb. 15)

The escape of the *Calliope* during the great storm at Samoa, 1889.
(ch. 21)

The launching of the steamer *Portland* by the New England Company, 1889. (*ch. 24*)

James I. Wilson holding wreckage from the *Portland* and Edward Rowe Snow with a stateroom door key. *(ch. 24)*

A family is separated during the great Massachusetts flood of 1874. *(ch. 26)*

Photo by Robert Dixon

Hurricane Carol at its height at South Boston, 1954. *Boston American* photographer Gene Dixon scrambles to safety after a huge wave knocked him down. (*ch. 26*)

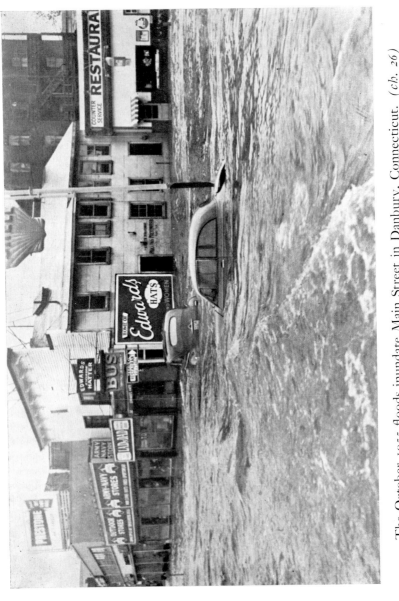

The October 1955 floods inundate Main Street in Danbury, Connecticut. *(ch. 26)*

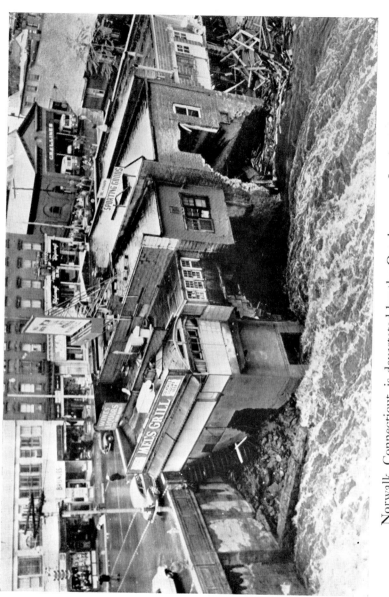

Norwalk, Connecticut, is devastated by the October 1955 flood. *(ch. 26)*

Photo by Daniel J. Sheehan; © The Boston Post

The stranding of the *Etrusco* at Scituate, Massachusetts, 1956.

and at dawn the mat was passed under the stern and made fast.

At first the leak continued to gain, but it soon slowed up. On December 24 at 11:00 in the morning the height of the water was measured at nineteen inches, and the relieved men at the pumps felt that they had made substantial progress.

The weather now became stormier. Possibly the rough water had opened more seams, for by noon the depth had gained eight inches, and another sail was thrummed and fothered.*

Hoping to locate the leak, the captain sent several men into the hold. As they were unable to find the aperture where the water was coming in, Riou ordered a hole cut in the stern deck so that men could get below more easily and pass up cargo to be jettisoned.

Officers and crew worked constantly at their tasks, and the captain labored with the others until a roll of the ship threw a heavy cask against his hand and smashed it badly.

At 5:00 the water was up to four feet again. A short time before midnight the starboard pump broke down, and the leak gained rapidly from then on.

At 6:00 the next morning, Christmas Day, the water was seven feet deep in the hold. The exhausted men, extremely cold, bitterly discouraged and hungry as well, began to feel that the task was an impossible one. The crew began hiding in the hammocks so that they could avoid what to them was now a hopeless task. Captain Riou realized that he would have to get them back to work.

"I'll throw overboard any of you who are hiding away," he shouted out, "for you are no better than useless lumber if you crawl to your hammocks."

The men returned one by one, appearing forlorn and dejected, but they continued to pump.

The water was now gaining a foot an hour. When it

---

* Passed under the ship.

reached the orlop deck, Riou realized it was the beginning of
the end, and the men gave themselves up for lost. A few in
their terror slipped away to break into the liquor room and
became drunk and mutinous. Finally the crew made formal
application to abandon ship, and the captain reluctantly consented. For the next hour the men busied themselves placing
masts, sails, water, provisions and compasses in the available
boats, but it was then discovered that there was not enough
room for all.

By this time Riou had already determined to remain aboard
and go down with his ship in the best tradition of the sea. He
decided to write a full report to his superior officer in England and give it to Mr. Clements, one of his officers who was
to leave the ship. From the letter one may gather that the
captain did not expect to survive.

> H. M. S. Guardian
> 25 December 1789

Sir:

If any part of the officers and crew of the *Guardian*
should ever get home, I have only to say that their conduct,
after the fatal stroke on an island of ice, was admirable and
wonderful in everything that relates to their duties, considered either as private men or in His Majesty's service.

As there seems to be no possibility of my remaining many
hours in this world, I beg leave to recommend to the consideration of the Admiralty of a sister, together with a widowed
mother, to whom their favour might be shown, if my conduct or services should be found deserving of any remembrance.

> I am, Sir,
> With great respect,
> Your ever obedient servant
> E. RIOU.

Philip Stephens, Esq.

At 7:00 the *Guardian* began to settle by the stern, with the
men below forced up on deck by a sudden inrush of water.

As the ship was apparently sinking fast, the crew hoisted out the boats. The first craft capsized while being lowered, but the launch, cutter and the jolly boat got away safely.

Those aboard the latter approached the launch, asking for provisions and water, and when refused attempted to board the larger craft. Suspecting that this might occur, those on the launch pushed away rapidly, but watched with horror as the jolly boat then filled and sank with all hands.

The cutter was equally unfortunate for she was never heard from again. The launch, with Mr. Clements, the purser, the master's mate, the chaplain, one midshipman and nine seamen aboard, was picked up on January 3, 1790, by a French merchant ship which landed them at the Cape of Good Hope. When he reached England, Mr. Clements took the captain's letter to the Admiralty, and the *Guardian* and Captain Riou, together with those who stayed behind on the ship with him, were given up as lost.

By 10:00 every boat from the *Guardian* was over the horizon, and Riou and his fellow survivors were left alone on the man-of-war which was expected momentarily to plunge forever under the stormy sea. At this time she was floating with the water at the level of her upper deck ports.

Instead of sitting idly by while his vessel sank, Riou now set his men to work repairing the pumps. Still aboard with the captain were six officers, the three warders, the daughter of one of them, a surgeon's mate, thirty sailors and boys and twenty-one convicts—sixty-two in all. And so these oddly assorted people spent Christmas of 1789.

The day after Christmas the thrummed foresail was slipped over the side and fothered. To his amazement, the captain discovered that the repaired pumps were able to keep the water from gaining. Then, hoping to lighten the *Guardian* still more, he ordered everything movable thrown overboard from the decks with the exception of two horses.

The Australian-bound convicts, feeling that otherwise death would claim them, asked permission to build a raft from the ship's timbers, but Riou had other plans. He put the convicts to work making a jury rudder from the jib boom and spare jib boom. When finished, this was let down over the stern and put in place. It was found to steer the man-of-war much better than might have been expected.

Although completely waterlogged, the *Guardian* seemed to be sinking no lower, and an investigation revealed that she was being kept afloat by innumerable casks in the hold floating up against the lower deck. Greatly relieved and encouraged the captain now headed toward the coast of Africa. Slowly but surely the ship sailed on and finally came in sight of the Cape of Good Hope. Another vessel approached in close and spoke to the *Guardian*. Her captain agreed to tow the wrecked craft the rest of the way into port. The arrival of the *Guardian* at Table Bay on February 22, 1790, concluded one of the most miraculous escapes from the sea's vengeance on record.

While in Table Bay Captain Riou again wrote the Admiralty, the second letter reaching its destination on April 28, 1790, long after Riou and his ship's company had been given up for dead. When it was brought before King George III, he expressed "uncommon satisfaction" at the wonderful news.

Meanwhile the *Guardian*, with a great hole in her bow, was driven ashore in a gale and sold as she lay, a wreck on the beach.

For his feat of daring in sailing the wreck to Africa, Captain Riou was made a commander. He was in charge of the *Amazon* at the Battle of Copenhagen in 1801, where he was killed. Nelson acknowledged his worth by saying that his country had "sustained a great loss." His tomb in Saint Paul's still is visited by many young, inspired midshipmen.

CHAPTER SEVEN

THE *Lady Hobart* AND THE ICEBERG

And what of the ship, the great brave vessel,
Buffeted, howled at, patient, dumb,
Built to withstand, and manned to wrestle,
Fashioned to strive and to overcome?

AROUND THE BEGINNING of the last century so many disasters
were taking place at Sable Island that for a time every craft
leaving Halifax, Nova Scotia, took extra precautions to avoid
being wrecked there.* Five ships, the *Princess Amelia, Francis, Hariot, Union* and *Hannah and Eliza,* were lost at the
island within a short period of time, causing the death of almost 300 persons. On June 22, 1803, the packet *Lady Hobart,*
commanded by Captain William D. Fellowes, departed from
Halifax for England, taking great care to sail sufficiently south
to avoid Sable Island.

---

* Having landed at Sable Island twice by airplane, I can realize the full
significance of the dangers of this unusual strip of sand far off the mainland
of America. Called the graveyard of shipping, the island with its three
bars—Inner Bar, Middle Bar and Outer Bar—has a record of five hundred
shipwrecks which took place on or near her shores.

However, the war with Napoleon was then being waged with great fury, and the *Lady Hobart* also had to watch out for enemy cruisers. Finally, with Sable Island far behind, Captain Fellowes concentrated on keeping clear of French warships by setting a new course directly north. But, having escaped stranding on Sable Island, the packet was sailing into even graver danger.

On June 26, reaching latitude North 44° 37′ and longitude West 51° 20′, in the vicinity of the Grand Banks, those aboard the vessel saw a large French schooner standing toward them. Her decks were crowded with men, who appeared ready to board the *Hobart*. Coming within range an hour after sighting her, the gunners on the packet fired a cannon shot at the Frenchman, whose colors were lowered at once in surrender. The *Hobart's* captive was the *l'Aimable Julie*. Laden with salt fish and sailing for Port Liberté from the island of Saint Pierre, the *Julie* was commanded by "Citizen" Charles Rossé, who had no intention of trying to take the *Lady Hobart*.

After giving the affair due consideration, Captain Fellowes decided to turn the prize over to John Little and William Hughes, two lieutenants of His Majesty's Navy, who were passengers on the *Hobart*. The lieutenants, together with two of the French crew and two Canadian seamen, sailed the French ship back to Halifax. A short time later Fellowes put the remaining prisoners aboard two Canadian schooners, but allowed Captain Rossé and two others to stay aboard his craft.

The next day the wind began to blow hard from the west and was accompanied by a heavy sea and a thick fog. At 1:00 the next morning the *Lady Hobart* was proceeding through the haze at the rate of seven knots, when she suddenly crashed into an iceberg with such violence that many of the men below were thrown out of their hammocks. The gigantic mass of ice was a quarter mile long, with great underwater shelves projecting far out from the visible part of the berg, which was so large it was referred to as an "island of ice."

When the crash occurred Fellowes ran up on deck and ordered the helm hard-a-port, but the ship struck again on the chess-trees,* and then swung round on her keel. Her stern post was stove in and her rudder soon carried away, but finally she was hauled off.

The *Lady Hobart*, still under the projecting mountain of ice and in danger of being hit by falling ledges of the berg, slowly began to sink. The waves were crashing into the ship and then into the iceberg in a wild, spectacular manner which filled the hearts of everyone aboard with an awed fascination. Each person knew that death in the sea was close at hand.

The captain ordered the anchors cut away, the guns hove overboard and two sails thrummed under her bottom. But it was of no avail, and within fifteen minutes, in spite of both pumps' working desperately and all hands bailing buckets of water from the main hatchway, the ship settled down to her forechains in the sea.

The desperate Fellowes now consulted a navy captain aboard named Thomas and his own master,** Mr. Bargus, as to the proper course to follow. Captain Fellowes was aware that the ship should be abandoned, but he did not see how both the people aboard and the mails could be saved. His fellow officers agreed with him in the decision to put forth every effort to save lives.

Wonderful discipline prevailed as Fellowes ordered all boats made ready. "Although the danger of perishing was every instant increasing, each man waited his own turn to get

---

* Two pieces of wood bolted perpendicularly, one on each side of the ship, to hold the clews of the mainsail for which purpose there is a hole in the upper part, through which the tack passed that extends the clew of the sail to windward.

** The title given the navigating officer in the navy of that period.

into the boats, with a coolness and composure that could not be surpassed."

Several members of the crew were put to work lashing the ballast of iron pigs to the mail, which was then thrown overboard. The cutter and the jolly boat were hoisted out, and the three women aboard were ordered to get into the cutter. A Miss Cottenham was so terrified that she leaped into the bottom of the boat with great force. The jump might have killed her, but for some reason she was not even injured. Finally, all except Mr. Bargus and the captain were aboard.

By now the main deck forward was under water, and Fellowes planned to drop from the end of the trysail boom into the sea. Fearing that the cutter might be stove in, he called out to the men to pull away from danger and await him.

"Ready, Mr. Bargus. You go first," said the captain.

"I am sorry, sir, but I beg leave to disobey. I must see that you are safe over before I start myself," Bargus replied. In that order the two men left the sinking packet, dropping into the sea to swim over to the cutter. With great haste the crew hauled them aboard and hoisted sail.

Just as the cutter pulled away, the *Lady Hobart* lurched heavily to port, and all hands watched as the packet went down bow first into the sea. Her colors, union downward, were still flying at the main topgallant masthead as she disappeared forever beneath the ocean waves.* Captain Fellowes stated that "we narrowly escaped being swallowed up in the vortex."

At the very moment the ship was plunging below the sea to her doom, the surrounding ocean seemed crowded with whales, which continued to play around the cutter and the jolly boat long after the vessel had disappeared. All hands

---

* The position of the *Lady Hobart* when she sank has been estimated as less than 150 miles from the area where the *Titanic* went down more than a century later.

shouted at the monstrous mammals every time they approached too close to the boats, but the cries did not affect the creatures, and after an hour fraught with danger the whales took off for other areas perhaps more plentifully supplied with capelard,* for which they were said to travel hundreds of miles.

It had been scarcely an hour from the moment the vessel struck the iceberg until the time she disappeared, and now the entire ship's company was distributed in two small boats. Aboard the cutter were the three ladies, the captain, Captain Richard Thomas of the navy, the French captain and twelve others, making eighteen in all. The supplies, added to their weight, brought the gunwhale of the twenty-foot cutter to within six inches of the water! In the fourteen-foot jolly boat were Master Samuel Bargus, Lieutenant-Colonel George Cook of the first regiment of guards and nine others, making eleven in all.

The only provisions were fifty pounds of biscuit, part of a barrel of spruce beer, a five-gallon bottle of rum and several bottles of port wine. The principal water supply was a five-gallon bottle which John Tipper had emptied of rum and then filled with water while the cutter was being made ready. Two compasses, a quadrant, a telescope, a small tin mug, the deck lantern, several candles, a tinderbox and matches kept in a bladder for steering by night comprised the remaining articles taken from the shipwreck.

For several days the wind continued to blow steadily from the west with a heavy sea. One morning at daylight it was estimated that they were now approximately 350 miles from Newfoundland. With no knowledge of how or when they would either sight land or be seen by a passing ship, Captain Fellowes stressed the need for great economy in the use of

---

* Now known as capelin, a small smeltlike fish.

food. Each person, therefore, was served a biscuit and a glass of wine during a twenty-four-hour period, with everyone agreeing not to begin using his meager water supply until later.

Soon after daylight the cutter made sail with the jolly boat in tow, standing close-hauled to the northwest. It was hoped that they would reach the island of Newfoundland within a relatively short time.

The next day brought light variable winds from the southeast. The biscuits had become soaked during the night, which forced a further curtailment of rations. A thick fog then came on, followed by a heavy rain which wet all hands to the skin. At noon it was estimated by dead reckoning that Saint John's, Newfoundland, bore 310 miles away. One of the ladies at that time read prayers to the gathering, stressing those applicable to their situation.

By morning the passengers were so benumbed with dampness and cold that Fellowes ordered half a glass of rum and a mouthful of biscuit for everyone. The sea was now calm, but the June air was raw and cold with thick fog all about.

The men took turns at rowing in both craft, day and night. The jolly boat, unfortunately, had put off from the ship with just three oars and had only a small sail, so the cutter was forced to tow her constantly.

On June 30 a fragment of ham was found in the jolly boat, and a small morsel was given each person, but it made them so thirsty that the captain threw away the remainder.

The next morning a gale of wind began from the west northwest with heavy fog and sleet, and the spray froze as it hit the boats. It was a depressing day for everyone aboard. A short time later the cutter shipped so much water and wallowed so low in the heavy seas that it was agreed each craft should operate independently. Those aboard the cutter cast free the line to the jolly boat, which was soon lost sight of in the fog.

Afterward, throughout the day, person after person in the cutter announced the sighting of a sail. All were mistaken, but Fellowes finally was forced to put the boat before the wind to prove them wrong. When he had done so, he enforced a strict rule of refusing to go after every supposed sail which the passengers thought they sighted.

From time to time prayers were given. In spite of heavy fog, pouring rain or driving sleet all the men removed their headgear and remained silent during the readings.

On Saturday, July 2, at 11:30 A.M. during a partial clearing a sail was actually sighted. She was to the eastward and standing to the northwest. All hands became encouraged, and a prayer was offered.

Captain Fellowes now raised himself as high as he could and waved the boathook to which was tied a lady's shawl. The distance between the two craft narrowed appreciably, but the captain now realized the other craft was the jolly boat on the same general course as the cutter. The feelings of disappointment were mingled with relief that the other craft was still afloat.

A breeze sprang up and the cutter's sail was raised. Since the jolly boat now had to row hard to keep up, the men in the cutter tossed a line aboard the other craft and towed her, the two boats proceeding as before.

Sometime after 8:00 that night, the French captain leaped into the sea to his death. He had become such a good friend of Fellowes that his loss was felt severely. When the ship had gone down, he implored Fellowes not to let him drown, and the captain assured him that he had no such intention. Another man in the jolly boat went mad and had to be tied to the gunwhale.

The sea now continued to break over both craft. It was so

crowded in the cutter's stern that "it was difficult for anyone to put his hand into his pocket," while the greater part of the crew lay in water in the bottom of the boat.

The very next morning a gale began from the southward, accompanied by a tremendous sea which would have swamped the cutter had the least deviation been made by the man at the helm. Toward evening the storm quieted down, and the cutter soon passed several pieces of floating rockweed, after which a hackdown flew by them. A short time later a beautiful white dovelike bird came over to attempt a landing on the masthead of the cutter, and all aboard considered it a favorable omen.

The survivors had now been six days and nights constantly wet and cold, getting as a ration a quarter of a biscuit daily and one wine glass of liquid every twenty-four hours. With the coming of the two birds, many of the men who had appeared indifferent to their fate took up their oars again and showed renewed interest in living. The jolly boat's towline had been cut to induce those who had ceased to care whether they lived to start rowing again.

But when Monday, July 4 dawned, it brought a fog so thick that the jolly boat was soon out of sight, and this fact depressed everyone. Tempers were now getting short, and the "most trifling remark or exclamation agitated us very much."

Then came a period when every new fog bank brought cries of land, after which several of the men swore that they could either hear breakers or the firing of distant guns. A short time later several whales appeared blowing repeatedly, making the noises previously attributed to breakers.

When daylight came the sun rose full in the east for the second time since the shipwreck. As soon as the fog burned off Captain Fellowes sighted land about a mile away, which proved to be Conception Bay between Kettle Cove and Island Cove, a little more than fifty miles from Saint John's, Newfoundland. At almost the same moment the jolly boat came into view, together with a small schooner which was standing off toward them from shore.

Fellowes now opened his prayer book and offered thanks to God for having preserved them through their sufferings.

The schooner drew near, received the survivors on board and took both boats in tow, but because of an offshore wind they did not land until 4:00 in the afternoon. By this time the entire community was down on the beach awaiting the arrival of the schooner. The inhabitants helped the victims make their way over the rocks which led to their homes.

After a few days spent in recuperating, most of the survivors recovered in part. Captain Fellowes discovered the natives had neither medical aid nor fresh provisions as they existed on salt fish and potatoes. He decided to start for Saint John's, and the group left at 2:00 that same afternoon. The captain had hired a small schooner to which the jolly boat was tied, and the cutter sailed alone. Toward dusk squalls came up, and the hired vessel anchored outside of Saint John's Harbor. The cutter was without a grapnel, and fears were entertained that she had drifted out to sea.

A party including the three women left the schooner in the jolly boat that night and reached shore at 12:00 P.M. After considerable wandering, they were able to find lodging with beds for the women and chairs for the men to sleep on that night.

In the morning the schooner and the cutter were sighted from shore. The latter had fallen in with a fishing craft to which she tied during the night. Hundreds of people crowded down to the landing, and when they saw the tiny craft which had taken the twenty-nine survivors from a shipwreck far at sea to the coast of Newfoundland, they could scarcely believe it.

Brigadier-General Skerritt, Commander of the Saint John's garrison, on being informed of the survivors' plight, ordered a party of soldiers to assist the crew and passengers from the boats. Within an hour they were comfortably quartered in the barracks. The following days brought most of them back to health, and Captain Fellowes, anxious to reach England with his wife, engaged a cabin on a small vessel bound to Oporto, Portugal. He arranged for the ship's company to return to Halifax, but took Colonel Cooke, the colonel's servant, Captain Thomas and Mr. Bargus aboard the Oporto-bound ship.

Leaving Saint John's on July 11, their craft fell in with an American ship, the *Bristol Trader* of New York under William Cowley. On being informed of the six shipwreck passengers, Cowley offered to take them on board his ship and sail them to Bristol, where they all arrived on August 3, 1803.

Duke of Cumberland

I would fain die a dry death.

QUITE OFTEN a hurricane is remembered because of an important ship which was lost or a location along the shore which suffered intense damage. Thus it is that the Minot's Light Storm of 1851 is identified by the lighthouse which crashed into the sea in that tempest, while the Portland Gale of 1898 is distinguished by the loss at sea of the steamer *Portland* with all on board.

Then there was the Long Island Hurricane of 1821. This unusual storm began on Turk's Island, September 1, and continued up the Atlantic coast to hit New York with such fury that more damage was sustained in two hours than ever before in the city's history. The tide came in with incredible speed, gaining thirteen feet in one hour's time! Continuing out over Long Island, the mighty wind caused such devastation that the gale ever afterward was called the Long Island Hurricane of 1821.

Other great hurricanes with unusual names include the Racer's Storm of 1837, the Daniel Webster Gale of 1856 and the Great Bahama Hurricane of 1866. The *Racer* was a British sloop-of-war caught in the 1837 storm off Yucatan, while the ship *Daniel Webster* was in the hurricane of 1856 for two full days.

Also well known are the Great Hurricane of 1780, the Tobago Hurricane of 1790, the Galveston Hurricane of 1900 and the New England Hurricane of 1938.

But of all the storms and hurricanes which have hit America since earliest times, and the recorded number is more than 1500, the gale which smashed into the Virgin Islands on September 3, 1804, is one of the few which include the story of a shipwreck with a happy ending. Because of the very nature of storms and shipwrecks not many fall into this category.

This hurricane, which on Monday, September 3, 1804, was centered over Antigua, swept across the West Indies to become one of the great storms of the nineteenth century, reaching Boston on September 9 to weaken the Old North Church to such an extent that its steeple finally toppled over in the gale of the following month.

At the start of the storm the packet *Duke of Cumberland*, under command of Captain Lawrence, was lying at anchor in the road at Saint John, Virgin Islands. On that same Monday morning the H. M. S. *Serapis* was two miles out to sea from the *Cumberland*. Toward noon a distress signal was sent across to the *Serapis* from the *De Ruyter*, a venerable seventy-four gun man-of-war which the government had planned to have fitted as a prison ship.

The wind grew in strength, and the *Cumberland* was obliged to strike her topgallant masts. At that moment a boat came alongside requesting sailors to help the crew of the *De Ruyter*, but Lawrence realized that he would need every man aboard his own craft to handle the sails and refused to send a single midshipman.

Because the packet was straining at her moorings, the captain ordered the *Cumberland's* best bower anchor to be put over. Four hours later, at six o'clock, the wind came in from the northwest. Almost immediately the bower parted, and they bent the remainder of the cable to the stream anchor. It did little good, and later they were forced to let go the two remaining anchors.

By ten o'clock that night the storm had become a wild, howling hurricane. The wind raged with a fury seldom seen in the tropics, and the torrential rain was overwhelming. The giant waves were crashing against the *Cumberland's* hull, and the ship pitched and rolled. At one moment her forecastle was under water, while the next it pointed sharply toward the skies. Vivid flashes of lightning added to the awesome scene, illuminating a ragged ledge of rocks immediately to leeward of the vessel.

Just before 11:00 there was a terrific crash aboard ship, and it was found that the windlass had given way. The sailors clapped stoppers on the cables and secured them to ring bolts on the deck, but because of the great wrenching strain they were subjected to, time and again the ring bolts would pull free.

Shortly after midnight there came a terrific blast of wind, and one after the other the cables parted. Many of the sailors cried aloud in terror. Overcome by the storm, Captain Lawrence could see no hope left and shouted, "All is now over! The Lord God have mercy upon every one of us!"

The *Cumberland* then began to drift broadside in the trough of the sea, and each man instinctively chose for himself a place of relative safety. Around 1:00 o'clock the ship grounded and then came off again. Out of the darkness loomed a dark object directly in their path, and the men feared that it was Rat Island off the Harbor of Saint John, but it proved to be a ship. They passed safely under her stern without identifying her.

Suddenly the wind changed from north northwest to west, and then began to blow with even greater fury, pushing them out into deep water again. Eventually the *Cumberland* started to drift toward the shore at a point where high cliffs and ugly rocks awaited. After several billows had surged by, one mighty wave seized the packet and threw it heavily upon the rocks at the base of a towering precipice, smashing a great hole in her side through which water began to surge.

The foremast and the mizzenmast were cut away at once, but it was decided that the mainmast should be left standing, for the time being. Shortly afterward the water pouring in had risen to the long deck.

After three more hours of darkness dawn appeared. In the light of day the *Cumberland* presented a hopeless sight with every sea making a complete breach over her. She had piled up on the rocks at the worst possible location, with not the slightest chance for the men either to launch a boat or scramble ashore to a sandy beach. High in the cliffs above the wreck a tree could be seen, its branches extending out over the precipice. The sailors looked up and wondered how they could possibly reach it.

Then the waves began to smash the packet apart. First a comber carried away her stern boat, and when the next breaker unshipped the rudder, her quarterboats, binnacle and roundhouse crashed into the sea.

The mainmast now canted toward land, and the sailors attempted to bridge the gulf by pushing the topmast across the chasm. They wedged it into the maintop so that it slanted against the cliff itself. But only one sailor could be found who would attempt to negotiate the dangerous journey. This hopeful midshipman climbed across to the tip of the topmast after which he threw a rope up around some large bushes at the top of the precipice. When he put his weight on the line, however, it brought down the shrubbery and a large rock as well, and he gave up his efforts.

The failure of the first sailor did not prevent another ambitious midshipman from climbing the mast with the idea of leaping across the six-foot gap which separated the tip of the mast from the top of the precipice. Inch by inch he worked his way out to the end of the span. Just as he was about to jump, however, the pole of the mast snapped, dropping him forty feet into the raging seas. A moment later he was seen still clinging to the broken fragment as he was tossed about in the surging waves. A tackle was quickly lowered to rescue him, and after several fruitless attempts the sailor was finally hauled aboard the *Cumberland*.

The storm continued to rage, and the ship showed further signs of breaking up. Completely exhausted by their exertions, one by one the discouraged members of the crew gave up, slipping helplessly down to the deck where the water repeatedly engulfed them.

Suddenly, at the top of the precipice several heads appeared. The ship had been discovered by the natives of Saint John who lived in the vicinity. Several hopeful sailors scampered up the mainmast with lines which they attempted to throw across to the people on the precipice. Strangely enough, it apparently made no difference what the sailors did, for the onlookers completely ignored the lines as they were tossed across at their feet, and finally, after gaping at the shipwrecked men, they walked away from the scene. They left the crew shouting and cursing at them in their own helplessness. Either from fear or stupidity the men of Saint John had decided not to help the survivors of the *Duke of Cumberland* and did not return to the scene.

This sudden chance for rescue followed by complete rejection left the sailors one and all with a feeling of despair. Still, there was one man with a glimmer of hope. He was the chief mate, Mr. Doncaster, who without telling anyone of his plan, now edged his way out to the end of the bowsprit. When he reached the tip of the jib boom, he was noticed by the captain and the sailors.

"Don't risk your life for us," cried the captain, but he was too late. Without a word the chief mate leaped from the end of the jib boom into the boiling tumult of surf. A great wave, much higher than the rest, appeared providentially, and seizing Doncaster in its grasp, it bore the mate right up the side of a towering rock to deposit him on its pinnacle. Clinging with both hands to a small ledge there, he managed to hold on while the wave receded. This miracle which had taken place before the eyes of the other survivors caused them to give a rousing cheer. But the mate had not yet reached safety, for there was a chasm of twenty feet between the pinnacle and the lowest part of the precipice across from the rock.

Studying the surf carefully as it hit the opposite cliff, Doncaster saw that several of the giant billows were reaching the top of the precipice at that point. He decided to get ready for a wave which might possibly deposit him atop the cliffs.

Realizing his plans, several of the survivors gave a great shout as a giant breaker roared in toward the rock. Doncaster stood ready, and as the surge of the sea began to roar up the side of the boulder he was on, he released his hold and leaped into the foaming water. Higher and higher the gigantic wave took him, with Doncaster praying every moment that he would reach his goal. He knew that the life of all aboard the *Cumberland* depended on his getting across the chasm.

With great force the water smashed him ashore. Hit on the head, he lost consciousness, but when he awakened several minutes later he was safe on top of a projection of the precipice, with the men below on the wreck calling for him to get up and climb to the tree.

After recovering his senses sufficiently to stand, he climbed slowly to the brow of the cliff, finally reaching the location where the natives had been seen. He was now less than thirty feet away from the maintop.

A line was thrown across by the eager sailors still aboard, but it failed to reach him. A second and then a third attempt were equally unsuccessful, but the fourth try succeeded. Doncaster grasped the line and carried the end of it to the tree at the top of the cliff where he secured it. Waving to his companions that they could now attempt a crossing, he watched tensely as the first survivor started out hand over hand along the strand of rope.

Halfway between the mast and the precipice the sailor changed his method of travel, and throwing his leg over the rope for greater security, he finished his journey to the cliff by working his way along the line with both arms and legs.

The next one to attempt a crossing tied one end of a heavier rope around his waist. Slowly but surely he warped his way over the chasm between ship and cliff. Finally, arriving on the rocky ledge, he and the others carried the new line to the tree, and signaled for the tackle to be tied on and sent across. In this way an endless line was run between ship and tree, and the survivors could be pulled over the chasm by the efforts of both those on the ship and those ashore in the manner of a breeches buoy.

Now that an impromptu rescue arrangement had been set up on the cliff, the three passengers were sent ashore, followed by the surgeon, the owner of the vessel whose name was also Lawrence, Lieutenant Webber of the artillery, Mr. Verchild and Mr. Wood. Then one by one the remaining seamen landed safely on the cliff.

Finally only three men were left. Captain Lawrence and the two seamen preceding him were forced to warp themselves along the line without assistance from the wreck. The

captain was the thirty-first and final survivor to cross from
the maintop to safety on the cliff, and with his arrival on land
a great cheer went up.

Unfortunately, the troubles of the ship's company were not
over, for the entire countryside had been flooded to a depth
of more than five feet by the torrential rains which were still
falling.

Working their way down from the precipice the party of
thirty-one found themselves in water up to their shoulders,
and only by joining hands and proceeding slowly were they
able to make any progress toward the village of Saint John
which lay about three miles distant. Their path crossed fields
of sugar cane whose tops were barely visible above the flood.

After wading more than three hours through the deep
water, they reached Saint John, where they again found a
complete apathy among the natives who didn't seem to care
that the shipwrecked mariners were in need of help. Finally,
in desperation, Captain Lawrence invaded a tailor shop and
demanded dry clothes and shelter. The tailor gave them
clothes and took them to his home a short distance away,
where he furnished the sailors with temporary sleeping quarters and later with provisions.

While they were in the tailor's home waiting the ending of
the storm, the wind veered around again, this time to the
south, from which quarter it proceeded to blow with the same
force and violence as before. All the remainder of the fourth
of September and well into the morning of the next day the
gale continued, and by the time the storm came to an end the
wind had made a complete swing around half of the compass,
beginning from the north and ending from the south.

On the day the blow was over the destitute survivors again
made the journey to the shore which they found littered with
wreckage from the De Ruyter, the Serapis and their own craft,
the Duke of Cumberland. The thirty-two-gun De Ruyter,

with Captain Joseph Beckett in command, had gone ashore at Antigua, and not a soul of the 250 aboard was lost. The *Serapis*, although riding out the gale successfully, had much of her upper works destroyed.

For the next few days the men of the *Duke of Cumberland* hiked and scrambled along the beach and the rocky shores, retrieving their garments and supplies. They located their vessel, incidentally, high on a rocky shore on her beam ends, and every man who saw her knew that but for the daring of Chief Mate Doncaster most of them would have perished in the gale.

CHAPTER NINE

CAPTAIN RILEY

O God! Have mercy in this dreadful hour
On the poor mariner!

DOWN THROUGH THE CENTURIES the great coast of Africa has not been kind to the scores of American vessels wrecked along its shores, and there are those who feel that this section of the world's surface has united in a particular conspiracy with the sea to wreak vengeance on the luckless sailor. One memorable example was the brig *Commerce*. When her master, Captain James Riley,* sailed her from Middletown, Connecticut, on May 6, 1815, the *Commerce* was bound for New Orleans. While proceeding off the Florida coast, she hit on Carysfort Reef but was able to continue her journey.

Captain Riley regarded this as an ill omen, for he had sailed for many years and had never run aground before. Nevertheless, the *Commerce* reached New Orleans successfully,

---

* His great-grandson is Commodore James Riley Hodder who now lives in Framingham, Massachusetts. He is the senior ex-commodore of both the Winthrop Yacht Club, 1899-1901, and the Boston Yacht Club, 1926-1928.

took on a load of freight for Europe, and sailed for Gibraltar a short time later.

Leaving Gibraltar on August 23, 1815, the brig passed Cape Spartel the next day. Fog set in shortly afterward, and not until the twenty-eighth could the captain get another observation. At 10:00 that night he estimated that the *Commerce* should be about thirty miles north of Cape Bojador.

Then with the vessel running at ten knots in a strong breeze and high sea, Riley heard a great roaring from the ocean and found to his horror that breakers were forming under their lee. Before his orders to change course could be carried out the brig grounded.

It was soon apparent that the *Commerce* couldn't be saved. The captain ordered all possible provisions to be brought on deck with as much water as possible drawn from the large casks.

By this time the seas were making a clean breach over the ship, but the shore was not far away. Telling the others to stay aboard, Riley took his mate, Mr. Porter, with him and started for land in the small boat. Swamped almost at once, they drifted toward the beach but were swept along by the current 300 yards at least when a great wave caught them and threw them up on the shore.

The captain now signaled for those on the wreck to send in a hawser. Before long Riley pulled the line out of the surf, secured it to a rock on the beach and then ordered the survivors out on the wreck to come in one by one.

Sailor John Hogan was the first to volunteer. He fought his way through each successive wave which engulfed him, pausing to get his breath after the billow swept by. But suddenly a terrific wave slid him against the hawser, loosened his grip and cast him near the shore several feet from where the captain awaited him. Riley and Porter rushed into the

surf and pulled the struggling sailor high above the reach of
the next breaker where he soon revived.

One by one the others of the crew came in over the line.
Their next task was to gather the provisions which had
washed ashore and carry them to a place of safety.

A short time afterward a native Arab appeared from the
south and slowly approached the party on the beach. He was
soon joined by others, including a girl whom Riley called
"not ugly" and five or six children, entirely naked. Finally
there were enough natives to overwhelm the Americans. Realizing their numerical superiority, they openly defied the white
men and fell to work plundering the spoils from the wreck,
breaking open trunks and chests.

Meanwhile the captain divided $1,000 among the crew,
hoping that if they were separated in some way the money
would help them to reach their homes. He then buried the
remaining $800 in two different locations in the sand.

The next decision was to repair the longboat and use it to
sail away from the country of savages, but the crew had
broken into a cask of wine and were in no mood for work.
Eventually the craft was repaired, but by this time night had
fallen and the natives had gone away. As there seemed to be
no immediate danger, Riley resigned himself to waiting another day and took stock of his situation. He was on a barren and inhospitable coast; the sea at the moment was too
rough to escape in that direction, and the natives were probably to return the next day and take them into slavery. He
awaited the coming of dawn with misgivings.

When daylight arrived, surely enough, the Arabs appeared
again, one old man ordering the captain away from the wreck.
Brandishing a twelve-foot spear, the savage tried to enforce
his wishes, but Riley fought him off as best he could until
two of the strongest natives seized him and he saw that further resistance was useless.

At low tide his crew had retreated to the vessel, and when the old Arab asked for money, the captain shouted to the men on the wreck to put their silver dollars into a bucket which he would send out. The sailors dropped scores of dollars into the receptacle until finally it was three-quarters filled. Then the bucket was sent ashore. The natives grabbed the money and began dividing their loot.

Captain Riley's arms were pinioned to his sides, but when the spoils were being divided the natives forgot to guard him. Watching his chances, he made an effort to escape. But he was seen, and the savages quickly captured him and brought him back.

His next move was to signal out to the brig. He asked one of the men to come in part way on the hawser and then stand in the surf out of reach of his captors but still close enough to discuss a plan the captain was formulating. Mr. Savage, the second mate, at length consented to come in on the hawser.

Riley shouted to Savage to send in the Negro lad, Antonio Michael, who might be able to reason with the natives. Antonio soon came in over the line, but when the natives found that he had brought no money, they beat him cruelly and would not listen to his entreaties for mercy.

The captain then told the natives by sign language that he had buried a considerable amount of money near the tent which had been erected on the beach. The natives literally fell over one another in their efforts to reach the shelter and start digging. Riley knew that when they found the $400 in Spanish currency which he had buried there the excitement would give him the last chance he would have to escape.

He later wrote in his journal: "I carefully drew up my legs under me, but without exciting suspicion, in order to be ready for a start. The place where they were digging was partly behind us on our right, and upon their making a noise near the tent both my guards turned their heads and eyes from me toward them, when I instantly sprang out from beneath their weapons, and flew to the beach. I was running for my life, and soon reached the water's edge. . . . I plunged into the sea with all my force head foremost, and swam under water as long as I could hold my breath; then rising to the surface, I looked round on my pursuers.

"An old man was within ten feet of me, up to his chin in water, and was in the act of darting his spear through my body, when a surf rolling over me, saved my life, and dashed him and his comrade on the beach.

"I was at some distance westward of the wreck. Swimming as fast as possible toward her, while surf after surf broke in towering heights over me, I was enabled, by almost superhuman exertions, to reach the wreck, when I was taken into the boat over the stern by the mates and people."

Captain Riley, overcome by his exertions, did not witness the terrible retribution for his escape on shore, when his crewman Antonio was beaten and cut by the natives. The victim begged for his life on his knees and then indicated to his captors that he had other knowledge of buried pieces of eight. Antonio took the Arabs to the other burial spot, and they dug up in rapid succession a new spy glass, a handsaw and a bag of 400 coins. But despite finding all the silver, they decided to avenge themselves on him for the escape of his captain. One of the savages was chosen to dispatch Antonio. Walking to the horrified seaman, the native plunged a spear clean through his body, and the lad died shortly afterward.

Captain Riley recovered his senses just in time to see the savages dragging the lifeless body of Antonio along the sandhills.

A conference was held on the wreck, and the captain suggested that there were only two plans possible. Both offered the risk of death. They could launch their longboat, now without either rudder or keel, and hope to make their way out to sea, or they could attempt to land on shore again before the natives returned in the morning. They agreed to leave by sea.

Meanwhile, as night wore on, the wind began to blow again. The surf soon was roaring in, hitting the *Commerce* and leaping up twenty and thirty feet high. Captain Riley realized that the wreck could not hold together indefinitely under such terrific battering. All that long night the waves smashed against the wreck.

Just before sunrise the deck and the outside timbers started to break off. The tide turned and began to come in rapidly, each wave jarring the wreck and separating more planking. A volunteer swam ashore to bring out two broken oars which had been placed above the high tide mark, and he was able to return before the natives appeared on the beach.

The captain realized that if they were going to sea in the longboat, drinking water was vital. Since the *Commerce* was at an angle on the ledge, he decided to attempt reclaiming one of the water casks between decks. Watching his chances as the waves roared by, he dove into the flooded hatchway, swam a few feet under water and then came out in the imprisoned air under the deck. Locating a water cask in the semidarkness, he tied it securely and swam back under water, pulling the cask behind him through the hatchway where the others on deck took it from him.

Then a live pig was discovered in the galley, and another bag of pieces of eight was located and put in the longboat.

Using a spar for a mast and the brig's foretopmast staysail, they rigged a sail. The tide now came in higher than ever. The men stood by their decision to leave the wreck and proceed to sea although the waves at the time were roaring in seven and eight feet high.

Then a miracle took place, described as follows in Captain Riley's account: "There appeared no possibility of getting through the breakers, and everyone trembled with apprehension. Each imagined that the moment we ventured past the vessel's stern would be his last.

" 'Let us pull off our hats.' I then said.

"It was done in an instant, when lifting up my eyes and soul to heaven, I exclaimed:

" 'Great Creator and Preserver of the Universe, who now see'st our distresses, we pray Thee to spare our lives, and permit us to pass through this overwhelming surf to the open sea; but if we are doomed to perish, THY WILL BE DONE! We commit our souls to Thee our God, who gave them. . . .'

"At this very moment, the wind, as if by divine command, stopped blowing, and the waves went down, only in one place, for a space which was about twenty yards wide, through which we rowed her out as smoothly as if she had been on a river in a calm, while on each side of us, the surf continued to break twenty feet high with unabated fury."

Then the captain observed that the wind was veering to the eastward, so that they passed the point of the Cape. Two days later on August 31, 1815, they killed their pig and divided it.

That night the weather was dark and threatening, and as Riley recorded, "the sky seemed big with an impending tempest." Before midnight another storm had hit the region, and the water swept into the longboat with such frequency that the men had to bail with their hats. The boat let in water at every seam. Sharp flashes of lightning now swept across the sky, making the scene even more horrible.

Morning came—the first of September, and thirst began to tell on the survivors. The wind blew all day long with violence. Worn out with fatigue, hunger and thirst, scorched by the tropical sun, and with no prospect of a vessel's appearing to rescue them, the men decided to go in toward shore again and take another chance with the savages.

It was on the morning of September 7 that land was discovered again, and the longboat's bow was turned toward it. Nearing shore, the survivors observed a high surf breaking on a rocky beach, but around sunset they noticed a small sandy shore and decided to land there.

A tremendous wave caught them and rushed them on toward the beach. Riley maneuvered the longboat right through the surf, and the craft smashed ashore so far up on the sand that it was left high and dry when the breaker receded.

The exhausted mariners clambered out of the boat with their belongings. They ate a few leftover fragments of pork and divided the pint of water which remained. Then they all lay down to rest and sleep.

On the morning of September 8 they started out to hike for a settlement, whatever it might be, because they knew they could not last more than a few days.

The captain now came to a decision. He still had many hundreds of the pieces of eight and agreed with the others that every bit of the money should be buried in the sand. He felt that the treasure had been the cause of their ill-treatment at the hands of the other natives and wished to avoid a similar occurrence.

Now they began their journey in earnest. Eventually they reached a region of great towering cliffs 500 and 600 feet high, and in their weakened condition the barriers presented almost insurmountable problems.

Vast masses of rocks, gravel and sand had given way and tumbled into the sea, and the men attempted to climb up the cliffs at this point. The sharp stones cut their shoes leaving their feet lacerated and bleeding. The rays of the hot sun on their bodies were unbearable. That afternoon Riley suffered an accident. "I broke my bottle and spilled the little water it contained, and my tongue, cleaving to the roof of my mouth

was as useless as a dry stick until I was able to loosen it by a
few drops of my more than a dozen times distilled urine."

Two days were spent in clambering among the rocks. Not
a single object of shelter was found. There was not a tree,
shrub or even spear of grass.

At sunset on the second day a sailor exclaimed, "I think
that I see a light." Surely enough, there was a gleam in the
distance. All the survivors were heartened at the news, but
it was decided to await the coming of morning before visiting
the source of the light.

Thus, early on September 10, 1815, the sailors started to
hike for the area where they had seen the glow of what evidently had been a great campfire. But before they were
within a hundred yards of the settlement which they could
see, a swarm of shouting natives started to rush for them.
Within the hour the sailors were seized and stripped of all
their clothes and possessions.

The Americans had momentary freedom while the savages
quarreled among themselves for the white men's belongings,
fighting each other with scimitars and clubs until the blood
ran down their bodies in streams. But finally all quieted down,
and the white men realized that what they had come upon
was a camp site of traveling camel dealers. The sailors were
told by gestures that they were prisoners who were to be
taken to the nearest village and sold as slaves, if they lived
that long.

The party now began to work its way into the great Sahara
Desert. As the survivors walked they found the burning sand
so soft that they sank below their ankles at every step. Meanwhile, the sun beat down relentlessly on their stark-naked
bodies.

The expedition continued all day long. Finally, when sunset came, camp was again made for the night.

The Arabian natives had been amused at the blundering

attempts of the New Englanders to walk through the sand, and it was agreed the following morning that the white men should travel on the camels. To Riley this was worse than before, for the camel chosen for him was extremely thin. The captain later stated:

"The backbone of the one I got on was only covered with skin, and as sharp as the edge of an oar's blade. His belly, distended with water, made him perfectly smooth, leaving no projection of the hips to keep me from sliding off behind, and his back or rump being as steep as the roof of a house, and so broad across as to keep my legs extended to their utmost stretch. The camel, extremely restive at the sight of his strange rider, was all the time running about among the drove, and making a most woeful bellowing; and as they have neither bridles, halters, or anything whereby to guide or govern them, all I had to do was to stick on as well as I could!"

Eventually Riley became so miserable from his cut feet, the bruises all over his body and the general hopelessness of his situation that he decided to commit suicide. Falling behind the caravan, he hunted for a large rock with which he could bash in his head. Unable to find a stone of any sort, he recovered his senses enough to give up his plan. By this time the caravan was far ahead, but in spite of his bleeding feet, the miserable mariner ran as fast as he could and rejoined the group as they were stopping for dinner.

On September 21 about the middle of the day, two strangers were sighted approaching the caravan and soon made contact with the group. It was learned that the two men were brothers and that they were returning to their homes in Morocco. The captain now saw a golden opportunity to escape from the natives and staked everything on a ten minute interview which he gained with the two men.

Explaining that he was worth heavy ransom should he be delivered at Mogadore, the great African seaport, and that his men were likewise valuable merchandise, Riley stated that the minute they arrived in that city the entire ransom money would be paid at once in gold. Of course, he was bluffing, but he had enough faith in himself to believe that he could arrange the ransom within a reasonable length of time after they arrived in Mogadore.

The two camel traders, whose names were Sidi Hamet and Seid, did not have money enough to purchase all the crew, but they bought Captain Riley, Savage, Horace, who was the cabin boy, Clark and Burns. The other members of the crew, because of the camel traders' limited funds, were left behind and "scattered in different parts of the desert." Not one was ever heard from again.

On October 1 the trip toward Mogadore began, and Riley soon found out that his new masters were much more humane than his former captors had been. Realizing how hungry the Americans were, Hamet bought an old camel, killed it and allowed all of his group to enjoy a sumptuous meal, after which he made shoes for the men from the camel's skin, and gave each one a coat of goatskin to protect him from the hot sun.

The days on the desert went by slowly. By October 17 the black tops of high mountains appeared in the distance to the eastward, and almost a week later the captain saw the ocean again. Here a band of wild Arabs attacked the travelers, but after much fighting, were beaten off. A short time later the two camel traders fell to blows while arguing about the division of their anticipated spoils, and the feud almost ended in death when each man grasped his pistol. However, Sidi Hamet, realizing that they had gone too far, discharged both his guns into the air, after which he presented his naked breast to his brother and dared him to fire. Seid declined, but "wreaked his vengeance" on the boy Horace, whom he seized and dashed to the ground, knocking the lad unconscious. He later recovered, however.

After suffering great hardships, the band arrived at Widnoon, or the River Noon, in the southern section of Suce. Three days later they entered Mogadore.

Fortunately for Captain Riley, the English Consul at Mogadore, Willshire by name, agreed to the suggested terms of ransom which the captain had outlined to the two camel traders, and the six sufferers were taken to the consul's home. There they were washed, clothed and fed, and no expense was spared in procuring for them every comfort.

"At the instance of Mr. Willshire I was weighed," stated Riley later, "and fell short of ninety pounds, though my usual weight for the last ten years had been over two hundred pounds; the weight of my companions was less than I dare to mention, for I apprehend it would not be believed that the bodies of men, retaining the vital spark, should not have weighed forty pounds!"

The British Consul was so good to Captain Riley and his party that the American never forgot it. Years later, when the captain became a land agent and moved westward, he settled at Celina, Ohio, where he named a town Willshire after the man who rescued him, and Willshire it is still known today. Many of his descendants today are named Willshire, in honor of the British Consul of Mogadore, Africa.

CHAPTER TEN

ELIZA BRADLEY'S SUFFERING

Till all exhausted, and bereft of strength,
O'erpowered they yield to cruel fate at length.

THE STORY OF Captain Riley, related in the previous chapter, was not the last time that the English Consul at Mogadore, Mr. Willshire, was to figure in the rescue of one of his countrymen from the hands of the Arabs, as the following tale will illustrate.

There are those who believe that the presence of a woman aboard a sailing vessel is a challenge to the sea. In the month of June, 1818, the ship *Sally* had an encounter with the ocean, and the subsequent sufferings of the wife of her master, Captain James Bradley, represent an epic that bears out this belief.

On May 18, 1818, Eliza Bradley left Liverpool aboard the *Sally* with her husband in command. They were bound for Teneriffe, with thirty-two members of the ship's company and Eliza the only woman on board.

A storm hit the ship five weeks after her departure, a terrible gale which lasted six days. Gradually the ship succumbed to the sea. First she developed a leak, and both pumps were put in operation. Then other leaks were detected, and soon the pumps were barely able to keep the water from gaining. The frightened members of the crew, aware that unless something were done the vessel would sink, appealed to Captain Bradley. The master agreed that the cargo would have to be thrown overboard to lighten the ship. This was done at once, and the vessel now appeared to be holding her own.

By the fifth day, as a reckoning was impossible in the storm, they had no idea of their position on the ocean, and Bradley knew that they were at the mercy of the sea.

In the evening of June 24 the gale began to subside, but a thick fog had developed. Shortly afterward breakers were heard, and the captain decided that the *Sally* should be put before the wind until land was sighted through the fog.

Just before midnight the roar of breakers increased, and without warning the ship struck with great force on a chain of rocks which ripped open her stern and she began to go to pieces.

The storm then returned in violence, and all the remainder of the night the survivors clung to the wreckage hoping that dawn would allow them to get ashore to safety.

But morning only made clearer the dangers ahead of them, for the gigantic waves were roaring in on the shore with such violence that no one would have survived had he cast himself into the ocean. All that day the thirty-two shipwrecked victims hoped for a lessening of the wind or calming of the seas, but afternoon gave way to night without the weather's improving, and not a single attempt had been made to leave the ship. Somehow, all survived through the long night, and when the following morning came, prayers were offered to God in thankfulness.

A short time later the wind and sea started to moderate, and Captain Bradley ordered the small jolly boat made ready for the dangerous trip to shore. All were anxious to go on the first journey through the surf, but finally the captain, his wife and several others started out. The jolly boat was swept through the terrific surf to a point high on the shore. Later the boat was taken out again for the remainder of the survivors to get aboard, and eventually all thirty-two were landed safely.

The coast was rocky, with cliffs more than 200 feet in height stretching in both directions, but the first efforts were spent not in trying to reach civilization, but in reclaiming as many articles from the wreck as possible. A barrel of flour, a keg of salt pork and some planking were secured before the wreck broke into pieces, but when the tide started to come in no further salvage was possible.

The captain realized that the ship had been wrecked on a dangerous part of the Barbary Coast, and that the survivors would probably be subjected to attack by the natives. As they had not rescued any weapons from the shipwreck, their position was grave.

Nevertheless something had to be done. Their greatest need was for drinking water, and so Bradley decided to hike with the others along the coast toward the southeast, hoping to locate a well or a stream. Mile after mile was traversed. Suddenly one of the sailors, who was walking out ahead, discovered a large bed of mussels, and the entire party stopped to satisfy their hunger.

They spent the night at that location and ate their fill of mussels again the next morning before they started walking. Thirty miles they traveled before stopping again for the night, but they found no water at all, and they had reached the great desert of Africa.

Finally, on the eve of the fourth day a brakish pool was discovered, and the members of the group quenched their thirst. Later, when the tide went down, they found another bed of mussels, and again feasted on the shellfish. In the same location a sailor discovered a dead seal, from which they cut slices of meat.

The journey in search of help continued, and cutting inland from the sea, which up to then they had followed, the survivors made some progress. The trip had been an exhausting one, and Eliza Bradley suddenly found herself unable to continue. The captain, deciding that he would stay with his wife, had the others go on in search of water, which was so sorely needed.

About two hours after they had departed, the sailors who had been hunting for water burst into the Bradley camp, out of breath and terribly frightened. They explained that they had been pursued by natives mounted on camels, who were even then close behind them. Hardly had they finished their tale when the savages appeared. Armed with muskets, spears and scimitars, they quickly took possession of the thirty-two white people.

Dismounting from their camels, the captors ripped off the clothing of the prisoners. The Arabs soon began to fight among themselves for the various articles of wearing apparel as well as for the survivors themselves. Soon many of them were severely wounded, and if it had not been for a sudden sharp order from their ancient sheik to stop, the natives might have annihilated each other.

Captain Bradley now implored the chieftain to furnish a drink for his thirsty party, and some slimy water was poured into a calabash and given to the sufferers. It was apparent to all of the survivors that they were now to be considered as merchandise too valuable to suffer hunger or thirst. Evidently they were to be sold into slavery for a handsome sum of money.

Mrs. Bradley was now mounted on a camel and given the privilege of riding astride a seat secured to the animal's hump. In this manner a jolting, swaying, exhausting ride began which was to be of several weeks' duration. Her husband and the other men were forced to stumble along in the heat of the desert day after day.

After intense suffering and the killing of one of the camels for food, the Arabs and their prisoners reached a small village where the Bradleys were put in separate quarters.

One afternoon Eliza watched with acute dismay as her husband was taken out of his prison, given to another group of natives and forced to hike with them away from the village and out of sight. She expected never to see him again. In her anguish she resorted to reading verses of scripture from a small Bible which her captors had allowed her to keep. Her favorite reading was from *Psalms* 50:15. "And call upon me in the day of trouble: I will deliver thee, and thou shalt glorify me."

A short time later her Arab captors ordered a new trek through the sands and broke camp at once. After further weeks of hardships, Eliza and the Arabs reached another village several days' journey from the remotest civilization. It had now been more than five months since Eliza had last seen the captain, and she had given up all hope of rescue. One day in the village, however, her attention was attracted by the approach of a strange Arab who introduced himself to her.

"How de dow, Christiano," he said as he gave her a letter which he had brought to the village. Stunned for a moment, Eliza stared at it and then happiness lighted her face as she recognized her husband's writing on the envelope. She almost fainted with joy before she could open it. Excitedly she ripped off the envelope and read as follows:

MOGADORE, December 10, 1818

My dear Eliza—

This will inform you that I am no longer a slave—by the blessing of God, I once more enjoy my liberty—I was brought to this place with three of my crew by the Arabs, a few days since, and humanely redeemed out of their hands by our excellent consul (Mr. Willshire) who resides there. I have informed him of your situation, and he has kindly offered me his assistance in effecting your redemption and restoring you to liberty—the bearer of this letter (should he be so fortunate as to find you) is a man in whom you may place the utmost reliance, and who will conduct you in safety to this place, should your master be pleased to comply with the proposals of Mr. Willshire, to whom he has directed a letter written in Arabic, offering seven hundred dollars for your redemption, provided he conveys you in safety to this place.

I am affectionately yours, &c.
JAMES BRADLEY

After reading the letter she asked permission to enter a nearby tent, where she offered her prayers of thankfulness to God. Returning to the men, she was told that a caravan would start immediately for Mogadore, 700 miles away.

Finally, seated on a fresh camel, Eliza began the tortuous journey back to civilization. Almost twenty days went by before the caravan reached the outskirts of Mogadore. Tears of joy came to her eyes when she saw the great harbor with the ships of many nations. Within an hour Eliza was in the arms of her husband, and the long separation had ended.

Two weeks went by before she was well enough to sail for Liverpool, but on February 1, 1819, the Bradley family, together with the six sailors who had been ransomed, left Mogadore for home. Forty days later when they landed in England their hardships were but memories.

CHAPTER ↕ ELEVEN

GEORGE FRAKER

Hark! Pity, hark!
Now mounts, now totters on the tempest's wings,
Now grounds and shivers the replunging bark!
Cling to the shrouds! In Vain!

ON WASHINGTON'S BIRTHDAY, 1817, the ship *Ocean* lay at anchor in the Plata River in South America. Shortly after sunrise Mr. George Fraker of Boston, one of the crew, observed a strange freak of weather.

It was then 7:30 in the morning, and a great dust cloud, called by the natives a pampero, was sighted proceeding along the coast about two miles away. The chief mate knew what to expect, however, and shouted a command.

"Stand by the cable tier; jump down and be ready to pay out; bear a hand, my hearties, for there's a pampero coming, driving all the world before it!"

And even as he spoke the huge black mass grew larger and larger, soon extending like night itself over almost half the horizon. A moment later the entire ship, lying broadside to the shore, was engulfed in total darkness.

At the moment Fraker was moving from the amidships section to the helm so that he could help bring the ship into the wind. But before he could reach his objective, a tremendous gust struck the ship, nearly capsizing her, and Fraker clutched the rail in desperation. The anchor cables began to drag, and all aboard thought that drowning would be their fate.

Fraker looked across toward shore where brilliant sunlight was still shining and then glanced in the other direction where everything was buried in impenetrable darkness.

Suddenly, as rapidly as it had come, the darkness lifted. George could now see the one shoreline again brilliant with sunshine, while the other which had been bright and visible was now wrapped in darkest gloom.

Twenty minutes later the wind went down and the chief mate discovered that no serious damage had been sustained. Every member of the ship's company was now covered with thick, black, heavy soot, however. The day continued to be boisterous and rainy after those few minutes of brilliant sunshine which followed the pampero, but except for occasional claps of thunder there was no real storm.

George Fraker had joined the crew of the *Ocean* as a mate in order to see the world, but when the ship's destination was changed in April and plans were made to sail back to Boston, George decided to obtain a release, and stayed in Buenos Aires to await a berth which might bring him adventure and travel of an unusual nature. It did!

In the month of May, 1817, he signed aboard the English ship *Jane* as second officer with Captain William Seaboth, bound from Buenos Aires to Brazil. Unfortunately, while the local pilot was in charge, the *Jane* struck on the bar, and the ship was forced to return to port for rudder repairs which took six weeks. Then, after a passage of twenty days, the *Jane* arrived in Rio de Janeiro.

On the third of September, 1817, the *Jane* sailed for Montevideo with a great cargo of rum, sugar, tobacco, flour, butter, rice and dry goods. On board as passengers were two Spaniards, a German, an Englishman and an American. Four slaves, who belonged to the last three mentioned passengers were also on the ship, and there were fourteen members of the crew, making twenty-three in all aboard the *Jane*.

Two weeks later they reached the Island of Flowers, fifteen miles away from Montevideo. As a gale began to blow, the *Jane* anchored. When Fraker came on deck at midnight, he went forward to examine the state of the cables in the hawse-holes, and then looked out on the sea. Observing breakers which had not been sighted a short time before, he concluded that the *Jane* was slowly moving. He expressed his opinion to the boatswain who thought it was merely the curl of the waves, not real breakers on a lee shore.

Fraker, however, was certain the ship was pulling her anchors and was working toward her doom in the breakers. He rushed below to arouse Captain Seaboth and all hands. At 12:15, as the captain reached the deck, the *Jane* struck heavily in the surf, and immediately waves began to smash into the ship.

All hands were now on deck, some in nightclothes, others completely naked and still others half-dressed. Everyone was struck with horror because of his own immediate peril.

"Cut away the masts!" shouted Seaboth, but it was discovered that the carpenter was sick below in his hammock, and there wasn't an ax available, so that the others were helpless to act.

The sea was now making a complete breach over every part of the ship, and George believed that the craft would soon break up. He threw off his pea jacket and hat and took a position in the mizzen top.

As his wet feet had lost circulation, he took off his shoes and slapped his hand repeatedly against his numbed toes, trying to regain feeling in them. Down below him he could see his shipmates being swept one by one to their death in the waves.

Fraker, from his perilous position in the mizzen top, watched in fascinated awe as the great ship began to go to pieces. The long boat was shattered and the small boat carried away. Then the mainmast crashed into the sea, and George felt the mizzen top starting to fall. Soon he was plunged into the ocean.

Swimming back, he scrambled aboard the ship where he made his way along the rigging as he found that every plank of the main deck had washed away. A great wave surged into the wreck pinning a beam against George's knee and trapping him under water with his head barely free. Another wave lifted the timber overboard and swept George also into the boiling tumult of the ocean.

While struggling to keep afloat, Fraker was suddenly grabbed from behind by a passenger whom he recognized as Señor Monasteria, a Spanish engineer. Terrified, the engineer clung desperately to George's neckerchief, choking him and forcing him down under the water. To save his own life he tried to untie the neckerchief. After a few frantic moments he succeeded in undoing the knot, slipped the silken tie off and watched horrified as the engineer sank to his death still clutching the neckerchief. While he was able to swim himself, George knew that both would have perished unless he had broken the Spaniard's hold on him.

Fraker swam toward shore through the tremendous waves, dodging timbers from the wreck. Struck from behind by a bale of goods, he pulled himself on top of it with difficulty. The improvised raft began dipping and pitching under his weight and when a particularly vicious breaker upset the bale to force George under water, the Bostonian realized that his strength was slowly leaving him.

Struggling desperately, he managed to reach the surface, and breathed deeply of the pure air, but a moment later another wave forced him under and this time he knew he didn't have the strength to fight for survival.

"Lord Jesus, receive my spirit," he thought to himself, and then his senses forsook him. At that very instant his mind was filled with the most singular and delightful sensation. When he came to again, he found himself floating on the surface of the sea. Close at hand was a large crate filled with straw, to which he attached himself.

As he clung to the crate the seas continued to break over him and push him toward shore. Then minutes later he found that the waves had carried him inside a relatively quiet lagoon. When his foot touched a sandy bottom he stood up waist deep, but the pain from his injured knee was too great, and he fell back. Crawling into shallow water he finally reached the shore where he lay for some time getting back his strength and his breath.

An hour later he again tried to stand, but the pain still prevented him. He toppled over on the shore, blood gushing from several of his wounds. It was then that he prayed for death. "His stroke would have been welcome," Fraker confided later, "not as the dread king of terrors, but as the hope-inspiring countenance of meek-eyed mercy."

Surveying the area, he found himself on the shores of a desolate country with no signs of habitation. As he lay shivering on the beach he saw a large cask of wine which had washed ashore from the cargo. His first instinct was for protection from the cold. The idea came to him that he could break the cask open and crawl inside to protect himself from the wind and cold. He stove in the wood, allowing the wine to flow out over him as he drank the liquid. Then, with the barrel empty, he crawled inside, arranging his body as best he could on two pieces of the head staves. The fumes of the wine overwhelmed him, and he fell exhausted into a deep sleep.

It was not until the following afternoon when he awakened. He crawled out of his shelter and decided to explore the area. George found that while he was unable to proceed normally forward because of his knee, he could walk backward, lifting his injured leg with his right hand. In this manner he climbed up over a sand dune to the other side, out of the wind. Here he dug a hole in the side of the dune, covering himself over with the wet sand as soon as the hole was deep enough, for the weather was intensely cold and raw.

After sufficient rest he awakened to find himself thirsty and hungry, and immediately began to explore the locality for water. In the distance he saw what appeared to be a pond, and finally he reached it and quenched his thirst.

Returning to the scene of the shipwreck, Fraker discovered another large cask of wine still unopened, and approached it slowly. It had been thrown far above the normal tide during the storm and had fallen in a sheltered place. George took it for his home after emptying the wine from it. Later he discovered some rolls of cotton bagging a great distance down the beach, and after much effort separated about ten fathoms from one of the rolls and carried the material back to his cask.

Arranging the cotton on the circular bottom of the huge barrel, George crawled inside and pulled half of the cloth over him. Thus he was protected both from the curving insides of the cask and the cool weather as well.

He stayed in this shelter for the remainder of the day and the following night, but when dawn came hunger and thirst forced him to crawl out again. On the shore he found a small, empty keg which he carried to another full wine cask. He knocked out the bung and after rinsing the keg, he filled it with wine. Not until this was accomplished did he drink deeply from the bung hole. Then he set out with the keg of wine, eventually reaching his own cask where he had spent the previous night.

Fraker realized that he would never see his mother and father back in Boston unless he took steps to reach civilization. Far in the distance he had noticed the overturned small boat or jolly boat, and the following day he started hiking toward it, in spite of his injured leg. After suffering excruciating pain in his knee, he reached the side of the craft.

At that very moment he heard the clop-clopping of hoofbeats, and his thoughts went at once to the stories of the mounted cannibals of the vicinity. Deciding that come what may, he was ready, he sat down at once on the sand. A moment later he glanced up, and there was a horse and rider a few feet away from him.

When the horseman approached, George looked up at him and shouted in Spanish, "Amigo, friend!" The horseman was dressed partly in Indian costume. Apparently he was shocked by what he saw, for George's face, beard and legs were all heavily covered with sand, and covered by only a shirt, the survivor presented a sad appearance to the visitor.

His caller proved to be a Creole Indian. Dismounting, he walked over to George, observing that Fraker was covered with cuts and bruises and that his right leg had swollen terribly.

"You are lucky," he told George in Spanish, "that I found you first, for the cannibals are all around here and would have killed you at once had they known of the shipwreck and of you being here on the beach. They are merciless and terribly ferocious."

The Indian galloped away to search for some food for George, and within the hour he returned bringing a warm sausage and some moldy bread wrapped up in a towel. The sailor greedily seized it and took a big bite. To his amazement he found that he couldn't swallow a mouthful, for his throat was shrunken and sore.

Seeing this, the Indian then made plans to remove George to his hut, and rode away to get others to help him. While he was gone the injured man again heard the gallop of a horse and saw a murderous looking savage, or gaucho, who rode up to within a few feet and then dismounted, striding across to the survivor.

"Who are you?" he asked in Spanish.

"A shipwrecked mariner."

"The captain, perhaps?"

"No, I was the mate, and a person has just discovered me and gone for aid. He will be back right away."

"Which way did this man go?"

"Toward the south."

With this answer the gaucho sprang upon his mount and galloped away, but to George's dismay he soon reappeared with several other gauchos seemingly for the purpose of putting the shipwrecked sailor to death. Just in time the friendly Indian returned, bringing with him his father and several others.

At this show of strength the gauchos galloped away, deciding to plunder what remained of the cargo near another lagoon a mile away. His new friend, who introduced himself as Pedro, then opened one of the passengers' trunks, which had been cast ashore nearby, and pulled out a suit of clothes and underwear, advising George that he might lose caste unless he appeared as a ship's officer should.

George agreed and attempted to dress himself, but his leg was so terribly swollen by this time that he was unable to do more than don a pair of loose drawers, a waistcoat and a coat.

The others then lifted him on the back of a waiting pony. When they saw that he would fall off without some assistance, Pedro mounted the pony in front of him, suggesting to

George that he put his arms around him and hold tight as they rode.

At this moment General Ortigues, who commanded the troops in the vicinity, came riding up with a guard of soldiers. He questioned Fraker for some time about the ship and the disaster, and then rode across to the scene of the wreck itself.

Without further delay George and his party started for the cottage where his new-found friend lived. As soon as they approached, several fierce-looking dogs began to bark at them, but Pedro quieted them and everyone dismounted. Fraker was carried into the hut and introduced to Pedro's mother, who, after sitting him on a chair and stripping off his wet clothing, put him to bed.

The old woman went out into the yard where she seized a fowl and killed it and then made some excellent broth which she fed the patient. After this she washed his leg with hot vinegar and dressed his wounds as best she could.

That night George drank great amounts of wine and water. The old lady had wrapped two junk bottles * filled with boiling water and placed them in the bed against his feet, for he could feel no sensation in either foot. At first there was just numbness, and then the sudden shock of returning circulation caused excruciating pain.

When dawn broke the old lady came to him and told him it was the Sabbath morning, September 21, and that he was to rest and relax as best he could.

As he lay there in bed Fraker looked around the dwelling and discovered at the end of the hut a crucifix with two candles burning on each side. Outside a kitchen had been built. The room where he lay was quite comfortable. There were a few hidebound chairs, some hide sacks, baskets, a hide sieve and a table. The hut itself was made of cane fastened together

---

* Stout bottles of thick dark-colored glass.

with strips of green hide and plastered with mud. It had a thatched roof.

On the following afternoon the general visited the hut, bringing with him several more bottles of wine and cordial taken from the beach. George decided to ask his visitor to help him.

"General Ortigues," he began, "I would like to send a letter to Montevideo."

"I do not know," answered General Ortigues. "There is no mail service and I would have to send a special messenger. But you write the letter and I'll try to have it delivered."

And so the next day George asked the old lady for paper and pencil, and then began the tedious business of writing a letter giving the details of the shipwreck to W. P. White, Esquire, the only person he knew in Montevideo. He also wrote another letter to be sent to Buenos Aires where the owners of the cargo lived. Two days later the letters were delivered.

Meanwhile Pedro and his workmen were down at the wreck, removing articles and provisions from the beach. The shore, George was informed, was now literally crowded with natives from all around who were breaking open trunks, chests and bales of goods, staving in casks of wine, plundering, fighting and drinking to excess.

The Indians of the region were giants in size, with long black hair which hung down like so many snakes from their shoulders. They wore a coarse blanket wrapped around the middle and another, with a hole, through which they thrust their heads. Their boots were of horseskin, worn raw in the shape of their feet. They looked like a band of demons. All of them wore large knives stuck in sheaths, weapons which they used for every purpose, to kill cattle, cut up beef, eat meat and stab their fellow creatures.

General Ortigues decided to leave a guard of several soldiers at the hut to prevent trouble, for the savages seemed to be planning a raid. During the next few days George Fraker had several visitors, each of whom wished to see the sole survivor of the terrible shipwreck, whose patron saint must have favored him highly to allow him to live when all his shipmates had perished in the sea.

Several of his visitors were women, and three of them met one afternoon to confer as to how he should best be cured. The result of the consultation was that they recommended the use of the large leaf of a native bush with medicinal properties.

Copious applications of this herb, dipped in oil and vinegar, were made, and although the knee was acutely painful after each dressing was applied, the swelling went down after several nights. George claimed that his injured limb was so sensitive that for some time it responded with intensified pain to every change in the wind.

Now that he was improving, the patient began to eat tremendous amounts of food and drank everything which came within his reach, always keeping several bottles of wine under his pillow for the night's supply. He also arranged for a small boy to do nothing but carry water to him, of which he drank at least five gallons daily for ten days!

All this time his pain was so intense that he often sang to kill the ache. This caused the old lady much consternation, for she feared that he was becoming delirious.

One night the dogs set up a great howl, and the guards left at the hut by the general were alerted. Suddenly, five hideous characters armed with swords and bayonets presented themselves at the door. Amazed when the guards appeared, the ruffians beat a hasty retreat, rebuffed by the general's foresight in their attempt to kill the American.

On the eighth day of his confinement, two clerks arrived from Montevideo to visit the Bostonian. They attempted to secure some of the property from the shipwreck, but by this time everything of value had been carried away by the natives and the Indians. Since they had been roughly handled by the natives, the clerks vowed that they would not go near the wreck again for any amount of money, and they slept that night at the hut. In the morning they decided to take George back with them to Montevideo and sent for a cart to carry him.

When the transportation finally arrived, Fraker said good-by to his kind-hearted hosts as they placed him tenderly in the wagon and covered him with blankets. The trip to Montevideo began and at 2:00 that afternoon the cortege arrived outside the gates of the city. Word of disaster always travels quickly, and as the cart jolted through the streets, the sole survivor of the shipwreck became the center of attention.

The patient and his escorts stopped at the home of the English merchant who had owned much of the cargo. He came out at once and assisted by his servants, carried George upstairs to his bedroom. It was twenty long days before he was able to walk, even around the room, and another week before he was permitted to go downstairs.

During Fraker's convalescence one of the owners of the ship visited him to hear the account of the disaster. He immediately began collecting a fund for Pedro and the poor mother who had taken care of the survivor. But before the money could be sent to her, the shocking news came that Pedro had been murdered by merciless savages the very night that George had been taken away.

Nevertheless, $400 was eventually raised and presented to Fraker, who all this time was gaining in strength. Several weeks later he was able to take passage for Buenos Aires, 110 miles away, on the opposite side of the river. Arriving there the day after leaving Montevideo, he found a great number of friends who welcomed him as though he returned from the dead.

George still suffered from lameness, and it was not until the month of July, 1818, that he was considered well enough to attempt the long trip to the United States.

Leaving Buenos Aires on July 12, 1818, he arrived in Baltimore on September 12 and soon embarked for Boston. He sailed by historic Boston Light on October 4, after an absence of more than two years. Hastening to the home of his parents who had feared that they might never see him again, he told them of his terrible ordeals, and when he had finished, they thanked God for his return.

George Fraker went to sea for many years after his terrifying experiences in South America, but needless to say he never forgot the disaster which befell the ill-fated ship *Jane*, and the trick of fate which left him the sole survivor.

CHAPTER ♦ TWELVE

WRECK OF THE *Albion*

O! I have suffer'd
With those that I saw suffer: a brave vessel,
Who had, no doubt, some noble creatures in her,
Dashed all to pieces.

IT HAS ALWAYS been claimed by students of Napoleonic history that the wreck of the packet ship *Albion* on a lonely part of the Irish coast in the year 1822 was preordained. Others feel that it was the vengeance of the sea taking effect on the life of one Lefebvre-Desnouettes, trusted and gifted general on the staff of the great Napoleon.

On April 1, 1822, the *Albion* sailed from New York, bound for Liverpool, under the command of Captain John Williams. The voyage was uneventful for the first twenty days. Land was sighted at 1:00 on the afternoon of Sunday, April 21, at Fastnet Rock, Ireland. At 2:00 the vessel made Cape Clear, a distance of about two leagues.

The weather now came in thick and foggy, with the wind blowing fresh and heavy squalls sweeping from the southward, but Captain Williams was not carrying too much sail at the time. Nevertheless, two hours later when they were under double-reefed topsails, foresail and mainsail, a sudden squall carried away the foreyard and split the fore topsail. The gale then began to increase, and the mainsail and the mizzen topsail were taken in, with the main trysail set.

When night fell the wind lulled and the conversation returned to what would be done in a relatively few hours when port was reached.

Suddenly, just before 9:00, a gigantic sea which apparently came from nowhere struck the *Albion*, throwing her over at once on her beam ends. The wave carried away the mainmast by the deck and the heads of the mizzen mast and fore topmast. At the same time the breaker swept the decks clear of everything, including the boats, caboose house and bulwarks, staving in all the hatches and staterooms and filling the cabin with water. One passenger and six seamen were swept overboard as the wave roared across the deck reducing the *Albion* to a shattered hulk in one instant.

The captain was stunned by the suddenness of the disaster. To keep the vessel afloat he ordered all the survivors to take a turn at the pumps. There was no shelter for those not working at the pumps as the furniture in the cabin was afloat and the entire ship was in total darkness, and so the survivors huddled wherever they could.

At 1:00 in the morning of the twenty-second, the gleam of Old Head Light, Kinsale, Ireland, was seen in the sky, but the officers could not agree upon a proper bearing. An hour later the ship was embayed, now being battered toward shore at a rate of three knots. Nearer and nearer the sea pushed her toward the jagged cliffs which Captain Williams knew were awaiting them. Finally he could delay no longer. Gathering the survivors together as best he could, he revealed that there was no hope that the *Albion* could avoid hitting shore on a part of the Irish coast dreaded by mariners because of its high rocky cliffs. His listeners reacted in various ways to his terrible news, some with prayer, others with stoicism, anger or hopeless submission.

At 3:00 the vessel crashed against a rocky ledge some distance from shore, her upper works being carried over the outer reef to fetch up on the inner ledge immediately under a towering 200-foot cliff. The captain and two others were swept away to their death almost at once.

As the mighty seas began to smash the ship apart, the hopelessness of the situation soon became apparent to everyone. A wave would pick up a section of the deck and shatter it to pieces against the rocky cliff until nothing but kindling wood remained. There seemed to be little hope that anyone would be saved.

Finally Mate Henry Cammyer decided to swim to a projecting rock a few rods from the wreck. He succeeded in reaching the pinnacle and getting a handhold there. Other members of the crew followed him, until there were seven on the rock. Then a wave struck the ledge, and two men were swept off into eternity.

Many of the crew and passengers aboard the ship drowned on the deck itself, which was now under water, for the lower part of the ship had simply been smashed away.

A passenger named Everhart, who was from Chester, Pennsylvania, had been so ill that he remained below at first. Finally he staggered out on deck just in time to have a woman fall against him. She implored him to save her, but another wave billowing in over the deck forced him to release her and hold on for himself with both hands, and she sank under water on the quarterdeck, with the following wave drowning her before his eyes.

Meanwhile, across on the sea-swept pinnacle, the mate had recovered enough of his strength to discuss with the other survivors on the rock the possibility of scaling the perpendicular cliff above them. They agreed that if he would lead they would follow. Watching his chances, he began to climb up the overhanging precipice, and when nearly at the top he noticed that the others were starting up behind him. All five crew members reached safety at the pinnacle of the rocky ledge, the first to be saved from the sea.

After they had rested sufficiently they began to explore the country in the vicinity. A short time later they found a small cottage half a mile away from the wreck where they were cared for by the occupants. One of the residents was sent to the home of Mr. Purcell, a leading citizen of Garretstown, to notify him of the disaster.

Mr. Purcell immediately made plans to visit the shipwreck, which he reached shortly after dawn. He had brought hundreds of feet of rope with him, and in spite of the terrible seas then running he and several others descended over the cliff as close as they dared to the *Albion* which they found in terrible condition.

The cargo had spewed out of the hold, with cotton, rice, beeswax, turpentine, gold and silver scattered in all directions, and the dead bodies of more than a score of the victims littered the deck and washed back and forth around the nearby rocks. Five corpses were side by side on the deck. Four other victims also on the deck were still alive calling out feebly for assistance. One of them was a woman. About forty feet stood between them and their would-be rescuers who, because of the roaring seas, had no means of reaching them. Every few moments the waves crashed in with unbelievable force, first onto the wreck and then against the base of the overhanging cliff.

At the moment a large section of the ship was suspended against a sloping rock. Part of the stern where the woman clung projected over a narrow gully which divided one rock from another. A moment later the stern broke apart, and the woman went to her death in the sea.

One of three men, all members of the crew, who had been swaying back and forth on a suspended fragment of spar, now attempted to clamber down across to the rock below him. From above, Mr. Purcell attracted the man's attention and then threw him the end of a line. The man failed to grasp it. Again Purcell threw and again the man missed. It was only on the fifth attempt that he secured the rope. Fastening it around his waist, he leaped toward shore and was hoisted out of the surf to safety a minute later. A short time after this rescue a second man succeeded in clambering down on the spar and catching a line; he too was hauled to the relative security of the cliffs a moment later.

Unfortunately, an instant afterward the quarterdeck disintegrated before the startled eyes of the watchers on the cliff, and soon there wasn't a living person in the wreckage.

Another large fragment of the *Albion* had become wedged under a pulpit-like cleft some distance away, and there were many still alive aboard that wreckage. Among these people was the most distinguished passenger aboard, General Lefebvre-Desnouettes. Early in Napoleon's career the general had taken part in the combination against Louis XVIII, and when his old commander landed from Elba he joined wholeheartedly in the activities which followed. After Napoleon's final banishment to St. Helena, Desnouettes was able to escape to the United States. Retiring to the French grant in Alabama, he had labored vigorously in the fields, working so hard that he had ruined his health.

Finally, with the knowledge that his wife still awaited him in France, he petitioned the French government to be allowed to return to his native country in peace. Permission had been granted, and the general embarked for home on the ill-fated *Albion*. Having desired to remain anonymous during the voyage, the general had grown a beard. Just before the crash he had broken his arm. He and two others were still in the cabin at that time.

General Lefebvre Desnouettes probably felt that there was little hope of his being saved, because after the ship was dashed against the ledge he never appeared on deck again. It is believed that he later drowned in the cabin.

Another important personality aboard the wreckage of the *Albion* was Professor Fisher of Yale, an instructor in mathematics and natural philosophy, who was planning a speaking tour of Europe. Fisher was last seen by Mr. Everhart, who, when he left the cabin, noticed the professor standing as though he were trying to make up his mind about something. Everhart said later that Fisher never followed him out on the deck, probably drowning along with the brilliant French general in the ruins of the cabin.

Everhart had struggled desperately to gain a hand hold on the deck. He had been seasick every day of the voyage and had hardly come out of the cabin during all that period of time. Now, with the packet a hopeless wreck and fragments of the ship disintegrating rapidly, he was to accomplish a feat which would long be remembered.

After watching several of the other passengers lose their lives by being washed overboard, Everhart spoke for a moment to Major William Gough of the British 68th Regiment about their chances for survival.

"Death," answered the major, "come as He will, is never a welcome visitor, but we must meet Him like men!"

Impressed by the manner in which Major Gough expressed himself, Everhart gained renewed courage to fight for his life. While the others stood around waiting the expected breaking up of the *Albion*, Everhart made a solemn resolve to save himself when the crisis arrived.

At this moment the fragment of wreckage on which he

stood seemingly raised itself into the air, evidently projected
by some underwater force. Frantically Everhart climbed to
the very top of the remains of the *Albion*. The wreckage
began to shift, and the next wave lifted it bodily toward the
shore where it soon caught on another pinnacle of rock and
then began to go to pieces. Realizing his predicament, Everhart decided to get a firm hold on the rock before the timbers
disintegrated, and accomplished his purpose just in time. He
was now the only passenger on the pinnacle, every one of
the others having been washed overboard.

A moment later, however, he saw several heads floating in
the sea, together with a fragment of the stern which had
broken off, and then watched as the survivors grabbed at the
rock where he was clinging. One of them, Colonel Au-
gustine J. Prevost, remarked as he clambered up on the rock
that he "was another poor fellow."

Eventually there were several men on the pinnacle. Three
critical hours went by and all clung desperately to their
perch. Then the tide started to come in again, and the waves
crashed higher and higher. Soon the holds of those clinging
to the lower part of the rock were loosened, and one by one
they were swept to their death in the sea. At last there was
only one man left with Everhart on the pinnacle, a person
he did not know. As a wave crashed up the sides of the rock,
the man felt himself slipping and made a desperate grab at
Everhart's leg almost pulling the latter loose. Everhart determined to hang on. The man then lost his grip, slid down
the rock, dropped into the waves and drowned.

The hours went by. First Everhart would stand with one
foot on the ledge, and then the other, his hands always firmly
clinging to the pinnacle.

Finally, he noticed several men with ropes descending over
the precipice, and he shouted across at them. One of the
men, Mr. James B. Gibbens, tossed Everhart a line which

the stranded man tied around his body. Giving a signal that he was ready, Everhart was pulled across to land. Mr. Gibbens had the survivor taken to his home, where it was several weeks before he recovered from his grim ordeal.

On being notified of the disaster, the American consul, a Mr. Marks, had hurried to the scene of the wreck. As the bodies came ashore, he supervised the burial of the victims at the nearby Templetrine Churchyard, four miles from the disaster.

Among the bodies washed up on a neighboring beach was that of the beautiful Madame Gardiner of Paris, whose naked corpse came ashore with hardly a mark on it. One of the group assisting in the burial of the dead was so overcome that he removed his own overcoat and covered the remains.

After his convalescence Mr. Everhart sailed to Liverpool on the next packet and told his friends there that the Irish people could not have treated him more tenderly "had I been a brother."

Everywhere that Everhart went in Liverpool he attracted attention as the only passenger saved from the terrible disaster which befell the *Albion*.

CHAPTER THIRTEEN

WRECK OF THE
NEW BEDFORD WHALER *Mentor*

> *Full fathom five thy father lies;*
> *Of his bones are coral made.*

STRANGELY ENOUGH, not quite half a century after the wreck of the packet *Antelope* * survivors of another wreck came again to the Pelew Islands. The New Englanders who took refuge at the island were to receive far different treatment from the savages although they were met by descendants of the same tribe of natives who had been so friendly to Captain Wilson and his men.**

In the month of July, 1831, there cleared from New Bedford Harbor in Massachusetts the whaler *Mentor*, with Captain Edward C. Barnard her master. Her first stop was the Azores, after which the whaler doubled the Cape of Good Hope, sailing between Africa and Madagascar to reach the

---

* See Chapter Four.
** An East India Company ship on January 21, 1791, arrived at Pelew to tell Abba Thulle of his son's death. Abba Thulle died several months later and was succeeded by Arra Kooker who died about 1815.

Indian Ocean. The ship was unable to pass through the Straits of Timor because of adverse conditions, and ran down the Island of Mortay to its furthermost point, where her course was altered for the Ladrone Islands.

After leaving Mortay Island, the ship was struck by a violent gale which lasted three days during which time an observation was impossible. All sails were taken in except the topsail, which was close reefed, the foresail and the fore topmast staysail.

At 11:00 on the night of May 21, 1832, just as the watches were being relieved, the *Mentor* struck a coral reef which made out from the Pelew Islands. Smashing into the sharp ledges three times within a minute, the whaler swung around, bringing her starboard side to windward, and a moment later went over on her beam ends.

It was a critical moment for all hands. Captain Barnard stumbled out on deck to ask the second mate, in charge at the time, if he could see land anywhere. After a hasty glance around the mate answered that he believed that he could see evidences of land to leeward. He now ordered the larboard quarter boat lowered, and ten of the crew leaped into it, cut the lines which held the oars and pushed off from the *Mentor*. Not one of them was ever seen or heard from again! The next morning the remains of the mate's boat were discovered on several jagged rocks some fifty yards from the ship, bottom up, with all sides stove in.

A short time after the quarter boat pushed away, the captain ordered his own boat to be made ready, although several members of his crew implored him to wait until the great seas then running quieted down. The masts were first cut away, righting the ship slightly, and then the captain's boat was lowered.

Captain Barnard, Charles Bouket, William Sedon and William Jones clambered aboard. Around his waist the captain had tied a 400-foot line, the other end of which was secured aboard the *Mentor* so that he could be towed back to the ship should the boat meet with a mishap.

Just as they were about to push away, a mighty wave smashed into the *Mentor*, crushing the boat and breaking it into a hundred fragments. Jones was killed immediately. Bouket swam back to the *Mentor* and was helped aboard the ship in safety. Sedon also managed to get back aboard the wreck, but the captain had seemingly disappeared. Then the sailors, finding Barnard's line taut, started to haul it in. Peering through the darkness, they sighted him almost 400 feet away as they pulled him through the rolling seas. The men kept hauling away on the line, finally bringing the exhausted captain aboard the wreck, frightened but uninjured.

It was then agreed that the eleven survivors should await daylight before attempting another shoreward journey. But the coming of dawn revealed the discouraging fact that land was more than twenty miles away. While the sailors had only a few arms and a small amount of provisions, they agreed that the sooner they struck out for land the better chance they would have of getting there.

With a certain amount of misgiving, Barnard launched the remaining boat. The eleven men rowed three miles through turbulent seas until they came to a large rock which had about 300 feet of its surface exposed. Feeling that it would be foolhardy to continue rowing, they decided to camp on the rock for the night and managed to catch a few eels, crabs and snails, after which they cooked a meal over a driftwood fire.

At sunrise a war canoe with twenty-two natives came out to them from the distant island, and the appearance of the naked savages, each one armed with a spear and a tomahawk, frightened the Americans. The natives were heavily tattooed all over their bodies, and their hair, coarse and black, hung loosely over their shoulders, giving them a frightful appearance. Their teeth were jet black, made so because of their habit of chewing "abooak." Actually they were the descendants of the savages who had similarly greeted the sailors from the *Antelope* forty-nine years before.

The natives soon took charge and offered the survivors coconuts and a kind of bread made from that fruit, boiled in a liquor extracted from the trunk of a tree. But they also took possession of any debris from the shipwreck which they could find, after which they made signals for the Americans to follow them in their own craft toward the island.

Captain Barnard didn't like their looks in the slightest and determined to steer for the open sea. He was stopped in this plan, however, by the appearance of no less than thirty other canoes, whose occupants paddled rapidly toward them. After a brief skirmish, the Americans were allowed to row away from the natives, who paddled over to the wreck. Rowing desperately all that day and night, the Americans reached another island by late the next day, and hoped that they had eluded their pursuers.

But they were soon discovered and the savages who found them ordered their appearance at the headquarters of the tribe on a neighboring island. Helpless to do otherwise, the discouraged whalers finally gave in. As they approached the island they were met by more canoes, the occupants of which took them on shore with some violence.

The New Bedford crew found the dignitaries of the island seated on a platform about fifteen feet square located on rising ground between two buildings known as *pyes*.

Shortly afterward they learned that the island they had reached was known to navigators as Baubelthouap, the largest of that particular archipelago.

In the center of the square where they had been taken there stood a very efficient-looking chopping block. The Americans were moved to another village before any of them could be executed, and they found out later that a prophetess had interceded in their behalf after which they were all sent out to her residence. Arriving at her home, they were relieved to discover that she had prepared for them a banquet which they enjoyed to the utmost.

While they were eating, the survivors noticed a man of about sixty approaching them. There was tattooing all over his body, and he walked toward them with a firm, quick step, indicating that he was a man of no little authority. When within a few feet of the diners, he stopped suddenly.

"My God, you are white men," he faltered. "You are fairly safe now, but I do not understand why they didn't kill you out on the water! It is a miracle!"

He sat down with the Americans and after finding out the details about them, began to tell his own strange story.

"I have been on the island for twenty-nine long years. My name is Charles Washington, and I was a hatter by trade. In naval service I was a private, on board the *Lion*, British man-of-war. I committed an offense, and afraid of punishment, I fled ashore and deserted in 1802. I've been here ever since and have worked my way up to the sixth prince in power on the entire island. I've no wish to go back to England, incidentally. My authority is great here, and I would be a nobody back in England. So here I shall remain."

Evidently Washington had been appointed a prince by King Arra Kooker around 1815 when the latter was alive. But since Kooker's death conditions on the Pelew Islands had rapidly deteriorated, and Washington's advice to the sailors was to leave as soon as the could possibly do so.

The older man did everything in his power to make it easier for the mariners, but he also told them that it would be a difficult task to escape from the island.

Nevertheless, he also mentioned that he owned a compass

from the 1783 wreck of the British ship *Antelope*, given to
one of the other chiefs by Captain Henry Wilson of that
vessel shortly after her disaster. Although not in proper working condition it could still be used for general sailing directions. The Americans gladly accepted the gift.

On the following morning, October 27, 1832, the whalers
put to sea in a boat and a canoe. The two craft soon proved
unseaworthy and began to leak rapidly, so the voyagers returned to the island the same night. The following month
was spent in refitting the boats. A fresh start was made, this
time in company with two of the chiefs who were to serve
as seagoing guides and later were to be rewarded. Three of
the whalers, unfortunately, were forced to stay behind as
hostages.

A violent storm soon blew up, and the rudder of the canoe
was unshipped. In the morning the rudder was reset and
again proved satisfactory. Later in the day the boat's mast
went overboard and the canoe sprang a leak.

Three days afterward the canoe capsized, throwing its
occupants into the sea. By careful maneuvering of the whale
boat, those who had been in the canoe were transferred to the
boat, but in effecting the change many of the provisions were
lost. The compass was saved, however, and the supply of
coconuts. When the accident occurred the boat was far at
sea out of sight of land.

Nine days later, with actual starvation ahead, they sighted
a large island, but before they could get within five miles of
the shore a fleet of canoes was observed heading for them.
The Americans were anxious to be friendly to those in the
canoes, but the savages were in no such frame of mind. Paddling up alongside the whale boat the natives swung their
clubs to knock the Americans and the Pelew Islanders out of
the boat into the ocean. They climbed back in as best they
could.

Then came a concerted attack against the boat. The natives smashed it apart, each canoe grabbing a fragment of the remains for its own use. For some time the savages refused to allow the whalers into their canoes, but at last they relented and pulled the Americans out of the water. Ripping the clothes from the sailors, they then forced them to paddle the canoes ashore.

Seaman Horace Holden, who took careful notes on his experiences while a captive, stated that when they reached shore, conditions were worse than before.

"The reception we met on land was no more agreeable than that upon the water. Judging from the treatment we had received from the females of the island we had just left, it was hoped that the gentler sex would extend to us some proof of their commiseration; but in this we were sadly disappointed. If possible, they were more cruel than their inhuman lords and masters.

"We were soon separated from each other, and dragged from place to place; our brutal captors, in the mean time, contending with each other to see who should have us as his property. Frequent contests of this kind occurred; in one of which, during the first day I was knocked down. The question of ownership was at length settled, and we were retained by those into whose hands we had fallen.

"Some of us were taken to their house of worship, called by them Verre-Yarris, literally God's house, where they went through with some of their religious ceremonies, and we received a few mouthfuls of food, which was the first we had tasted through the day.

"The character of the inhabitants much resembles that of the island itself. Cowardly and servile, yet most barbarous and cruel, they combine, in their habits, tempers, and dispositions, the most disgusting and loathesome features that disgrace humanity. And what may be regarded as remarkable, the female portion of the inhabitants outstrip the men in cruelty and savage depravity; so much so, that we were frequently indebted to the tender mercies of the men for escapes from death at the hands of the women.

"The indolence of the inhabitants, which not even the fear of starvation itself can arouse to exertion, prevents their undertaking the least toil.

"We were captured and taken to the island, December 6, 1832, and on the third day of February, 1833, two months, wanting three days, Captain Barnard and Bartlet Rollins effected their escape. A ship was discovered a short distance from the island, and the natives immediately collected, and prepared to go to it, in order to obtain iron, or some other articles of value. Hope once more visited us.

"Accordingly, when the canoes put off, we attempted to go. Our savage masters interposed their authority, and by menaces and blows prevented us. Many of us were severely beaten, and all but two were detained by the brutal force of the savages.

"At length, Captain Barnard and Rollins, after being severely beaten, were allowed to accompany the natives to the ship, and succeeded in effecting their escape."

Holden and the others waited in vain for the sailors from the vessel to come ashore and rescue them as well, but as they found out later the captain was afraid of trouble if he attempted it.

Treated with much greater severity after the two escaped, the remaining sailors were forced to construct a stone wall around the coconut grove on the island. A storm brought down many trees and created a famine. Eventually the coconut trees which remained returned to health, and the chief source of island food was again plentiful.

The next ordeal for the sailors was tattooing. The chief decreed that all Americans be tattooed, and they were forced to submit to the process, administered with a sharpened fish bone.

After a year on the island whaler William Sedon became so emaciated that he resembled a living skeleton. Finally, with his strength exhausted, he was placed in a canoe and set adrift from the island never to be seen again. The next to die was Peter Andrews, executed by the natives for a trifling offense. Seven months later Milton Hewlet died and was committed to the ocean, while Charles Bouket had become so thin and feeble that he was also set adrift in a canoe and was never heard from again.

Finally only Nute, Holden and one Pelew chieftain remained alive. By the fall of 1834 they were unable to work, having become terribly feeble because of a lack of sufficient food.

Two months later, on November 27, they sighted a vessel approaching the island. The craft proved to be the British bark *Britannia* commanded by Captain Short and bound for Canton. The natives finally relented enough to allow the two Americans to accompany them in war canoes out to the vessel, but refused to let the Pelew chief go with them. They bade farewell to their friend and fellow sufferer on the shore, promising to do all in their power to effect his release so that he might return to his island home.

Paddling out to the bark, they found the sailors aboard frightened at the appearance of the great number of savages, but Holden shouted that he and his comrade wished to be taken off. The British captain removed the two Americans who, because of their skeleton-like figures seemed on the verge of death.

Taken to Canton, they were brought ashore at a factory there and placed under medical treatment for some time. Word then came that an American ship was soon to sail for the United States, and the medical director allowed them to be discharged from the hospital. Given passage aboard the ship *Morrison*, they soon sailed for New York where they arrived without further incident on May 5, 1835.

When the American government was notified of the wreck of the *Mentor*, the United States sloop-of-war *Vincennes* was ordered to the Pelew Islands and also to Lord North's Island. The American seamen left as hostages at Pelew were found safe and taken aboard, after which the *Vincennes* visited Lord North's Island. There they found the sole surviving Pelew Islander, Prince Kobac, still alive but terribly thin from starvation. Bringing the prince aboard the sloop, they cared for him as best they could and were able to land him in much better health at Pelew than when they had found him at Lord North's Island.

CHAPTER ⚬ FOURTEEN

THE CIRCUS SHIP CATCHES FIRE

Lo! o'er the waves a lurid light is cast;
Blood-red the ship pursues her burning way;
Devoured by fire, sore smitten by the blast,
Her doom is sealed ere dawns another day.

THE MARINE TRAGEDY of the *Royal Tar* is the first sea disaster of its type in American history. The fantastic story of the circus * ship was mentioned briefly in my *Storms and Shipwrecks* (published in 1943 and now out of print) and ever since then I have been receiving letters with additional information concerning this fire at sea. Now, for the first time, the entire story can be told.

The *Royal Tar*, named for King William IV of England, was a new 164-foot side-wheeler commanded by Captain Thomas Reed. On October 21, 1836, she left Saint John,

---

* Many people will undoubtedly recall the terrible Hartford, Connecticut, holocaust of July 6, 1944, when a great circus fire occurred. After the fire broke out a stampede began in the main tent, which ended with 168 dead and 487 injured persons. While this disaster was the worst tragedy ever connected with a circus, the story which follows was the first American marine tragedy connected with a circus fire.

New Brunswick, with a circus and menagerie aboard for Portland, Maine. The circus had a double billing and was known as Dexter's Locomotive Museum and Burgess' Collection of Serpents and Birds. On deck were an elephant, Mogul by name, two pelicans, two camels, several horses, lions, a Royal Bengal tiger, a gnu and many other animals and birds. There was also a fine brass band aboard. Unfortunately, in order to accommodate the large circus on deck, two lifeboats had been left behind at Saint John.

Soon reaching the open sea, the *Royal Tar* proceeded south. The weather was perfect in every respect at first, but before the sun went down that Friday a high westerly wind began to blow. Continuing for several days, the gale eventually forced the side-wheeler to seek shelter in Eastport Harbor where the steamer remained until Tuesday.

Leaving Eastport Harbor Tuesday afternoon, she was again hit by rising winds, and for a second time sought shelter, on this occasion finding a lee behind Fox Island in Penobscot Bay. While the steamer was anchored two miles off Fox Island Thoroughfare, orders were given to fill her boiler.

Pilot Atkins' son, attracted by the intense blistering heat of the wooden beams near the boiler, tested the lower cock only to find it dry. He told his father who mentioned the fact to Second Engineer Marshall, then in charge.

In no uncertain language the boy and father were made to understand that they were greatly mistaken in assuming that the boilers were dry and were told by the indignant Mr. Marshall that "Everything is in perfect order!"

Actually, as we later discovered, the regular engineer, who had been up all night working on the boilers, had retired to his bunk and given the task of filling them to his second engineer, who in turn had ordered the fireman to do this job, but the fireman had failed to carry out these orders.

A few seconds after the discussion the boiler became red

hot, setting fire to two wedges which had been inserted between it and the elephant cage. The flames soon spread, and the crew quickly organized to fight the fire.

Assembled in the cabin, the passengers were about to sit down to dinner when they heard a strange commotion outside. Captain Reed rushed to the companionway, took one look at the flames leaping up through the grating and realized that the *Royal Tar* was doomed. It was then blowing a gale offshore and the foresail caught fire immediately. The jib was hoisted, but burned through almost at once.

"Slip the anchor," the captain shouted, "and hoist a distress signal."

Captain Reed realized with sinking heart that the two lifeboats left behind in Saint John were going to be desperately needed. All that remained were the longboat and the jolly boat, both of which he ordered launched.

A great number of persons jumped into the longboat, cut the ropes to drop the craft into the water and soon were rowing away from the blazing steamer toward the distant shore. Captain Reed leaped into the jolly boat to prevent its being rowed away.

About twenty men still on the *Royal Tar* tried to tip overboard one of the great omnibuses which on land were used to transport the circus, but in this they failed.

A short time later the Revenue Cutter *Veto*, stationed at Castine, was sighted five miles away, and as she drew near Reed had a few survivors get into the jolly boat, after which he rowed them across to the *Veto*. The captain learning that the *Veto* was short-handed and without her regular commanding officer, volunteered to take the wheel briefly and explain to the helmsman what should be done. He also planned to send some of his own men over to help out the sailors on the cutter. Since the *Veto* had a load of powder aboard she could not sail too close to the burning steamer which was then drifting helplessly out to sea.

By staying far enough away from the *Royal Tar*, Captain Reed prevented the panic-stricken survivors from leaping into and swamping his boat. One by one he ordered the desperate passengers to jump into the water and grab his oar, and then he pulled them into the jolly boat. In this way he was able to transport a total of almost fifty persons from the *Royal Tar* to the *Veto*.

Some of the experiences both survivors and victims underwent were heartrending. The *Veto's* gig was launched under the command of the pilot who was afraid to get too close to the flames. Passing around to the stern, he noticed many passengers who could not swim hanging to ropes put over the side of the burning craft. When they shouted to him for help he lost his nerve completely, ordering the gig back to the cutter. Soon afterward the flames reached the ropes, burned through and dropped the unfortunate victims into the water to their doom. If the pilot had not lost his head, over twenty of those who met their death in this way would have been saved.

Feeling that otherwise they would perish, a group of men then began putting together a makeshift float which they managed to get over the side and into the sea. Just as they were clambering down onto the raft there was a terrific blast of hot air and burning embers from the blaze, followed almost at once by the sound of a frenzied elephant trumpeting in terror.

At the very moment that the men were aboard their raft and about to push off, the elephant appeared immediately above them. Placing his forepaws on the taffrail as he was accustomed to do during a trick he had performed in the circus, the huge beast smashed through the rail carrying several desperate humans with him, and hurtled down on the raft and its occupants submerging the men forever in the sea.

Minutes later the beast was seen coming to the surface, after which he started to swim for the nearest land, but as the *Royal Tar* was then more than five miles out to sea, Mogul evidently perished before he reached shore. His lifeless body was found floating a few days later near Brimstone Island.*

Aboard the ship were six horses whose duty it had been to pull the huge locomotive museum. They were released and backed into the ocean, after which three of them swam instinctively for the nearest land and were saved, while the other three circled the burning craft until exhausted and then sank beneath the waves.

One passenger who had carried aboard ship a tremendous number of silver coins decided to fasten his money belt around his waist with $500 in silver in it. Since he was a good swimmer he had no fear when he mounted the taffrail and leaped into the sea, but he had forgotten the heavy weight of the coins. He never came to the surface, dragged down by his wealth to his doom in the waters of Penobscot Bay.

Mr. H. H. Fuller, one of the officials in the circus, told of how he had been seasick in his berth when the fire broke out.

"When I reached the deck I saw the longboat full of people, a quarter of a mile to leeward; they were rowing hard and soon out of sight. The small boat, in which was Captain Reed, who took possession of it to prevent its following the longboat to the leeward, lay about fifty yards astern; three persons swam off, and were taken into her, though the wind was then blowing a gale, and a tremendous sea was running. He then bore away for the land, to the windward about two miles. At this time a great many persons jumped overboard

---

* Mr. Roy Coombs of Vinalhaven preserved a fragment of the huge skeleton for many years. In 1944 I received in the mail from a member of the Coombs family the skeletal remains of Mogul's foot.

and were drowned. The screams of the women and children, the horrid yells of the men, the roaring of the storm, and the awful confusion, baffle description. . . . The steamer then broached to, and was shortly afterward completely enveloped in flames amidships. The fire interrupted all communication fore and aft; and neither those in the bow nor those in the stern could see or know the fate of each other. All but myself fled from the quarter-deck. I sat on the stern rail, till my coat caught fire. I looked round, and seeing not a soul . . . fastened a rope to the tiller chain and dropped over the stern, where I found about fifteen others hanging in various places, mostly in the water."

As Mr. Fuller hung there, he saw several of the survivors drop off to their death, but he had fastened his rope to the chain, which was in turn fastened to iron bolts, and Fuller knew that the iron would not catch fire. He took a turn with the line around his "neck and thigh," and in this manner was able to bear the weight of four others, three men and a lady, "who hung securely to me."

A thrilling drama was enacted a short distance from Fuller. Pilot Atkins was holding a woman with his feet when her strength finally failed and she began to slip from his grasp. He let himself down a short distance and was able to grasp her again with his feet, holding her in the water against the ship. Then a terrific wave smashed against them, and she was washed away. For a minute it seemed as if she were lost. Miraculously the next wave dashed her against another man to whom she clung desperately.

At that moment the cutter's gig passed close by, but although pitiful entreaties were directed at its pilot, the gig went away without helping anyone. Finally Captain Reed came in and rescued her and the other survivors around the tiller, taking them across to the cutter.

William Marjoram, a deck passenger, remembered that

while passing the cage of the lion on deck he thought of psalmist David who said, "My soul is among lions, even those that are set on fire." He was encouraged when he noticed the cutter approaching, but his heart sank when she began to sail away. Later, however, he saw Captain Reed board her with some of his sailors to man her, and then the captain began ferrying passengers across from the burning *Royal Tar* to the *Veto*.

Marjoram's story follows:

"I was three hours on the wreck, and was taken off by the captain. The moment I got on board of the cutter, I begged Captain Dyer to carry her alongside, but he refused; saying the elephant would jump aboard. I then requested him to sail the cutter under the bows, and ask the keeper to lash his [the elephant's] leg to the windlass; but it was of no avail; he ordered me to go below, which I did for a short time. I again went on deck, and helped the people out of the boat as they came alongside, remarking every time that they brought no women with them.

"About six o'clock the boat came with only three persons on board—a Mr. Brown, late steward of the boat, and a colored sailor, that belonged to the steamboat, who was the means of saving a great many lives, having been in the boat a long time. He requested me to take his place, the cutter-master said he could stay no longer.

"I . . . jumped into the boat, and rowed away: on reaching the wreck there was one woman holding on the bowsprit, with a child in her arms, and another in the water, with her clothes burnt off, holding on by a piece of rope: she let go, and before I could get to her the child was drowned; but we saved the woman, who was nearly dead. . . . The cutter stood for the shore, where she landed the survivors, except the last woman; Captain Dyer and myself sitting up all night, endeavoring to bring her to, which we did."

The shore mentioned by Marjoram was Isle au Haut, where the Revenue Cutter *Veto* had taken the survivors. The inhabitants on the island cared for their needs.

Another passenger, Stimson Patten of Saint John, New Brunswick, was warm in praise of Captain Reed, saying that "to him all credit is due for his deliberate and manly perseverance throughout the whole calamity. It is impossible to describe the appalling spectacle which the whole scene presented—the boat wrapped in flames, with nearly 100 souls on board, without any hope of relief, rending the air with their shrieks for help; the caravan of wild beasts on deck, ready to tear to pieces all that might escape the flames."

Shortly before sunset the last rescue boat with a single survivor left the *Royal Tar*. Still blazing fiercely, the side-wheeler continued to drift out to sea, and the light of the conflagration was still visible at 7:00 in the evening, after which it suddenly disappeared. The steamer is believed to have gone down into the sea at that moment about twenty miles from the place where she had taken fire seven hours earlier.

Captain Reed was soon subjected to the usual criticism a sea captain faces after a disaster, but he came out of the ordeal with flying colors. As mentioned above, when the revenue cutter arrived on the scene she was under-manned and in charge of a Lieutenant Dyer, who was uncertain of what to do. With a cargo of powder aboard, which he could easily have dumped into the sea to leeward, Dyer was afraid to approach too near, and so Captain Reed put his own crew aboard and personally supervised the ferry service. More lives would have been saved if the man in command of the gig had not been afraid. But when everything is taken into consideration, the proportion of survivors was high. Thirty-two people perished, and only one person burned to death in the flames, an old lady who did not appear on deck at all. Of the ninety-three persons aboard, sixty-one, or almost two-thirds, were eventually saved. Most of the others lost their lives by leaping into the sea in panic or slipping to their death in the ocean when the ropes to which they were clinging burned through.

On October 26, 1836, while ashore at Isle au Haut, Captain Reed wrote a letter to Leonard Billings, steamboat agent at Portland. Part of his statement follows:

"I have no blame to attach to anyone—I think that it was pure accident. I am very stiffened from overexertion, but hope to be better shortly. The people here have been very kind, indeed, and we are as well off as can be expected."

The passengers at Isle au Haut soon obtained a schooner to take them to Portland, while the master and crew later returned to Eastport on another craft.

Captain Thomas Reed was highly regarded for the remainder of his life for his bravery during the burning of the *Royal Tar*. On November 3, 1836, he was presented with a purse of $700 for his heroism during the fire. Later he was appointed Harbor Master at Saint John, where for many years he was a picturesque figure around the waterfront, and was often seen walking from wharf to wharf with his faithful dog at his side.

CHAPTER FIFTEEN

THE BARK *Mexico*

O bitter sea, tumultuous sea,
Full many an evil is wrought by thee.

ON OCTOBER 25, 1836, Captain Winslow sailed the Bark *Mexico* out of Liverpool, England, bound for New York. On board were 149 persons, all of whom suffered from hunger during the last part of the voyage, for the bark had been seriously underprovisioned. To make matters worse, the craft had sprung a leak.

On December 20 the hungry passengers were so desperate for food that they wrote a letter to the captain:

20 December 1836
To Captain Winslow:
Sir:
We, the undersigned, passengers in the barque Mexico, under your command, being reduced to a very deplorable state, for want of provisions, and unable to bear the privation any longer, take this means of proposing the only plan that can be adopted to preserve the lives of ourselves, our wives and our children. We are fully aware of some provisions being on board, such as biscuits and herrings.

We propose to purchase a sufficient quantity of the same,

and to give you a deposit equal to their current price at New York; and this will secure you in the value of such part of your cargo as we may consume.

We respectfully submit this for your consideration, and request a reply in the course of the day.

Signed by WILLIAM ROBERTSON
(and forty others.)

Captain Winslow, while not replying, asked the messenger if he wanted to take command of the ship. Nevertheless, he did improve the menu from that point on until the New Jersey shore was sighted, when food ran out altogether.

At 11:00 A.M. on December 31, Winslow was able to sight the town of Woodland on the Jersey shore. Hoping that he would shortly pick up a pilot, he ran down the coast, heaving to when he saw the lighthouse on the Highlands of Navesink. Unfortunately, the New York pilots were not functioning properly at this time, and scores of vessels were waiting outside New York unable to enter the harbor.

Early on Sunday, January 1, 1837, the captain bore up to Sandy Hook with his signal for a pilot flying. Later, when no pilot appeared, he hoisted a signal of distress, for with his passengers starving and the bark leaking, he was frantic with anxiety at his situation. Several steamers passed him and must have noticed his call for help, but they all ignored it.

A snowstorm began shortly afterward, lasting all the following night, and the next morning the weather turned extremely cold. Nevertheless, Captain Winslow was able to sight Sandy Hook again, and fired several distress guns, but to no avail.

Fatigued from his long ordeal, Winslow finally had to go below for a rest and he asked the mate to take a sounding. The mate reported fifteen fathoms, which would indicate the bark was over ten miles out to sea. Someone blundered, however, because at 5:00 the next morning, Tuesday, the *Mexico* smashed ashore at Hempstead Beach, Long Island. It was four degrees above zero, a strong wind blew along shore and a high sea and heavy surf were then running.

A short time later the rudder smashed away, the main and mizzen masts were let go by the board and the spray began to ice entirely over the bark. Passengers visiting the hold found that their baggage was being submerged. They saved what they could, most of them fastening what money they had around their bodies. Across on the Long Island shore, news of the disaster had spread rapidly, and scores of residents were hurrying down to the beach.

For two generations a Mr. Raynor R. Smith had been saving people wrecked off the sands of Hempstead, and his sons and also his grandsons had grown up with the same benevolent spirit. He had never shirked what he considered his duty toward the mariner in trouble off his shore, and always cooperated with Wreckmaster Seaman, the local shipping representative.

Mr. Smith had a longboat some three miles from the scene of the wreck. Although it was one of the coldest days of the winter, he, together with two sons and two grandsons and one other man pulled the boat three miles down the beach until they were opposite the wreck. By this time the sun was low in the west, and they all knew they must act fast. The longboat was launched at once into a breaker, threatened to capsize and then righted itself. The experience of the lifesavers triumphed, and fifteen minutes later the Smith boat was nearing the wreck.

By this time all aboard the lifeboat were heavily iced over, the oars were becoming unmanageable, and the men's clothing was getting as stiff as boards. But the lifesavers fought their way to a position just under the bowsprit. After three attempts Smith was able to grab a chain hanging from the jib boom, by which he kept the boat at the wreck. With great urgency he shouted to the survivors to clamber out onto the flying jib boom and drop into the boat.

The cook was the first to try it and he landed safely in the sternsheets, followed almost at once by a sailor. Just as a wave forced the boat away, a third man dropped, falling into the sea to his death.

Another man landed on the gunwhale. Smith pulled him aboard, but in doing so he was forced to let go the jib boom chain, and in a moment the boat was driven twenty feet away. Here they found another man struggling in the water. Zopher Smith saved this survivor. Icing conditions were now almost hopeless, and the boys implored their father to return to shore or they would all be doomed.

Just then Captain Winslow of the *Mexico* clambered out on the bowsprit to hail the boat, and Raynor Smith decided to make a final effort.

"If we get the captain, he'll be able to tell us the entire disaster story," he told his family, and they reluctantly started the ice-covered boat toward the *Mexico* again.

After three more desperate attempts the chain was secured, and the captain made his way out along the flying jib boom, helping a young boy, brother of the bark's owner, as he did so.

"Jump, lad, jump," Winslow shouted, and the boy dropped into the boat. The captain followed him a moment later, and soon there were eight survivors in the Smith lifeboat. No more could be taken, and the ice-encrusted boat, now filled to capacity with human beings, left the ship.

The lifeboat was headed toward shore. After a cold, perilous journey it landed on the sandy beach behind a huge wave. All fifteen men had reached safety, but they were just in time. The lifeboat, now inches deep in ice and with the oars white with frozen surf, was so heavy after the occupants had left it that twenty volunteers could not move it up the beach.

When the tide dropped considerably, a horse was taken down on the shore. After much of the ice had been chipped from the boat, the horse was able to pull the craft above the high water mark. But for those unfortunates still out aboard the wreck when the boat was drawn up the beach it meant the end of all attempts at rescue.

The sun went down shortly afterward, and one may imagine the feelings of those on the doomed *Mexico* who realized that it was doubtful if any of them would live throughout the night. Wrapping themselves in blankets and whatever other garments they could find, they clustered together for warmth. But as evening came and then the blackness of night, one by one they died. Eventually all were to perish. Not a single person besides those who were brought ashore by the Smiths lived!

The *Mexico* soon began to break up, and that night the beach was littered with frozen bodies. The remains were gathered together and taken in carts and wagons to the great barn of Mr. John I. Lott, who ran the local tavern.*

The following morning the British consul visited the scene of the disaster and was completely overcome by what he found on the shore at Hempstead. His statement follows:

"I confess that I am utterly unable to proceed in the painful detail, of which I know no parallel; and the only consolation—while I am writing at the beach, so near the scene, with so many of the dead bodies, as it were, before me—is that their sufferings are ended; but I must proceed.

"The state of the tide, the violence of the surf and spray, the intense cold, that turned to ice every dash of the waves which touched the boat and oars, obliged the brave Smith and his heroic party to abandon all hope of returning to the vessel; and O horrible alternative! they drew the boat out of the

---

* I have in my files the entire list of passengers who sailed aboard the *Mexico*, should any reader have more than a passing interest in the disaster.

surf on the beach. And who saw this just as the sun was setting on that fateful day? One hundred and eight persons big with hope, that they had crossed the Atlantic—some that they were to embrace their parents, a wife her husband.

"Gracious God! What tongue can speak the misery, the despair, the suffering of one hundred and eight of our fellowbeings, twelve hours in the suspense described? And now, the sun declining, the people mournfully withdrawing from their cries, the spray and frost binding them to each other; all hope, all prospect of relief extinguished. Some of the humane people who lingered on the shore, say that the cries and supplications were distinctly heard; but they gradually died away, and at 11:00 P.M., not a voice was heard."

Weeks after the wreck a small silk handkerchief, frozen in ice, was picked up on the Long Island shore. When the finder thawed it out, he discovered two prayer books inside, indicating that the owner of one was a man of the Catholic faith, while the owner of the other was a lady of the same belief.

People who visited Hempstead at that time never forgot the terrible sights they witnessed. The remains taken to Lott's Tavern had been laid side by side in the inn keeper's great barn.

"I went out in the barn," records a visitor. "The doors were open, and such a scene as presented itself to my view, I never could have contemplated. It was a dreadful, a frightful scene of horror.

"Forty or fifty bodies, of all ages and sexes, were lying promiscuously before me all over the floor, all frozen, and as solid as marble—and all except a very few, in the very dresses in which they had perished Some with their hands clenched, as if for warmth, and almost every one, with an arm crooked and bent, as it would be in clinging to the rigging.

"There were scattered about among the number, four or five beautiful little girls, from six to sixteen years of age. their cheeks and lips as red as roses, with their calm blue eyes open, looking you in the face, as if they would speak. I could hardly realize that they were dead.

"I touched their cheeks, and they were frozen as solid as a rock, and not the least indentation could be made by any pressure of the hand. I could perceive a resemblance to each other, and supposed them to be the daughters of a passenger named Pepper,* who perished, together with his wife and all the family.

"On the arms of some were seen the impressions of the rope which they had clung to—the mark of the twist deeply sunk into the flesh. I saw one poor Negro sailor, a tall man, with his head thrown back, his lips parted, and his now sightless eye-balls turned upward, and his arms crossed over his breast, as if imploring heaven for aid. The poor fellow evidently had frozen while in the act of fervent prayer.

"One female had a rope tied to her leg, which had bound her to the rigging; and another little fellow had been crying and was thus frozen with the muscles of his face just as we see children when crying.

"One little girl had raised herself on tiptoe, and thus was frozen, just in that position. It was an awful sight; and such a picture of horror was before me, that I became unconsciously fixed to the spot, and found myself trying to suppress my ordinary breathing, lest I should disturb the repose of those around me.

"As I was about to leave my attention became directed to a girl, who I afterwards learned, had come that morning from the city to search for her sister. She had sent for her to come

---

* The passenger list includes William Pepper, Judith Pepper, Joseph Pepper, William Pepper, Jr., Rebecca Pepper, David Pepper, Miriam Pepper and John Pepper.

over from England, and had received intelligence that she was in this ship. She came into the barn, and the second body she cast her eyes upon, was her sister.

"She gave way to such a burst of impassioned grief and anguish, that I could not behold her without sharing her feelings. She threw herself upon the cold and icy face and neck of the lifeless body, and thus, with her arms around her, remained wailing, mourning, and sobbing, till I came away. When some distance off I could hear her calling her sister by name in a most frantic manner.

"So little time, it appears, had they to prepare for their fate, that I perceived a bunch of keys, and a half-eaten cake, fall from the bosom of a girl whom the coroner was removing. The cake appeared as if part of it had just been bitten, and hastily thrust into her bosom, and round her neck was a ribbon, with a pair of scissors.

"And to observe the stout, rugged sailors, too, whose iron frames could endure so much hardship—here they lay, masses of ice. Such scenes show us, indeed, how powerless and feeble are all human efforts, when contending against the storms and tempests, which sweep with resistless violence over the face of the deep.

"And yet the vessel was so near the shore, that the shrieks and moans of the poor creatures were heard through that bitter, dreadful night, till toward morning, when the last groan died away, and all was hushed in death, and the murmur of the raging billows was all the sound that then met the ear."

After the relatives and friends of the known dead had taken away the three bodies of those who were to be buried elsewhere, the local residents found that they had no less than forty-three bodies in the great barn, and a committee decided that they would all be given a funeral together at the Methodist Church.

A procession was formed on the day of the funeral, with

no less than 300 carriages in line as the funeral cortege went from the inn to the church, a distance of three miles.

Clergymen from every faith were in attendance, and included the Rev. Mr. Carmichael, the Rev. Mr. Crane, the Rev. Dr. Shoomaker, the Rev. Mr. Law and the Rev. Mr. Floy. After simple but impressive services, the victims were interred in the nearby cemetery.

Later, when $300 found on the bodies had not been claimed, the New York legislature authorized the erection of a monument over the remains, using the money for the purpose.

Mr. Samuel Broome of New York was the owner of the eleven-year-old 280-ton *Mexico*. He was so grateful that his young twelve-year-old brother was saved along with the captain that he gave $50 to each member of the boat crew who had rescued the eight survivors.

The New York piloting system, which was to blame for the eventual disaster to the *Mexico*, was entirely reorganized as a result of the wreck. While there may be those who think the captain should have remained aboard the *Mexico* following the best traditions of the sea, the hard facts of the case are that because he was saved he could explain why the *Mexico* was wrecked, and thus lend his weight to the movement which eventually changed the New York piloting system into the efficient machine it later became. In this way his rescue probably saved scores of lives by preventing similar disasters in the future.

Another result of the wreck was that new laws were passed compelling the owners of passenger ships to provide them with far more than an adequate amount of supplies and provisions, so that if the craft were delayed several weeks, they still would have enough food to eat, and "starvation should not stare them in the face."

CHAPTER SIXTEEN

THE EXPLOSION OF THE *Pulaski*

God rest the brave,
Who 'neath the Atlantic wave
Have sunk to their last home!

ON THE THIRTEENTH day of June, 1838, the steam packet *Pulaski*, a side-wheeler, sailed away from Savannah, Georgia, forever. On board were the master, Captain Dubois, the crew and ninety passengers. The steamer arrived at Charlestown, South Carolina, that afternoon and sailed from there the following morning with sixty-five more passengers.

Late that day the wind freshened from the east, bringing high seas within a few hours. This change of weather slowed the ship's progress, causing the engineer to use a full head of steam. By 10:30 that night there was a high wind, but a clear starry sky gave every promise of a fine night.

Half an hour later, without any warning, the giant starboard boiler exploded with a terrific concussion, blowing sky high part of the promenade deck and smashing to pieces the starboard amidships section. The explosion also stove in the bulkhead between the boilers and the forward cabin, blocked up the companion stairway and swept away the bar room.

The larboard boiler was found intact. The *Pulaski* began to list in that direction, the result being that the starboard side remained out of water except when she rolled badly, and then the waves swept into the breach caused by the blast. Gradually the water rose and in about three-quarters of an hour had reached such a depth that the ladies' cabin was entirely submerged. All the women and children were told to assemble on the promenade deck. The ship filled rapidly, however, and when the water reached the promenade deck, the vessel broke in two.

The bow and the stern rose briefly and then settled gradually, the stern splitting into three separate sections, each of which capsized to throw its occupants into the sea. As the fragments of the stern continued to break up, scores of impromptu rafts were assembled by crewmen and passengers.

Many now gained the relative safety of the bow, while others busied themselves in lowering the "side boats," as they were called. First mate Hibbard took the lifeboat on the starboard side, while Mr. J. H. Cooper chose to operate the larboard lifeboat. There were also two deck boats available. Several members of the crew launched one of them and clambered in, but the seams were all open from exposure to the sun so that she filled instantly, and they scrambled out and back to the bow.

A short time after the explosion one of the survivors jumped toward a boat but, because of the dark night, missed and landed in the water. His wife, hearing his screams, shouted out to him, "Where are you? Where are you?"

"I am here," he cried from the water, whereupon she leaped on the rail and plunged headlong into the sea, both of them drowning a short time later.

The handful of people in Mr. Hibbard's boat were anxious to start out for land at once, but he refused to leave until the lifeboat was filled. Finally he picked up enough survivors to complete a load of passengers and started for the distant shore. It was then 3:00 in the morning.

Nine hours later, after exhausting, strenuous rowing, those in the lifeboat sighted land, and at 3:00 that afternoon they were just off the shore. Mr. Hibbard refused to land as the breakers were too high, and when the other boat came alongside, Mr. Cooper agreed with Hibbard's decision. But the two in command were voted down. Hibbard then gave in to the rule of the majority and started for shore. The boat was caught in a breaker and swamped at once, disappearing from the view. Six of the occupants of the lifeboat eventually saved themselves, but five others drowned. Mr. Hibbard was among those rescued.

The survivors in the second boat, realizing that five in the first craft had drowned, were now reluctant to try their chances in the surf. At sunset, however, Mr. Cooper decided that they would have to attempt it or risk the possibility of capsizing in the darkness. There were many problems to consider, but the most serious one was the presence in the boat of a seven-months-old baby, the child of a Mrs. Nightingale.* Cooper lashed the infant securely to Mrs. Nightingale's body and assured her of his help when they should land. Then he told the others that it was now or possibly never, and started the lifeboat into the breakers.

The first great comber caught the craft, but Cooper held it back and the wave went roaring on toward the beach. Then a second wave, with a breaking crest, came surging at them. Picking up the boat, the breaker capsized it and everyone went into the sea. When Cooper came to the surface he counted heads, and all except Mrs. Nightingale and her baby were accounted for. Then he felt a woman's dress touching his foot. Without hesitating he dove down and grasped Mrs.

---

* Mrs. Nightingale was the daughter of John A. King, Esq., and the granddaughter of the well-known Massachusetts congressman, Rufus King.

Nightingale's hair. A moment later he pulled the woman to the surface, her baby still tied to her. After a terrific struggle he brought the two up on the beach, where he met the others in the party, and all were saved.

The men agreed that for protection against the bitter wind they should bury the women and children up to their necks in the sand to keep their bodies warm, and this was done at once.

Meanwhile, one of the number went for help, and after a time he located the home of Mr. Siglee Redd about three quarters of a mile away. The entire party was soon inside Mr. Redd's warm house where all the women and children were put to bed and given hot food. After the men were fed they received additional clothing.

Back out on the wreck the bow stayed afloat. Aboard it were Major James P. Heath and twenty-one others. A short time before the explosion one of the passengers had mentioned to the major that the gauge then showed thirty inches of steam. The engineer, when questioned, boasted that the gauge could show forty inches without danger. The boiler had burst a few minutes later, sending live steam into the cabin to kill instantly everyone it contacted. Major Heath hid from the steam under the steps with a Mr. A. Lovejoy of Georgia, and both were thus shielded from the worst of its effects. Going out on deck shortly afterward, Heath was hit by a wave and sent overboard, but a line caught his leg and he used the fragment of rope to haul himself back to safety.

The mast soon fell, crushing to death a French gentleman named Auze of Augusta, Georgia. Half an hour later Major Heath heard a wild scream as the huge promenade deck capsized, and he estimated that there must have been 100 people on the deck at the time. Almost every one of them perished including a majority of the women and children who were aboard. When dawn came, the major found that a Captain

Pearson had joined the group on the bow. The captain had been blown out into the sea by the explosion, and finding a plank, he had kicked his way back to the wreck.

All twenty-three of the survivors on the bow were in immediate peril as that section of the ship appeared to be about to go to pieces. The heavy mast lay across the deck where it had fallen, and the planking was separating rapidly. Captain Pearson suggested that they all attempt to bind the mast to the deck with lines and thus tighten the entire mass before it broke apart. This was done, and two large boxes were lashed on the deck to serve as seats.

Friday came and departed. No vessel had appeared, and the hot sun poured down on their heads, blistering their faces and backs. Some of the survivors were entirely naked, while others had merely the most abbreviated of costumes. Major Twiggs of the U. S. Army had with him his twelve-year-old son, and the lad suffered intensely from lack of water and the hot rays of the sun.

Just before sunset of the following day, their makeshift raft drifted within a half mile of the shore, and Mr. Greenwood, an expert swimmer from Georgia, volunteered to swim in for help, but Major Heath would not allow it, saying that Greenwood should not risk his life. Shortly afterward an offshore wind took them out to sea again.

It began to rain on Sunday. Every effort was made to catch some of the precious water, but they were only able to secure a tiny amount. Although it did cool them off somewhat, the shower merely brought temporary relief.

Monday dawned, and by noon four vessels had come into sight. They raised the hopes of the survivors, but in spite of everything the sufferers could do to attract attention, the distant craft did not notice them and continued on their way. Without food and water now for four days, their tongues were dry and their brains fevered. Many of them began to exhibit signs of approaching madness, but Major Heath still attempted to keep a firm hand on the situation.

On Tuesday morning they sighted another vessel, and for a time they thought the ship was bearing down on them. Then it appeared that she was going to pass them to continue down the coast. Actually her captain had sighted the survivors and was merely swinging in to approach them to leeward. The ship proved to be the schooner *Henry Camerdon*, bound to Wilmington, North Carolina.

As soon as he was within speaking distance the captain shouted across through his trumpet, "Be of good cheer. I will save you!"

This was the first utterance from a stranger they had heard in five days. Then minutes later they were all aboard the *Camerdon*, and Major Heath lost no time in telling the captain of another portion of the wreck which had been seen that very morning. The captain sailed at once in the direction of the other fragment of wreckage and soon sighted it. Five persons were on the improvised raft, and the men on the *Camerdon* quickly got them aboard. All the people rescued were placed on water rations so that they would not drink too much and die.

As they recovered the survivors recounted their experiences:

Captain Hubbard had been asleep at the time of the explosion. Jumping from his bunk, he wandered through the steam toward the ladies' cabin, found his wife there and went to the promenade deck with her. When that deck capsized, his wife clung desperately to him. Two other women then grasped him, and a short time later a wave swept all of them overboard. When Hubbard came to the surface, he saw neither his wife nor the others again.

After searching in vain, he and several men built a raft, and on it attempted to repair the leaky boat which had been abandoned. Finally the captain decided that the boat would hold six of them and he put off for shore with five others. They rowed for several hours, and night caught them adrift at sea. With the following day they began to row again, eventually approaching land.

Entering the surf, the boat soon was caught by a wave and rode it at breakneck speed for 200 yards "like a duck." The craft eluded a second wave, but the third caught the craft and capsized it at once, not far from the beach. By helping each other all six survivors were able to get ashore. They found that they had landed at Onslow Bay, a mile and a half south of New River.

Back at the wreck, a Mr. Merritt of Mobile was able to support his wife and child in the water until a heavy man grabbed him from behind. An expert swimmer and diver, Merritt allowed himself to sink under water with the man, who finally released his hold. Coming to the surface, Merritt looked in vain for his two loved ones, but he never saw either of them again.

Merritt now joined forces with a Mr. Stewart, and they gathered wreckage together so that they were able to form an impromptu raft. It proved a good one, and they floated on it for some time.

On Saturday evening they saw land, and several hours later were caught in the breakers, but both managed to get to the beach alive.

Mr. B. W. Fosdick of Boston helped build a small raft on which he was able to float until he reached the breakers. As the great waves smashed ashore he managed to escape the undertow and save himself as well as rescue several others from the surf. Excerpts from his statement follow:

"I was one of the number that did not feel exactly well, and went to bed in the after cabin about 8:00, and had slept for several hours, when I was awakened about 11:00, by a loud report, followed by a tremendous crash.

"My first impression was, that we had gone ashore, or had run into some vessel. It did not occur to me that the boiler had burst; and finding myself uninjured, I dressed myself entirely, putting my watch in my pocket, and taking my hat, and from the pocket of my cloak a light cap, which I put into my hat, thinking it would be of use, in case I could not keep my hat upon my head.

"Before I had finished dressing, a person ran down into the cabin, exclaiming, 'The boat is on fire—come up and bring buckets to extinguish it.' This person, I believe, was Mr. Sherman Miller. I never saw him afterward.

"I immediately started for the deck, and as I approached the cabin stairs, found that a number of planks of the cabin floor had been torn up; as it was quite dark in the cabin, there being but one or two candles burning, I came near falling through into the hold.

"When I reached the deck, I found that the boiler had burst. The confusion was very great: men and women were running from one part to the other; some calling for their wives, others for their husbands. On going forward, I found I could get no farther than the shaft. Beyond that, as far as the wheel house, all appeared to be in ruins and in darkness; and at every roll of the boat the water would rush in.

"There was one solitary lantern near me, and this I lashed to the ceiling. In doing so, I saw a person among the ruins of the engine, trying to get out, and moaning and crying aloud, 'Gone—gone—gone—fireman, help me—fireman, help me.' In a few minutes some one came to his assistance and extricated him. This person, I afterwards learned was one of the firemen.

"I then went aft again, and with some others assisted in removing some of the rubbish in the gangway, for, at this time, I think no one supposed the boat would sink, and we thought it best to have as clear a place as possible on deck. But we soon found this of no avail, for the water was rushing in rapidly, and everyone began to turn his attention to preparing something to support himself upon the water; such as lashing settees together, and tables, &c. A Negro was discovered preparing something of this kind, and on being asked what he was going to do, said, 'I am going to try to save my master'; appearing perfectly regardless of himself.

"The two quarter-boats were lowered into the water; but when, I do not recollect, though I have an indistinct remembrance of seeing one of them lowered by two or three persons. The boat now appeared to be sinking pretty fast, and I climbed to the promenade deck, (the only way to get there, for the stairs were at the forward part of the boat,) and there I found some forty or fifty persons, many of whom were ladies. There was also a yawl boat, which was filled with women and children; and among them the family of G. B. Lamar, of Savannah. Himself and two or three other gentlemen were standing near the boat, to keep it in an upright position, when the promenade deck of the steamboat should sink, which, as the boat had broken in two in the middle, it had begun to do; and one end was already immersed in the water. For the purpose of assisting in keeping the boat upright, I took hold of the bows.

"The water was now rushing on deck rapidly, and the forward part of the promenade deck sank so fast, that the bows of the yawl-boat filled with water, and a wave washed me from my hold, and I sank. When I rose, I found myself near a piece of plank, to which I clung; but this not being large enough to support me, I left it; and after getting from one fragment of the wreck to another, (and the water all around me was filled with fragments,) I succeeded in finding a piece large enough to support me sitting, and upon this I remained some ten minutes, and took off my boots and loosened my dress, for my clothes were so full of water that I could scarcely move. While upon this piece, I saw, near me, Mr. George Huntington, of Savannah.

"Here I will mention what was told me by a person, (Mr. Eldridge, of Syracuse, N. Y.,) who was upon the promenade deck after I was washed from it. He says that nearly all the females in the yawl-boat were drowned at the time it filled.

"After removing my boots, I remained quiet some ten or fifteen minutes, when I heard some persons calling out not far from me, and concluded they were in one of the boats; but upon inquiring, found it was a part of the ladies' cabin, (the side,) and that there were two persons upon it, (Andrew Stewart and Owen Gallagher, deck hands,) and that there was room enough for another, and that they would take one upon it, if I could get up to it—but that they had no means of coming to me. I knew the only chance of safety was to reach it—and I made a desperate effort, and succeeded, by swimming, and by getting from plank to plank, which were scattered all around me, in reaching it, and was pulled upon it almost exhausted.

"This piece of the ladies' cabin was then about ten feet wide, by forty-five feet long; but in the course of the night we lost ten or fifteen feet of it—leaving us a piece of thirty feet in length. Upon this we sat all night, with the water about a foot deep. The wind was blowing quite fresh, in a direction toward land, and our raft, being long and narrow, made very good progress; and in the course of two hours after the bursting of the boiler, we were out of sight of the wreck.

"About this time we discovered, approaching near us, a portion of the deck of the steamboat, with an upright post near the centre of it—and upon it were Mr. George Huntington and two other persons. They said they were all from

Savannah. We lashed the two rafts together with a rope, which they threw us—but finding that the sea dashed our rafts together with a considerable violence, we concluded it would be better to separate again—and we did so. Mr. Huntington wished me to take a passage with them, but I concluded to remain where I was. I saw them no more.

"Friday morning came, and discovered to us our situation. We were out of sight of land. Three rafts we saw at a distance. They were too far off for us to discern the persons upon them, but they all had signals flying. Upon our little raft we found a small chest belonging to one of the firemen, and which afterward served us as a seat; two mattresses, a sheet, a blanket, and some female wearing apparel.

"The mattresses we emptied of their contents, and with the covering of one of them we made a sail, which, with a good deal of difficulty, we succeeded in putting up, but which did us much service, for by noon we had almost entirely lost sight of the other rafts; and in the afternoon nothing was seen, as far as the eye could reach, but sky and water.

"But our spirits did not flag, for we thought that by morning we must certainly fall in with some fishing boats. We had also found on the raft a tin box, the cover gone, containing some cake, wrapped up in a cloth. This was completely saturated with salt water, but we took a mouthful of it in the course of the day, and found it pretty good. There was also a keg, which floated on to the raft, containing a little gin; but this was of little service, for, by some means or other, it was mixed with salt water.

"The night came; the wind and sea increased, and we were obliged to take down our little sail. During the night the waves were constantly washing over our raft, and the water, at all times, stood a foot deep upon it. We sat close together upon the chest, which we lashed as well as we could to the raft, and wrapped ourselves up in the wet blanket and clothes, for the night air felt very cold, after having been exposed, as we were all day, to the broiling sun. We were much fatigued, and once, during the night, we fell asleep, and were awakened by the upsetting of our seat, which nearly threw us overboard.

"Anxiously we watched the rising of the moon, which rose some hours after midnight; and still more, the rising of the sun, which we hoped would disclose to our weary eyes the sight of some distant sail. The sun at last *did* rise, *but there was nothing in sight.*

"For the first time we began to feel a little discouraged; still the hope that we should soon see land impressed itself upon us, and eagerly we cast our eyes landward, every now and then, as the sun continued to rise. And, joyful sight! about six o'clock we *thought* we did see land, and in another half hour were sure of it.

"Now we redoubled our exertions; we paddled; we held up in our hands pieces of cloth—we did everything to propel our little craft, for we feared the wind might change, and blow off shore, and then all hope would be lost; for our raft, we felt sure could not hold together another day. As we neared land, we found the surf was running pretty high, but there was a sandy shore, and we felt no fear of this, for we *saw the land*, and we knew that soon our suspense would be at an end.

"About 4:00 P.M., on Saturday, we reached the breakers. The first breaker came over us with great violence, and so did the second; the third broke the raft in pieces, but we clung to the fragments, and soon found we could touch the bottom with our feet; and in a few minutes we were safe upon *terra firma*, considerably bruised and sun-burnt, but with our lives. And grateful did we feel to that Almighty Arm, which, in the hour of danger, was stretched over us to save and protect. And it was only by the mercy of a Divine

Providence that we were thus saved from a watery grave. I forgot to mention that, on Saturday, a *shark* was following us nearly all the morning, but we frightened it away.

"Near the shore, which was at New River Inlet, N. C., we found the house of Mr. Henderson, who received us in the kindest manner, and did all in his power for us. And from every one we met, we have received the utmost hospitality especially from some gentlemen of Newbern, who furnished us with money to pay our way home. But we found that it was not much needed, for neither the conductors of the railroad cars, nor the captains of the steamboats, would receive anything for our passage."

Of the 183 who were aboard the *Pulaski* when she blew up and later went down off Cape Lookout, North Carolina, only fifty-nine eventually were saved.

People rescued from drowning or disaster at sea have often been embarrassed because someone else saved their lives and they do not always show the gratitude one might expect. However, Major Heath issued a statement which was a masterpiece of appreciation for those who had helped in saving him from the wreck of the *Pulaski*. He closed his acknowledgment with the following:

"To all, finally, who aided and befriended the undersigned, in the extremity of their misfortunes, they offer the feelings of hearts which the tongue cannot express, and, without stopping particularly to name each benefactor, beg that one and all will receive this as the sincere return of thanks from rescued, and now grateful fellow-beings.

"James P. Heath,
"For himself and others."

CHAPTER SEVENTEEN

GRACE DARLING

The young, the brave!
The heroine of the wreck and storm!

WHILE ALMOST EVERYONE has heard of Grace Darling and the fact that she rescued several people from the sea's vengeance, very few know the details of her great feat of daring which has caused mariners from all over the world to honor her memory.

Her father, William Darling, was the son of a lighthouse keeper as was his father before him.* Grace's grandfather kept the Staple Island Light when her father was a small child. One day the lighthouse keeper, his wife and son were down at the southern side of the island where the lighthouse stood. Suddenly, without warning, a gigantic wave was seen rushing at the island. The keeper grabbed his boy and told his wife to run. They barely escaped to higher ground before the wave hit, toppled over the lighthouse and washed away the keeper's residence. Without shelter and food, the family was in dire straits until finally rescued by a relief boat.

---

* A relatively short time ago in the present century there was a Darling registered as keeper of Farne Lighthouse in the British Isles.

Sometime later William had another escape. Fourteen years of age at the time, he was in the tower of the Brownsman Light playing on the upper platform when he fell off. Fortunately he was caught by a projection halfway down the outside of the lighthouse. When his father discovered the boy, he feared that he was dead. Taking the lad inside, he cared for him until he regained consciousness.

By the time he was eighteen William was a tall, strong young man who had decided to go into the lighthouse service as his father had done. He married a girl named Thomasin Horseley, who was twelve years older than he was, and soon was given the care of the Longstone Light on Farne Island. They had several children, and Grace was born at Bamborough, Northumberland, on November 24, 1815.

As she grew up the girl quickly learned how to handle a boat, and her parents taught her the fundamentals of education. She took an active part at the station, often lighting the lights at night and putting them out in the morning.

On September 5, 1838, a fisherman had brought packets and letters out from North Sunderland to the Longstone Rock with Grace as usual meeting the vessel in her small boat. The day was a relatively pleasant one, but toward evening heavy masses of clouds started to build up, and shortly afterward a high wind began to blow. All the next day a great storm raged. That night when Grace went to bed she was filled with anxiety for those out on the ocean.

Early the next morning, long before dawn, there was a lull in the storm, and Grace awakened. Something other than the roar of the sea had aroused her. She listened and then heard a chilling sound. It was the shrill, piercing shriek of a woman in mortal terror, and Grace knew instinctively that someone was in trouble out on the angry ocean.

Dressing hastily, she aroused her father and told him what she had heard.

"Nonsense, Grace!" was his answer. "What makes you so sure that you heard a human cry above the roar of the sea?"

"Father, there's no question in my mind, and I am going to help whoever is in trouble!" In spite of the protests of both her mother and father, Grace put on her outer garments and told her father she was rowing out alone or with him, but in any case she was going.

Realizing that his daughter was in earnest, William Darling dressed hurriedly and went with her down to the rocky shore.

There in the gathering dawn, they could faintly discern the outline of a steamer wrecked on a ledge half a mile from the lighthouse. By this time the mother had joined them, and she implored her husband not to row out.

"Oh, William," she began. "There's been a shipwreck, and lives are lost, but don't add your own to the number. Your boat wouldn't live ten minutes in such a sea!"

But father and daughter both explained that they couldn't stand idly by and let everyone drown. Grace then seized the oars and sprang into the boat, and her father followed her at once. The distraught mother watched with fear as they met the first breakers. Within five minutes the first dangerous line of combers was behind them and they were making fair headway toward the ship.

The wreck was the steamer *Forfarshire*. The 300-ton steamer had sailed from Hull under Mr. John Humble on a voyage to Dundee, Scotland, at 6:30 on the evening of Wednesday, September 5, 1838, in company with the *Pegasus* and the *Innisfail*. The *Forfarshire* was a combination freight and passenger steamer, having on board bale goods, sheet iron and forty passengers besides Captain Humble and his wife, ten seamen, four firemen, two engineers, two coal trimmers and two stewards.

Just before leaving Hull, the steamer's boilers had been inspected and a small leak was revealed. Temporary repairs had been made, but when the vessel was off Flambro Head the leak started again. According to Fireman Daniel Donovan it became so bad that two of the boiler fires were extinguished. Eventually they were relighted after the boilers had again been repaired. Nevertheless, a passenger named Mrs. Dawson stated that "even before we left Hull, my impressions that all was not well were so strong that had my husband, a glassman, come down to the packet before she sailed I'd have returned with him on shore."

While the boilers were being repaired at sea the *Forfarshire* had slowed down, and three steamers passed her.

Proceeding through the Fairway between the Farne Islands and the mainland, the steamer entered Berwick Bay at 8:00 that following Thursday evening. By this time the wind was blowing strong, creating an ominous swaying motion aboard the ship, and soon the leak increased to such a degree that the firemen could not keep the fires going. Two men were then ordered to keep water pumping into the boilers, but they emptied through the leak as fast as they were filled.

Increasing steadily, the storm was a raging gale by the time that the *Forfarshire* limped by St. Abb's Head. Shortly afterward the engines became utterly useless and almost all control of the steamer in the sea was at an end. The *Forfarshire*, with sixty-two persons aboard, was now adrift on a raging sea off a dangerous part of the coast with no immediate hope of rescue.

She did carry a limited number of sails, which were hoisted fore and aft, enabling her to get around before the wind. In this manner she was kept off shore, but no attempt at anchoring was made.

The storm soon increased to such a degree that the sails slatted away. The steamer then became unmanageable and began to drift rapidly, caught by the strong south tide. The rain was now a downpour, and a thick British fog had come in, making visibility less than ten feet.

Later, however, the fog lifted a trifle, and what those aboard the *Forfarshire* saw filled them with stark terror. The steamer was drifting in toward heavy breakers, which showed to the leeward, while in the distance the gleam of Farne Light could be discerned. A desperate attempt to run the ship between the Farne islands was made, but the *Forfarshire* failed completely to answer her helm.

Drifting slowly but surely, all hope of rescue gone, the side-wheeler was soon caught in the dreaded grasp of the Longstone breakers. Pushed steadily shoreward, she crashed heavily on the rocks. It was then 3:00 in the morning of September 7, 1838.

Already several members of the crew had lowered the larboard quarterboat. They now jumped into it to abandon the ship. From the moment of striking the captain apparently lost all ability to retain command, and the shrieks of his distraught wife were heard at times even above the roar of the breakers and the whistle of the wind.

At the moment the steamer struck many of the cabin passengers were below, still asleep, and the steward rushed down to awaken them. In spite of his efforts only one person was able to leave in time. He was Ruthven Ritchie, a farmer of Hill, Perthshire, who was making the journey with his aunt and uncle. Every other cabin passenger drowned. Ritchie had seized a pair of trousers when awakened, rushed naked out on deck and leaped into the waiting boat, where he donned his pants.

His aunt and uncle, who had stopped to dress, managed to reach the deck just as the boat was pulling away. They also attempted to get in, but narrowly missed the jump and fell into the sea. Both were drowned.

After the craft left the wreck, Ritchie borrowed a shoe

from another occupant and used it as a howskelly or bailer. The escape of the boat was amazing, for there was only one outlet by which it could be saved, and without knowing it the oarsmen steered through that very area! The nine occupants were picked up the following Saturday morning by a craft from Montrose, and taken into Shields. Luckily, Ritchie had several gold sovereigns in his trousers pocket and purchased additional clothing on landing.

Back aboard the *Forfarshire* the survivors had watched the boat disappear, not knowing its fate. They were now afraid that the steamer would go to pieces. Striking just aft of the paddleboxes, she had broken apart. The stern, quarter deck and cabin were carried away with those who were aboard that part, while the bow and the amidships section remained pinioned to the rock. The captain and his wife, adrift on the stern, soon slipped off and were drowned.

One of the most heartrending incidents occurred shortly afterward. Mrs. Dawson, a steerage passenger, was with her two children, a boy of eight and a girl of eleven. At the time of the wreck she had managed to cling to a rail on the deck, her two children holding desperately to her. But the exposure was too great for the youngsters, and both soon perished. Nevertheless, Mrs. Dawson refused to believe that her young ones were dead, and when finally rescued, had to be led away into the waiting lifeboat.

Another survivor was Fireman Donovan, who had managed to hang on to a spike on the deck for three hours, his hands bleeding and raw.

It was at daybreak that morning that Grace and her father launched their tiny boat into the tempestuous sea. The keeper and his twenty-two-year-old daughter realized that the chances were slim of their ever reaching the steamer in the coble * through the breaking, surging seas. Again and again

---

* A short flat-bottomed rowboat.

the breakers smashed into their craft, but each time they started anew for the wreck. Reaching the scene of the disaster, the father jumped out on the sloping deck of the side-wheeler, while Grace was forced to row back into the shelter of the rock itself to prevent the giant waves from swamping the boat. Keeper Darling arranged with the nine survivors on the wreck that four men and a woman should go back with them on the first trip and the others should await a second attempt.

Grace then brought the tiny boat alongside the wreck, and her father helped the five persons aboard, after which both father and daughter rowed strenuously for the safety of Farne Island. After battling the waves they finally reached the lee of the island, and the five survivors were brought ashore and taken up to the keeper's home where Mrs. Darling was already preparing for their relief and comfort. Another trip to the wreck resulted in the removal of the last four survivors, and when they also were landed safely and taken into the home of the Darlings one of the great lifesaving feats of the century had been accomplished.

The storm did not go down until the following Sunday. At that time all nine survivors were taken across to the mainland to begin the journey to their respective homes. Mrs. Dawson and Fireman Donovan, however, had been so battered by the great waves which swept the wreck that they were unable to travel and were cared for at Bamburgh Castle for several days until they recovered.

It was not long before news traveled all over England of Grace Darling's courage, and before the year ended the girl was receiving letters and honors from everywhere in Britain. Subscriptions were started by various organizations to reward her properly for her accomplishment and in a short space of time she was the recipient of more than £700.

Grace became ill in the summer of 1842, and growing

worse by the fall, she was taken ashore to Bamborough. There, on October 20, at the age of twenty-five, she died and was interred in the local Bamborough churchyard.

Since her death two unusual memorials have been erected in her honor. The one on Farne Island is a simple tablet while the one in the Bamborough churchyard is an imposing tomb showing a recumbent figure of the heroine.

At least one hundred poems have been written in Grace Darling's memory. That she saved nine persons from the vengeful sea in such heroic fashion is something which the world has remembered through the years. From scores of stanzas written in her honor, I have chosen the following from the pen of William Wordsworth:

> Shout ye waves!
> Pipe a glad song of triumph, ye fierce winds!
> Ye screaming sea mews in the concert join!
> And would that some immortal voice,
> Fitly attuned to all that gratitude
> Breathes out from flock or couch through pallid lips
> Of the survivors, to the clouds might bear—
> (Blended with praise of that parental love,
> Pious and pure, modest and yet so brave,
> Though young, so wise, though meek so resolute)
> Might carry to the clouds, and to the stars,
> Yes, to celestial choirs, GRACE DARLING'S name.

CHAPTER ∘ EIGHTEEN

AIDED BY A MADMAN

Though this be madness, yet there is method in't.

THE SEA ITSELF is both wonderful and terrible. Whenever a ship sails away from land the powerful ocean holds the vessel firmly in its grasp. A hundred years ago the deep exerted even more influence on those who chose to challenge its supremacy than it does today, and strange and remarkable events often took place far out on the broad marine highways. At times, however, the ever-alert sea, always waiting to avenge itself on man for his audacity in daring to venture afloat at all, has been materially assisted by some unworthy representative of the human race.

And so it was that on September 23, 1845, during a voyage of the bark *Tory* from Hong Kong to London, began as cruel and as cold-blooded an episode as any in marine history.

On that particular date the crew of the *Tory*, hungry and discouraged, realized that Captain George Johnstone was not going to stop at Ascension Island for more supplies. Short of both food and water, they decided to have one of their number appeal to the captain for more substantial fare.

Johnstone, known as a terror when in his cups, apparently had exhausted his available liquor supply some time before, as he was more or less tolerant of their demands for better meals. He also agreed to attempt to obtain additional stores from the first passing craft.

A short time later the *Tory* spoke to the French bark *L'Avenier* from which she obtained fresh water, provisions and a plentiful stock of brandy and wine for the captain's cabin.

Johnstone soon became intoxicated and stayed in that condition most of the remainder of this voyage. A relatively mild man when sober, he now began to suspect the other members of the ship's company of plotting to take his command away from him.

On September 28, 1845, he called Chief Mate Rambert before him, accusing Rambert of planning a mutiny. Rambert vehemently denied any such activity, but the crazed captain, disbelieving the mate, smashed the officer to his knees with a broadsword. For three hours Johnstone kept him there during which time he wounded him several times. Abandoning the mate for the moment, he called for three members of the crew—Reason, Cone and Lee—and when they came into his cabin he assaulted them severely.

While the sailors were still bleeding from their injuries, the captain sent his terrified victims aloft, ironed and shackled, one to the maintop and two to the mizzentop, still cutting at them with his sword whenever they were in reach.

Realizing that Johnstone was maddened with liquor, the mate decided to prevent further bloodshed. Taking advantage of his absence, the wounded officer secretly implored the other members of the crew to seize the captain and put him in irons. Unfortunately for Rambert they discussed it with a seaman named French who was a special favorite of Johnstone's, and he vetoed the idea. Thus the mate's fellow crewmen went forward to their quarters and did nothing to help him.

Rushing at once to his commanding officer, French told him of Mate Rambert's plan to confine him, and the captain had Rambert seized and placed in irons after which he began cutting the officer again with his sword, one of his swings nearly severing Rambert's ear. Then, ordering the prisoner released, he chased him around the deck, cruelly slashing at him with his weapon.

The amazing part of this story is the apparent passiveness of the passengers, who witnessed the wounding and killing of the sailors from various parts of the ship. We can appreciate the fact that a seaman on a British ship during this period had no rights at all and would often suffer the most heartless indignities without starting a mutiny, but it is hard to understand the attitude of the passengers, not bound in any way by the traditions of the sea.

Mrs. Mary Blewett, a cabin passenger, was on the poop deck on the afternoon of September 28. Earlier she had seen the three men—Reason, Cone and Lee—in irons in the rigging and wondered about it.

At 3:00 Mrs. Blewett heard the captain bellowing for the mate to be brought to him and, unknown to Johnstone she observed what followed. With a pistol in one hand and his sword in the other, the skipper struck and stabbed Rambert time and again. Begging repeatedly for mercy, the mate groveled on the deck, shrinking from each blow.

The frenzied captain gave the same answer each time: "No, you overgrown monster! No, you cowardly brute!"

"Ask the sailors," implored Rambert. "Ask them if I ever said a word against you."

This only enraged Johnstone further, and with renewed fury he struck the officer again and again. Finally Rambert shouted out in despair that there was no hope left. He staggered to the rail, climbed over, and plunged to a merciful death in the sea.

The wounded men were taken out of irons a few days later, and except for an occasional outburst from the intoxicated captain, the bark reached Fayal without further incident.

While ashore at Fayal with the British consul, Captain Johnstone drank an excess of wine, after which he confided in a lad named Stephens, a passenger on the *Tory*, that he was planning to kill every member of the mutinous crew when he returned to the bark.

On the way out to the *Tory* he wounded one of his men. Going aboard, he appeared to be heavily intoxicated and suddenly exclaimed, "Here I come, like a seven-bell half struck."

He then called for Second Mate Mars whom he also accused of plotting mutiny. Mars denied the accusation. Nevertheless Johnstone swung his sword at the man cutting him several times.

"That will show you, Mars, that you made a mistake in planning your mutiny. Now jump into the sea from the stern windows!"

Mars refused to commit suicide, whereupon the captain sent him out of the cabin, but recalled him almost immediately to assault him further.

"I'll fix you, you mutineer!" he shouted.

Mars now made a final appeal to his master. "Please have me tried by the law of my country if I am a mutineer," he begged.

"I will not, for the only trial you'll ever have is board-of-ship law! I'll cut you up into inches before I finish!"

Mars was then allowed to go up on deck again, with a fifty-pound shackle around his neck and his hands manacled with cuffs.

When the captain ordered the mate to come back once

more into the cabin, it was now occupied by a sailor named Spence, Harry Slack, the carpenter, and Cordiviallo, a seaman. Still in irons, the defenseless Mars appeared at the cabin door. Immediately Johnstone began swinging at him with his sword, slashing at the poor man until he was a mass of bleeding cuts.

"Don't ever call this man Mr. Mars again, for from now on his name is just Mars," shouted the enraged master, as he continued to slash away, until finally his victim slid to the deck unconscious.

"Pick him up," he shouted at the others. "Can't you make him stand up?"

When the others were unable to force the unconscious man to remain standing, the captain ordered them to tie him around the middle and suspend him to a cleat in the bulkhead. The men were reluctant to do this, and Johnstone glared at them. At this moment Mars gained consciousness.

"Tie him to the cleat, or else you and Harry shall be punished together," he bellowed at Cordiviallo, and the two sailors quickly obeyed.

The captain then amused himself during dinner by throwing his sword at Mars. Finally, his passion satisfied, he ordered the man taken up on deck, laid prone, and pressed with heavy weights. This was done and as the torture continued the unfortunate mate suffered more than he could bear. Losing consciousness again, he died shortly afterward.

Johnstone next decided to concentrate his diabolical fury on Reason, who had also been placed in shackles. Stepping up to his victim, he ran him through several times. Savagely attacking the man, he hacked away until it was apparent that the sailor was dying. Just before his death the captain appeared momentarily remorseful, and went to the man to hold his head up.

"Tom, dear Tom," he said, "speak just two words to me."

But the sailor died without regaining consciousness. Apparently this further enraged the drunken maniac, for he wounded several others immediately following the death of Reason.

The liquor was now again exhausted, and Johnstone seemed to have become remorseful and also not a little worried. Realizing his position, the scheming master planned his moves carefully. He ordered Seaman Spence, a good writer, to appear in the cabin, where the captain dictated entries into the log. Excerpts from the dictation follow:

"Chief Mate Rambert became mutinous, and to save himself from the consequences, jumped overboard, giving three cheers as he leaped.

"The crew killed Mars and Reason. We have come to the conclusion that Mars was a mutineer of the darkest dye."

Later the master told Mrs. Blewett that he was going to put her in irons for the remainder of the voyage for witnessing what happened, and he vowed he would have her hanged at the Old Bailey upon arrival in London. He did not carry out his threat, however.

Just before entering Plymouth Harbor Johnstone called Seaman Harry Yelverton into his stateroom off the main cabin. Taking a strand of rope, he tore Harry's shirt off and began lashing the bare back and shoulders of the seaman. Finally the captain finished the abuse and allowed Harry to go up on deck.

The following morning, when Johnstone realized that all the wounded men would present an odd sight to the pilot when he boarded the *Tory*, he decided to get Yelverton and French to help him.

"Yelverton," he began, "I am truly sorry for what I have done to you. It is a wonder I have not killed you. I did it because of what you said at dinner. You remember that you asked me not to kill any more?"

"Yes, sir, I remember."

"Well, Harry, when the crew comes aft, speak up and tell how the crew had you lashed against the mizzenmast with a rope around your neck, and then Mr. French and I'll start firing on them."

The crew now reported aft. The captain had already armed his new mate, Mr. French, with a pistol, and without warning the two officers started firing at their hysterical men, continuing for three-quarters of an hour, after which Johnstone began swinging his sabre. Although the pistols did not at first contain shot, the powder burns were very painful, and then the captain loaded his weapon with shot. A Frenchman named Reulau, a seaman named Gair and several others were shockingly mutilated. When this carnage ended, thirteen in the crew had been severely wounded.

Even after the pilot came aboard Captain Johnstone continued to abuse the crew, cutting and jabbing Peter Curtis in several places about the head and body, after which the victim hid under the longboat to save his life.

Later Johnstone sent for another sailor, Franklin Neckar, and ordered him to his knees in the cabin. Calling his newly elected mate, the captain instructed him to fire with powder directly at Neckar. Neckar was then released but within an hour was sent for again. This time, possibly to impress the pilot, who was within hearing, Johnstone cried out, "Mutiny, to arms!" Then French and Johnstone blew out the lights and smashed at Neckar in the darkness, after which they locked him up.

The captain now put every other member of the crew in irons, and as soon as he reached port lodged a complaint of mutiny against them. In turn the men accused the captain, and the tables slowly began to turn.

And so it came about that Captain Johnstone was eventually charged with the murder of Rambert, Mars and Reason and brought before Mr. Broderip at the Thames Police Court in London.

Johnstone was represented in the police court by a solicitor, Mr. Jervis, who advised his client not to take the stand and to remain silent. The solicitor had discussed the case carefully with the captain who apparently was quite rational when not under the influence of liquor. After hearing all the details, the lawyer planned to plead insanity for the defendant. One by one the crew members told their strange story of violence, cruelty and murder essentially as I have described it. Then with a confident air Captain Johnstone stood up when he was ordered to do so by the police judge, Mr. Broderip.

"Prisoner at the bar," began Mr. Broderip, "it is now my duty to send you to take your trial at the next session of the Central Criminal Court for the wilful murder of Thomas Reason, also for the wilful murder of William Mars, and also for the wilful murder of William Rambert. I have, moreover, to commit you to take your trial on the charge of feloniously wounding Stephen Cone, Thomas Lee, David Johnson, Thomas Gair, Ronilleau, William Burton, Robert Thompson, Andrew Nelson, William Beresford, and Peter Curtis."

Captain Johnstone had not expected this, for he thought he would be freed because of his claim that the men had mutinied against him. Broderip's statement was too much for him, and he collapsed, being removed from the bar "in a very feeble condition."

The trial was held early in 1846, and on Friday, February 6 of that year Mr. Jervis, speaking on behalf of his client at the regular session of the Criminal Court, stated that it would be impossible for the jury "to find the prisoner guilty," because the defendant was out of his mind.

Justice Williams summed up the strange case as follows: "The mere fact of a crime being committed under most atrocious and revolting circumstances ought not to be taken as a proof of the insanity of the person who committed it. Nevertheless, the members of the jury should weigh all the facts and make their decision accordingly."

The jury retired and returned in twenty-five minutes. The foreman stood up.

"We find the prisoner guilty, but that he was not in a sound state of mind."

Mr. Justice Williams then told the jury that they would either have to state him guilty or not guilty, and if they thought that the captain was not in his right mind that would suggest a Not Guilty verdict on the grounds of insanity. Confused as they were, the members of the jury were finally ordered by the justice to retire and return another verdict. At last they returned with a Not Guilty verdict on the grounds that the prisoner was in a state of insanity at the time of his acts.

The verdict, of course, allowed the prisoner to be removed and placed in safe custody. His future life is a mystery, for he completely disappeared behind the walls of an institution.

At the time the verdict was not received with favor by the public. One writer of the period made the following statement:

"It is difficult to restrain one's indignation, it is impossible to abstain from bitterness, in beholding the first principles of law perverted and made to work the grossest injustice. . . . It is become a fashion, of late years, to presume the existence of this disease in every criminal whose offense is characterized by extraordinary atrocity. . . . The commission of a great crime without apparent motive is supposed to be in itself a proof of insanity. Once admit it, and you give a premium to enormous crimes.

"The master of a merchant vessel sails from China for an English port. Midway on his homeward voyage the water and provisions run short. The crew are placed upon short allowance, and, of course, show some symptoms of discontent. These are conveyed to the captain's ears by meddling, sneaking rascals, such as are always to be found on board ship, ready with any act of meanness to curry favor. The captain is alarmed (we put the matter in the most favorable light for himself) for the safety of his valuable cargo. He determines to crush the spirit of mutiny in the very outset; and to do this by a system of intimidation. In order to wind up his feelings to the necessary point of savage barbarity, he seeks the usual resource and incentive of crime—the bottle.

"An unfortunate occurrence—the meeting with another vessel on the high seas—supplies him with an unlimited means of intoxication. . . . He commits, with a reckless, indiscriminate atrocity, and a barbarous exultation, repeated acts of cruelty upon his trembling crew. He perpetrates murders wholesale, cuts and slashes men as though they were senseless stocks, then drinks again to deaden the stings of remorse, and returns to the attack.

"He arrives at length in port, and, having had ample time for deliberation, resumes the initiative, and charges his crew with mutiny.

"The charge is investigated, but in the course of it, such tales are told as throw the guilt upon the master, instead of the men, and the Crown is impelled to intervene. The captain is placed at the bar of his country on a charge of murder.

"The case is proved against him, with all the attendant horrors of a cold-blooded and motiveless inhumanity. He offers no defense—not even an attempt is made to prove his insanity. On the contrary, it is admitted that up to the moment of the supposed mutiny, he was quiet, and sufficiently inoffensive.

"His defense is rested solely on the unaccountableness of his conduct, on the fashionable idea, *that a crime without a motive is no crime at all*. The jury find him guilty and insane. They are told the verdict is a contradiction. They are puzzled at first, and no wonder. At last they acquit him on the grounds of insanity.

"And this trial takes place in 1846, in the heart of London, in the center of enlightenment and civilization, before a jury sworn 'to give a true verdict, according to the evidence.' That they have not done so, we do not hesitate to affirm. They may have decided according to the evidence. The contest lies between their judgment and their honor. The one has failed. We will not suppose it to be the latter."

CHAPTER NINETEEN

THE BURNING OF THE *Austria*

Then rose from sea to sky the wild farewell;
Then shriek'd the timid and stood still the brave,
Then some leap'd overboard with dreadful yell,
As eager to anticipate their grave.

ON SEPTEMBER 2, 1858, Captain Heydtmann sailed the passenger steamer *Austria* from Hamburg, Germany, bound for a stop at Southampton and then the trip across the ocean to America. When the steamer left England there were 538 persons aboard.

It was a beautiful, calm day on September 13, and the *Austria* was far at sea. All doors and portholes were open to let the warm fall air blow through the ship. As conditions were ideal for the purpose orders were given to fumigate the vessel. The fourth officer, who was in charge of fumigation plans, directed the boatswain's mate to obtain a bucket of tar and a piece of hot iron chain after which he was to go into the forward steerage and fumigate it by dropping the chain into the tar. Although the boatswain's mate did as directed, something went wrong, and the tar caught fire. To make matters worse, the mate released the end of the chain because it was too hot to hold, and it fell on the bucket, upsetting the burning tar, which started to flow in all directions.

Berths and mattresses were soon aflame, and the blaze spread at almost unbelievable speed along the deck. In a relatively short time the flames leaped through the gangways to the hatchways at the entrance to the first and second cabins toward the stern, and soon the fire was shooting up through the areaways like a blast furnace, cutting off all retreat for passengers who were below.

As it was a calm day, orders had gone out to open all portholes, all stateroom doors and all bulkhead doors for ventilation so that a breeze now fanned the flames. Consequently, the entire upper amidships section of the *Austria* was ablaze within five minutes after the boatswain's mate had upset the bucket of tar.

A wild panic resulted, with men and women running back and forth, unable to escape the fire leaping toward them. Some began to pray, while others screamed or fainted dead away. A few people, took careful stock of the situation to see what they could do about it.

All ships customarily carry hose to extinguish fires and boats to be launched for the purpose of escaping from a sinking ship. Unfortunately, in this instance, the hose was out of order and the boats had been permanently riveted to the chocks by a thrifty carpenter who was afraid that they would wash overboard in a storm.

The captain did not help matters by losing his head and shouting that they were all lost. He ran to the quarter-deck, but in doing so he had to pass through the flames, burning himself severely. He was seen by the first officer, standing on the quarter-deck in a dazed condition, and a short time later he leaped to his death in the sea.

Masses of people were now trampling over one another in

their frenzy to get away from the heat, and many children were trodden on and suffocated. A few escaped to the rigging, hoping in some way the fire would not reach them there, while others prepared to leap into the sea.

At this time quiet, purposeful men were attempting to hammer off the bolts which held the lifeboats to the chocks, and finally one was freed. But before any of the starboard boats could be launched they caught fire. On the larboard (or port side, as it is now called) four boats were released and lowered. Three of them smashed as they hit the water, and only one finally reached the sea intact. It was a large metallic lifeboat and had been overcrowded when it left the deck. In the descent it tipped, spewing out nearly twenty persons. About thirty others held on and were still aboard when the craft put out from the *Austria*. It capsized again, and by the time it was finally righted, seven more men had drowned, leaving only the first officer, six of the crew, one steward and fifteen passengers remaining.

The engines of the *Austria* could not be stopped because of the fire, and the steamer soon outdistanced the lifeboat. Swamped to her gunwhales, the small craft was emptied of water by floating some of the people on the oars and mast, while the others bailed until she once more became seaworthy.

An hour later a sail was sighted far in the distance, and it came directly toward the survivors. It was the French bark *Maurice*, which soon picked up the grateful band of refugees. The bark had already rescued some passengers and the *Austria's* third officer.

After the lifeboat had gone, the fire aboard the burning steamer gradually forced many of the passengers toward the bowsprit, and before long there were more than a hundred people there. But the hungry flames began to burn those nearest amidships, and scores soon believed that there was no hope for them. One unfortunate mother was seen to kiss both her daughters, put her arms around them and leap with them into the sea. All three perished at once. Another woman had a girl of five, a boy of three and a baby in her arms. Her husband leaped overboard and sank to his death. She first took the little girl, kissed her and threw her into the sea. Then she grasped her boy, kissed him and dropped him overboard. Striking on his back, the lad floated for a long time, and his piteous cries could be heard aboard the ship. "Mamma, Mamma, Mamma," he sobbed before he sank never to rise. The poor woman now clasped her infant to her breast and jumped. She landed in the water and floated for a time, kissing her baby desperately as she did so. Then she began to sink, dragged down by her heavy wet clothing, and disappeared shortly afterward.

A young man and his seventeen-year-old sister were on their way to California. To prevent the fire's reaching her he tied a line around her body and lowered her into the sea, making the other end fast to a cleat on the deck. He put another line around himself and started down, but he slipped and the rope caught around his neck, choking him. His unfortunate sister, a helpless witness, cried out for someone to rescue her brother, but no one responded, and mercifully she soon followed him in death.

A fifty-year-old Englishman crawled out on the bowsprit with his wife, but when the flames approached and began to scorch them, they leaped into the sea together, where they were swallowed up at once.

Back on the quarter-deck, members of families which were separated attempted to locate each other, but as the relentless flames sought them out, they, too, were forced to the stern of the ship, where in groups or singly they leaped to their doom in the sea. As the distance to the water was twenty-two feet, many hesitated at first, but the blistering heat soon gave them no alternative, and within half an hour from the start of the fire, not a soul was alive on the poop deck.

The tragic deaths of those working in the engine room at the boilers are almost beyond contemplation. Several passengers who were afterward saved had jumped into the sea to grasp fragments of wreckage or simply swim. While in the water, they were within a few feet of the portholes of the burning ship, and there they had indelibly imprinted on their memory the terrible picture of frenzied firemen and engineers, with a wall of flame behind them, attempting the impossible task of jamming their burning bodies through the ports.

Personal experiences of many of the passengers were recorded immediately after the disaster. One boy, the son of a Mr. Rosen, had a particularly sad story to tell.

"My father and I ran forward to escape the fire, and were followed by the other passengers. I saw the fire pouring out through the skylights. In ten or fifteen minutes more the cry rang fore and aft, 'To the boats!' All hands then crowded into the boats. . . . The first mate mounted the rail near the forward boat on the port side, in which we were sitting with a large crowd of other passengers. He ordered all of us to get out so that it could be lowered. But as fast as one got out, others rushed into their places, and we also went back to our first seat. The first mate then took a knife, and cut the tackle, and the boat fell into the water.

"Falling from such a height, the boat filled and sank, and all the people were washed out. I came up under the boat, but I found my way out, and clambered into the boat. There were five or six oars lashed together, and they all floated out.

"My father came within reach of these, and seized hold of them with five or six others. He saw me in the boat, and called out to me, 'Oh, my boy, we are all lost!' In a short time, one end of the oar drifted near the boat, and I caught hold of it to haul him in. I also asked a passenger near to assist me in saving my father.

"We pulled together, but there were so many clinging to the oars, we could not move them. I then said to my father, 'Hold on and do the best you can.'

"He then drifted along near us, still clinging to the oars. In this way he held on for nearly four hours. I could not bear to look at him and we drifted in silence. During this time the boat rolled over several times, and many were drowned each time.

"My father by this time had drifted so near the boat that he caught hold of the stern. I was at the bow and could not reach him. Mr. John F. Cox said, 'Charley, your father has hold of the stern of the boat, and can get in.' I said, 'Oh, I am so glad that he is safe.' But he was so exhausted that he held on only about five minutes, and then sank. Just before he let go, he said to Mr. Cox, 'If my boy is safe, I am satisfied.'"

Professor Glaubensklee of the New York Free Academy was in his stateroom when the alarm of fire came. Noticing the many tragedies at the lifeboats, he decided not to trust himself there, but determined to stay aboard ship just as long as possible.

The professor went to the forecastle, where he helped in cutting down the jib so that it could be saturated with water to check the forward progress of the fire. Unfortunately, those who were assisting dropped the sail into the sea and it floated away.

Glaubensklee then went looking for some material from which he could build a raft. Finding nothing, he climbed out over the starboard bulwarks upon the plank sheer, a ledge some eighteen inches wide, and peered across the sea toward two vessels which he had seen earlier. The closer ship seemed approaching rapidly, but the other craft was now hull down and moving away. The bark *Maurice* under Captain Renaud was rapidly bearing down on the *Austria*, but when she was still some distance away the breeze died.

Meanwhile the foremast and the mainmast of the *Austria* fell, and the boiler exploded shortly afterward. Up to then the ship had been heading southwest, but now she swung around to the north, her engines silenced. Ten minutes later the powder magazine blew up.

A breeze now began to blow, and the *Austria* fell off before it. Those on the forecastle then were subjected to the hot flames, which forced them over the bow, and all who could took refuge in the bowsprit and the forechains.

Professor Glaubensklee shifted his position from the plank sheer to the forechains, and for a time actually clung to the beautiful double-headed eagle which formed the figurehead of the vessel. Realizing that at any moment he might be forced to leap into the water, he took off his boots, shirt and undershirt, and then he cut off his trousers above the knees.

He remained there with the others awaiting the arrival of the bark which was now making slow progress. Many who were clinging to the forechains became exhausted, let go their holds and fell into the ocean where they were swallowed up.

Far in the distance another sail could be seen, even as the *Maurice* came closer. All over the burning ship people had strung ropes and lines overboard, to which many of them still clung desperately, but there were many other lines dangling over the sides whose occupants had lost their holds and perished.

Now three-quarters of a mile away, Captain Renaud of the *Maurice* ordered his own boats lowered, and when the first lifeboat from the bark arrived on the scene, Professor Glaubensklee sprang into the ocean and swam to the rescue craft. Five others were taken from the water, and what appeared to be a dead man was found floating in the sea halfway back to the bark. The unconscious man, however, whose name was Theodore Eisfeld, revived under treatment.

A shuttle service of lifeboats was kept up until darkness fell, and Captain Renaud remained nearby all night long. By sunset he had picked up the *Austria's* single lifeboat.

When morning came a Norwegian bark was seen near the burning steamer, and Renaud now concluded that no living person remained on board. He had provisions for only a few days for the sixty-seven persons whom he had rescued, and so he decided to start at once for Fayal. Later they fell in with the bark *Lotus*, which took off twelve survivors and landed them at Halifax. The others who were taken from the *Austria* had been given shelter in tents on the deck and below wherever they could crowd, and all reached Fayal safely.

Thus it was that of the 538 persons on board the beautiful ship *Austria*, 471 perished in the sea.

CHAPTER TWENTY

THE *Dailey* AND THE *Kay*

The howling of the storm alone to hear,
And the wild sea that to the tempest raves.

DURING THE MONTH of January, 1956 there was a spell of nine days in which the coastal residents of New England did not see the sun once, and they began to question whether it still remained in the heavens. Only those who had flown above the closely packed clouds were able to give reassurance that that body was still shining above the clouds.

Long intervals of sunless weather are commonplace in America, but generally, as in that instance, they are forgotten unless directly associated with some unpleasant experience. One such memorable period occurred in January, 1883, in the mid-Atlantic states, when the sun was blanketed by fog and snow for four full days and nights during which shipping was plagued up and down the coast.

The first craft to suffer trouble in this storm was the two-masted schooner *Albert Dailey* from Augusta, Maine, which on January 7, 1883, was carrying a load of coal from Baltimore, Maryland, bound for Bridgeport, Connecticut, with a crew of six.

Because of a strong current and a dense fog the *Dailey* ran aground on Smith's Island, Virginia, hitting at a point three miles northeast by east of the Smith's Island Life Saving Station. At 1:30 in the morning there was a partial lifting of the fog, and a passing patrolman from the station caught sight of what appeared to be a phanton schooner an eighth of a mile offshore.

The patrolman immediately lighted a Coston flare, which spluttered out its red warning light, but there was no answer from the wreck. Another Coston flare brought a "faint halloaing" from the schooner, and the patrolman stabbed a third lighted flare into the sand and ran for the lifesaving station three miles away.

Reaching the station half an hour later, he reported the wreck to Keeper G. D. Hitchins. The crew started the surfboat on the beach-cart down the long stretch of sand, and after a three-mile haul they reached the Coston flare and launched into the sea. The fog now set in worse than ever, and the ghostly apparition of the schooner had vanished again.

The crew was unable to find the vessel. The fog was now so thick that all that Keeper Hitchens could see from the stern where he stood with his great steering oar were the outlines of his own men as they rowed for their unseen goal. Finally, at 4:30 in the morning, the vague bulk of the coal schooner was recognized and they pulled for her without any delay.

Going aboard the *Dailey*, they found the schooner in no danger and accepted the captain's invitation to remain on the vessel until noon. Then, with the tide coming in, the entire crew was rowed ashore and conveyed to the station where the men were soon made comfortable.

On the following day another trip was completed to the *Dailey*, where the captain bargained with Mr. Cobb of the Cobb Wrecking Company to get the schooner off the beach. The wreckers and the original crew were left on the schooner while the captain of the *Dailey* was quartered at the lifesaving station, uneasily awaiting developments.

When a great northeast snowstorm began, Keeper Hitchins made a visit to the vessel and implored the wreckers to leave. They refused, drawing attention to their sturdy surfboat alongside the *Dailey*. However, they did agree that if trouble developed, they would signal for help either by waving a flag in the daytime, flashing lights at night or sounding the fog-horn in poor visibility. But Keeper Hitchins, who knew the vicinity and what a northeast snowstorm could do, had his crew and lifeboat waiting opposite the vessel ready for service.

By 4:00 that afternoon all realized that a great snowstorm was upon them, and the keeper set up patrols, instructing the men to use the "utmost vigilance."

In spite of all the signaling plans, there was such a howling wind and driving snowstorm that no communication could be made with the wreck, for visibility at that time was less than ten feet and a fog horn could not be heard fifty feet away!

When, shortly after 11:00, Keeper Hitchins noticed wreckage coming ashore, he identified the schooner's hatches and a fragment of her boat, which indicated that she was breaking up. Arousing his patrolmen, and with the captain of the schooner and Lt. Failing, the local inspector of the Fifth Virginian Life Saving District, Keeper Hitchins loaded up the mortar cart with the wreck gun and apparatus. They all then set out through the terrible storm for the scene of the wreck. The going through the soft sand and snow was difficult. Every foot of the way the men encountered driving snow, sand and sleet which cut and burned their faces. With each step they sank into an eighteen-inch quagmire of snow, mushy sand, slush, thick tree roots and knobbly stumps.

It was 2:00 in the morning before they reached their post opposite the wreck where the lifeboat and crew waited. Now all hands peered through the darkness. As mile-a-minute gusts scattered the white flakes, the outline of the *Dailey's* masts could be momentarily discerned, and then the picture would fade away in a terrifying swirl of thick, wet, clinging snow. Only the masts had been seen, and it was realized that the schooner's hull was buried in the heavy, driving surf.

Meanwhile out on the wreck the men had sought refuge in the rigging, driven there by the suddenness of a storm which prevented them from signaling to the shore.

Hoping to reveal the schooner again by Coston light, the keeper burned six flares in succession, but it did no good. The watchers on shore were still unable to sight her again.

At 3:00, worried by the possibility that all the men aboard the wreck might soon be lost in the sea, Keeper Hitchins ordered the lifeboat launched, but it was a full hour before the oarsmen were able to pull the craft through the breakers immediately offshore. The lifesavers rowed desperately, but try as they would they were unable to find the schooner. As the great seas were rising even higher, the keeper now realized that if they did reach the vessel it would be next to impossible to get the survivors down from the rigging in the heavy, breaking seas. He also feared the danger of being struck by timbers from the wreck which would stave in his lifeboat and make all further chances of rescue impossible. Finally, aware of his own danger and inability to help those on the schooner, he guided the lifeboat back to land, beached it safely and awaited the approach of dawn.

Daylight came to aid the lifesavers, but the morning presented a dismal spectacle to the anxious coast guardsmen watching the rolling, tumultuous sea. They saw two masts of the schooner with the spars and cordage a weaving conglomeration of wreckage. The masts themselves were great white shapeless sticks of frozen snow and ice. Lashed to the fore rigging where they had been since the day before were the survivors, their clothing frozen to a boardlike consistency which held their arms and legs in awkward, abnormal positions.

The keeper counted the forms. All were there except one. He learned later that Edward Hunter, the vessel's steward, had been washed out of the rigging during the night. With the snow still as thick as ever, Keeper Hitchens decided that he would not launch his boat again, but would attempt to shoot the Lyle gun instead.

The first shot threw the line across the jib boom, but not a man moved from the rigging to secure it. After a short wait, the keeper hauled it in and fired a second shot. This time the projectile hit the bowsprit, but still the exhausted survivors did not stir. The third attempt did not hit the schooner at all, and on the fourth try the line broke in flight. It was later ascertained that even if the line had dropped into the very hands of the shipwrecked men it could not have been grasped. By this time they were so helpless from exposure and exhaustion that not one of them would have had strength to handle it properly.

Keeper Hitchins now decided that he would have to launch his lifeboat again in spite of the mountainous waves then hitting the Virginian shore. He announced that when the tide fell he would make a final desperate attempt to reach the wreck. It was then 8:00, but the wind was starting to back into the west, and Hitchins knew that with a falling tide the sea would go down a little.

And so it was that at 11:30 that morning, with what was still considered a terrible sea raging, the lifeboat was again launched, although it was white with frozen surf and snow.

The first launching proved a failure. Once beyond the breakers, the lifeboat was swept by the current past the wreck far to the leeward of that cluster of helpless humans frozen to the foremast rigging. The keeper then beached the lifeboat to prepare for a second launching, hauling the craft far up the beach to take full advantage of the current.

After a rest of a few minutes, a second attempt was made, and this time the crew rowed the boat near enough to lay a line aboard the wreck. The sea tore the line away, and the lifeboat was forced to row back to shore once more. But still Hitchins would not give up. He knew, however, that his men were only human and their endurance would allow just one more chance. Then if failure resulted every man out on the wreck would die, for there was no alternative.

Mincing no words as he told his men the desperate situation, he ordered the third and final launching, and soon the lifesavers were in the dreadful surf for what they felt would be the last try.

This time they reached the wreck, made a successful throw and uttered a wordless prayer of thankfulness as the line was secured aboard. Watching desperately, the keeper tested the line to see if it would hold, and then three men steadied the rope while the others clambered over the icy rigging to reach the survivors. The first two men they came to were apparently almost dead. They had lost consciousness tied in the ratlines as they were, and Hitchins knew the importance of getting them ashore at once if they were to be revived. Stopping just long enough to take two of the other survivors aboard, he ordered the lifeboat rowed ashore. Twenty minutes later the four survivors were being borne along the sand toward the lifesaving station where Lt. Failing, a sailor from the revenue sloop named Johnson, Keeper Goffigan and Assistant Keeper Coston of the Smith's Island Light rendered assistance.

Back on shore, heartened by their success, the tired crew decided to make still another trip to the wreck. They launched again, reached the schooner, removed the last four men and brought them safely ashore. As they landed on the beach, one

of the wrecking crew, a middle-aged workman named Richard
Gordon, died from the results of his long exposure.

Of those seven who survived the ordeal it took five hours
of nursing before two of them recovered enough to regain
consciousness, while all seven stayed at the station for many
days before they were able to leave.

The snowstorm had continued relentlessly throughout the
day of the rescue, the following day, the next day and the day
after that. On January 10, 1883, three days following the
wreck of the *Dailey*, another schooner met grief. The three-
masted two-decked *Sallie W. Kay*, with seven in the crew
and bound from Baltimore to Boston with a load of coal,
found herself embroiled in the same storm, which had had no
parallel for years before, nor would have for many years
afterward.

At 6:15 that January morning, when the snow was coming
down so hard that the schooner's lookout could see less than
eighty feet ahead, the *Kay* brought up hard and fast aground.
At the moment of striking, the watch below tumbled up on
deck, and Captain Smith ordered the yawl moved from the
stern to a position of safety in the lee of the bow, ready for
use should they have to leave the schooner in a hurry.

Before the command to move the yawl could be obeyed,
giant wave after giant wave smashed into and over the stern,
tearing the yawl from her tackles and sweeping it out of sight.
The last hope of getting ashore without outside help was
gone.

Again the waves thundered aboard the vessel, tearing the
top of the cabin off, bursting open the hatches and pouring
below.

There had been no time to lower sails, for the men were
forced to scamper up into the rigging immediately after the
ship struck, but the filling of the vessel added to her weight.
She now began to lift and fall so heavily that the crew feared

the masts would go by the board and take them to their death in the sea.

Deciding to seek another safety point, they climbed down one by one, between the waves, to reassemble on the bowsprit and the jib boom. They were all clustered on the jib boom like birds in a row, finally loosening the flying jib and wrapping themselves as a group in its folds.

They couldn't tell where they were, but the schooner had struck on a bar an eighth of a mile offshore from Ocean City, Maryland, about five miles north of the lifesaving station there. The steady fall of snow was uninterrupted, but when a clearing gust swept the area the men on the jib boom could see a single house just beyond the beach a short distance to the north.

A fisherman named Howard lived there, and it was his son, around 8:00 that morning, who sighted the wreck during a lull in the storm.

Conditions were then at their worst. The great tide which the prolonged snowstorm had brought to the Maryland shore was smashing across the outer barrier beach and in several places knifing eight and ten feet into the sand to reach the bay beyond. The pounding surf was opening giant gullies across the outer beach through which the sea rushed with the force of a torrent. When his son told him of the wreck, Howard realized that because of the high tide it would be impossible then to walk the more than five miles to the lifesaving station at Ocean City and notify Keeper William West of the disaster.

The tide began to fall shortly after 9:00 o'clock, making the beach relatively safe. At that time Howard dispatched his son on the five mile journey for help.

The boy had reached a point abeam of the schooner when a tragic event occurred. By this time the survivors had spent three hours on the jib boom. One of them, a powerful German lad named Anton, announced that he was going to wait no longer, for he had a plan. Several years before he had swum ashore from another shipwreck to spread the alarm. He now decided that he would slip overboard, swim to the beach and go to the house to get help for his shipmates.

Captain Smith attempted to prevent Anton from leaving by telling him that no one could live in such surf and that the lifesavers would soon see the wreck and come to the rescue. But the German, taking off his boots and his outer clothing, slid down the martingale and dropped into the swirling seas, where he struck out boldly for shore using the breast stroke.

A moment later Captain Smith, peering through the snow, saw young Howard hiking along the beach toward the distant lifesaving station. Anton, however, never knew that rescue was on the way. The German made several ineffectual attempts to stagger out of the undertow, but the icy waters had numbed him by now, and he was swept away toward the south by the powerful current to be seen alive no more.

Meanwhile, back at Ocean City, the patrolman who had started out at 4:00 that morning on his northward beat had encountered conditions that made walking almost impossible. After proceeding about two miles up the beach he was forced by the tide to return to the station, where he arrived at 8:00 o'clock. All during his patrol he had met nothing except snow and sleet, and at no time had visibility been more than fifty yards. In low areas he had waded waist deep through the flooded sands. Above the water was the snow piled in drifts six feet high.

After the Howard lad left the area opposite the wreck he also found his progress extremely slow. He continued fighting his way up the beach, at times forced to crawl along the sand and often to climb in and out of the gullies.

At 11:00 there was a definite lull in the snowstorm during which time the lookout at Ocean City had a chance to train

his telescope to the north. He saw the wreck and rang the
alarm bell. At once Keeper West called out the crew. But
West soon realized that no group of men could possibly haul
the beach apparatus through the gullies and ridges left by the
high tide and surf. When his efforts to secure horses failed,
he dispatched a patrolman for a pair of oxen.

After a delay necessitated by bringing the oxen across to
the beach, the lifesaving crew left the station just before noon.
It was an arduous journey. Every man had his own line with
which he was helping the oxen to pull the wagon, but the
load weighed more than 1500 pounds. The route to the scene
of the wreck was flooded with seas, clogged with snow and
strewn with great gullies. As the men and beasts made their
slow progress through the snow, sand and sleet hit them
head-on, half blinding them as they stumbled along.

Halfway to the wreck they encountered the little messenger boy, weary, footsore and disconsolate. He told his story
of the men hanging to the jib boom with the schooner liable
to break up at any minute, and this news gave the lifesavers
added strength to reach the shipwreck. Ultimately, at 2:15,
they arrived at a position opposite the stranded schooner.

In spite of the overwhelming need for haste, they had to
rest for a few moments to gain enough strength to continue.
Their first view of the wreck through the gusts of snow
showed them the desperate situation out on the *Sallie Kay*.
Speeding their efforts, they set up their apparatus and aimed
the Lyle gun for a shot at the schooner.

The first missile screamed out over the boiling waters to
hit just over the foremast stay, with the bight slipping down
within reach of the survivors. In spite of their exhaustion, the
sailors began to haul in immediately, cheered by the possibility
of rescue. Numb from the storm and the cold, their bodies
frozen with snow and spray, they worked feebly to gather in
the whip line. Although one end of it was anchored on shore

and the other on the schooner, the current took the center of the line far to the southward in a great arc.

At last the breeches buoy was rigged on and sent out, and the moment came for the first man to attempt the trip ashore. Stepping into the breeches buoy, he gave the signal that he was ready. He was hauled in through the surf to land safely on the beach above the reach of the waves. In forty minutes his companions were all on shore with him, safe and sound, and the wreck was alone in the great rolling ocean. Except for the German lad, the sea had on this occasion been cheated of its prey.

At this time twelve residents of Ocean City who had heard about the wreck reached the scene. They arrived just in time, for neither the survivors nor the lifesavers were in condition after their grueling experiences to attempt making their way back over the tortuous route to the station without additional help. The survivors were on the verge of death from exhaustion while the lifesavers could barely stumble along the beach with their heavy apparatus.

The operator of the nearby ship service, James Crawford, then arrived with his wagon. It was arranged that the seamen should take turns walking and riding. Three at a time they rested in the wagon under blankets. But even with the help of a landsman on each side whenever they walked, the sailors were so exhausted that they pleaded to be allowed to sit down on the sand and rest. Since it would have been a rest of death, the local inhabitants urged them on.

The day ended, and twilight came, followed by blackest night. It was after 6:00 on that winter's evening before the strange procession reached the Ocean City Life Saving Station. There the sailors were quickly stripped of their icy, stiffened clothing. Put to bed, they were given hot soup and coffee and allowed to go to sleep.

Two days later the men were up and about, making plans

to return to their respective homes when a messenger from far down the beach arrived at the lifesaving station. The body of Anton, the German swimmer, had just been recovered from the sea, sixteen miles to the south of the place where the schooner had been wrecked.

Although the official report states that Anton's death "must be charged to his rash, though gallant effort to swim ashore," I do not agree. Anton gave his life trying to get help for his comrades from the shore, and since he had succeeded once before, it was the only thing he could have done under the circumstances. "Gallant" he was, but never "rash."

CHAPTER TWENTY-ONE

SAMOAN HURRICANE

Sudden they see from midst of all the main
The surging waters like a mountain rise,
And the great sea, puff'd up with proud disdain,
As threat'ning to devour all that his power despise.

ON OCCASIONS the mighty sea apparently reacts to the conflicts of man and puts on a show of strength which dwarfs anything he might offer.

In the year 1887 several German officers in the Samoan Islands believed that the local king, Malieton by name, was so unfriendly to Germany that he should be forced off the throne. Therefore, surreptitiously they kidnapped the monarch, sending him into exile on another island thousands of miles away.

The Germans now set up a new king, Tamasese, who favored them, but the natives and what few American traders lived in Samoa attempted to install one of Malieton's relatives, Mataafa by name. Civil war resulted. Battle after battle was fought, and finally the German-favored monarch was forced from his throne at Apia, capital of Samoa, shutting himself up in a native fortress eight miles distant.

The Germans, during this period, had confined themselves to bombarding several unfriendly native villages. Early in December, 1888, however, German troops went ashore and assaulted Mataafa's small army. In spite of their modern weapons the invaders were thrown back, driven to the beach and eventually out to their warships, with a battle casualty list of fifty men either killed or wounded. This caused Germany to "declare war" against Samoa.

At the time there was one American man-of-war in the harbor, but as soon as the United States War Department learned of the German action, other craft were sent there. By March 15, 1889, the United States had off Apia the warship *Trenton*, the flagship of Admiral Kimberly, with Captain N. H. Farquhar in command; the *Nipsic*, Commander D. W. Mullan; and the *Vandalia*, whose captain was Commander C. M. Schoonmaker. The Germans had the warship *Olga* and the cruisers *Eber* and *Adler*, while the British had the man-of-war *Calliope*. Also in the harbor were about twelve trading schooners and vessels.

Those of you who have journeyed to Samoa may recall that the town of Apia lies around a small but circular bay. A coral reef, bare at low tide, extends across the mouth of the harbor. A break in the reef about a quarter of a mile wide forms the entrance to Apia Harbor, which is deep only on the western side. On that day of March 15 the harbor was especially crowded, with nineteen craft squeezed into the deeper section of the area. The *Eber* and the *Nipsic* were nearer than the other ships to shore. The schooners and other peaceful vessels were in relatively shoal water near a fringing reef on the western side of the harbor.

Apia itself is composed of low cottages easily swayed in the wind and well bound together so as to give in a moderate storm without blowing away.

For several weeks the weather had been threatening and a

storm was expected. And so it was that during the afternoon of March 15, with battleships from three nations assembled in tiny Apia Harbor, the sea itself decided to put on a show which would reduce to pigmy proportions any war the so-called civilized powers might be planning to fight.

The wind now began to increase, and the warships lowered their topmasts and secured their spars; two of them prepared stormsails for emergency use. The anchors were all out, and steam was raised to help the anchors hold.

Gradually the wind blew stronger. Each passing minute gave new strength to the gale then rising, until by 11:00 that fearsome night a mighty hurricane was unleashed. Realizing what was coming, the crews of most of the small craft in the harbor put out their spare anchors and went ashore, hoping but not in any way confident, that they would hold.

At midnight gigantic rollers began to sweep in over the coral reef, which is lower than in many other harbors. The rain now started to fall, a regular deluge, and the wind continued to increase.

By noon, March 15, the barometer had registered 29° 11', lower than it had been known to be in the region for a quarter of a century! The wind gradually swung around to the northeast, the hurricane quarter, and blew in fierce squalls.

Shortly afterward, the *Eber*, with all her crew and soldiers aboard, began dragging her anchors, and she started her engines to counter the force of the blow. By 1:00 the *Vandalia* also used her engines for the same purpose.

Two o'clock came, and still other craft were under power. But in spite of all precautions taken, by 3:00 in the morning every warship in the harbor was dragging, and, in that cramped area, collisions were inevitable.

Across on land the crashing of trees and the roar of wind awakened the natives. Roofs began to tear away, and groups of terrified inhabitants gathered together for mutual assistance.

They watched sand and gravel as it was swept off the beach and into their homes. The tide was still rising, and soon many of the streets of Apia, ninety-three feet above high water mark, were flooded. The spray smashed against the windows of the houses.

The natives now forgot their tribal fights and wars in the presence of something infinitely greater. The followers of both Tamasese and Mataafa were shoulder to shoulder again, overawed by what was taking place.

Toward dawn, those on the shore could see the confused mass of ships crossing and recrossing each other in unbelievable turmoil. Heavy black smoke poured from the furnaces of the warships as they attempted to avoid collisions.

Many of the sailing craft were already on the reef, and fragments of wreckage began to come ashore. Three warships, the *Eber*, *Adler* and *Nipsic* struggled just off the fatal shoal to avoid destruction.

Then came the *Eber's* final, desperate sally. Pushed toward the reef, she recovered momentarily. An instant later she dashed forward right into the storm. The current caught her and smashed her against the *Nipsic*, her bow carrying away a boat and part of the port quarter rail on the other craft. Dropping back, she fouled the *Olga*, carried away her own rudder and swung broadside to the wind where a gigantic wave caught her, hurling her with the full force of the hurricane up on the reef. There she heeled over, facing the sea, for a moment, and then completely disappeared.

The horror-struck natives, stunned into inactivity at first, recovered their senses and rushed down toward the scene of disaster. Reaching the shore, they dashed into the surf to aid the German sailors who a short time before had been shooting at them. But the natives were savages, failing to appreciate the finer points of civilization, and they did not consider the fact that the sailors were enemies, giving thought only to the saving of human life wherever possible.

For several minutes they could see no signs of survivors, and then a few struggling forms were visible in the surf. The natives made a human lifeline, hauling the German sailors ashore. Then, across on the piling of a small wharf, another figure was sighted. When the man was brought ashore, he proved to be the sole surviving officer. As he later explained, he had been officer of the watch when the wreck occurred. All the others were below and were either crushed to death or drowned.

Back out in the harbor the *Adler* had fouled the *Olga* and was then 200 yards away from the place where the *Eber* had met disaster. For the next half hour the *Adler*, broadside to the waves, drifted slowly toward destruction. Then, a huge billow pushed her against the reef on her beam ends, throwing almost everyone into the harbor. But the ship had gone over in shallow water, and those in the rigging were relatively safe, facing the shore.

The natives were able to attach a line to the *Adler*, but meanwhile the American man-of-war *Nipsic* was getting into further trouble. Still maneuvering in the harbor, the warship was being threatened by the giant *Olga* which was bearing down on her. At the height of this emergency a tiny schooner with three men aboard was cut down by the *Olga*. Two of the three men clambered across to the German craft in safety while the third perished.

Commander Mullane of the *Nipsic* now ordered the men to bend a heavy hawser to one of the eight-inch rifles and cast it overboard for an extra anchor, but just then the German vessel bore down on the *Nipsic* striking her a terrible blow amidships, overturning her smokestack and carrying away a boat as the rail was splintered. The stack then rocked back and forth with each roll of the ship. All who could climbed into the rigging, believing that the ship was sinking.

The *Nipsic* had now been forced to within a few yards of the location where the *Eber* had vanished, and Captain Mullane knew that with the smokestack gone they could not keep up steam. Realizing that his vessel would hit the reef unless something was done, Captain Mullane headed his craft toward the sandy beach where the American consulate was located. His steam was going down all the time, but he gambled with the chance that there might still be a small head left.

A great crowd of people assembled on shore to watch the maneuver. Captain Mullane's course led him parallel to the dangerous reef which could wreck him in a minute if his luck did not hold or his skill failed. Those on shore watched the *Nipsic* steam so close that faces of the men huddled in the bow could be recognized! Two of the crew who had all-night passes were among the watchers of the life and death struggle of their countrymen.

A few moments more and the American warship had escaped the reef. Now she aimed for the sandy shore. All aboard braced themselves as they tensely waited for the crash. Then with a final shudder, the ship drove up on the sand, swinging around diagonally to the storm shortly afterward.

Smashing into her stern, the breakers apparently were intent on beating the *Nipsic* to pieces. Five sailors manned a boat, but the falls worked improperly, and the men dropped to their death in the sea. A short time later the surgeon took five sick men and placed them in another boat, but at the moment of launching the craft capsized.

The natives now formed another life chain of clasped hands and saved several of the sailors. Six men, seeing the lifeline, leaped into the breakers, and two were lost.

All those on the warship who could do so crowded into the forecastle, which was higher in the sand than the rest of the ship. Two native chieftains, Seumanu Tafa and Salu Anae, sent out lines to the stranded vessel and eventually every man then aboard was brought ashore to safety.

The four larger men-of-war, well out in the harbor, were safe for the time being, but when a huge mass of wreckage struck the stern of the *Trenton* it carried away her rudder and propellor. At this moment the American *Vandalia* and the English *Calliope* started to drift shoreward. Getting up additional steam, the *Vandalia* began to pull away from danger. Suddenly, however, the iron prow of the English vessel loomed up ahead of the American craft, rose high in the air on the crest of a wave, and then fell with terrific force on the *Vandalia's* port quarter. The *Calliope* crushed the heavy timbers of the American ship as if it were an eggshell, at the same time smashing off her own jib boom.

There were those who feared that the *Calliope* had given a death blow to the *Vandalia*, but the frightened men on the latter craft who had been swarming from the hatches returned to their posts.

Realizing that if he stayed where he was, the *Vandalia*, his own ship, or both of them would be sunk by further collisions, Captain Henry Coey Kane decided to attempt a daring maneuver, the one remaining alternative to collision. At exactly 9:20 that wild morning at the height of the gale he announced to the other officers his decision to take the *Calliope* out to sea! He would gamble everything on the premise that his engines, boilers, rudder and steering gear could stand the strain, and trust God to allow him a clear sight of the quarter-mile opening in the reef.

Steam was reported ready in all six boilers, and with the engine room telegraph placed on full speed ahead, the last cable was slipped, and the *Calliope* began her epic run.

For at least two minutes, even with her propeller thrashing the water wildly at full speed, the *Calliope* did not make any progress against the overwhelming wind and sea, her screw being lifted out of the water with an ominous sound in the huge swells. Then there was a God-sent lull, and the *Calliope* slowly forged ahead, managing to claw her way around the bow of the *Vandalia.*

Engineer William Milton stood at the throttle-valve in the engine room turning off the steam as the propeller screamed out into the air and opening it to full when the stern submerged again.

The first half mile took the *Calliope* a full hour. She made a splendid, fearsome sight, at times pitching to such a degree that her keel was bare for half of her length! Out near the narrow entrance to the barrier reef the steam corvette *Trenton* lay blocking her path, but Captain Kane believed that with luck he could maneuver around the American ship. Since the *Trenton's* rudder and wheel had been carried away and she was flooded fore and aft, her men hoisted the signal "Fires extinguished." Lurching hopelessly to and fro in the wild seas which only a full scale hurricane can bring, she could do nothing to aid the British vessel, held only by her cables as she was.

Yard by yard the *Calliope* advanced on the helpless American craft until Captain Kane could see that the opening between the corvette and the reef itself was not quite closed and that he might, with luck, have a chance to gain the ocean through it.

He steered straight for the *Trenton's* stern, and then put the helm hard-a-starboard when less than forty feet away, the ships being so close that the *Calliope's* foreyard actually overhung the *Trenton's* port quarter as she worked her way past.

For a moment it seemed as though the sea would triumph after all, for both craft were rolling, and if they did so simultaneously they would have collided.

But fate decreed otherwise and the sea was cheated of its prey, for the bow of the *Calliope* slowly cleared the *Trenton.*

Captain Kane had the rudder put hard over in the opposite direction to swing her back once more on course, and she slid by the *Trenton* a few yards to starboard with the infuriated sea smashing over the edge of the western reef a scant one hundred feet away!

As the *Calliope* passed the *Trenton* something unpremeditated happened, which neither crew ever forgot. The entire ship's company of 450 men on the *Trenton* gave three rousing cheers, heard even above the gale, for the gallant officers and men aboard the British vessel, and those on the *Calliope* answered in kind. Despite their own predicament the Americans saluted the seamanship of those aboard the British craft who were escaping to sea.

Steaming steadily out beyond the reef, the *Calliope* won her gamble with fate and soon disappeared in the rain and mists of the storm.

The *Vandalia* meanwhile had settled in deep water close to the stranded *Nipsic,* and her submerged upper deck was swept angrily by the savage seas. They were just far enough from shore to prevent aid from reaching them. Gradually, the exhausted sailors were torn from their perches on deck and in the rigging and were drowned, one by one. Captain Schoonmaker was lost, together with three other officers and forty sailors.

At 3:00 on the afternoon of the sixteenth, the *Trenton,* whose lines had held steadily, began to pull away, and one by one her cables snapped. Hopelessly out of control, she started drifting into the harbor, and drove stern first to the inner anchorage where she smashed into the *Olga,* which until that moment had ridden out the storm in comparative safety. The *Olga* parted two of her cables and started drifting toward shore. Von Ehrhardt now set his fore and aft sails and went full speed ahead with his engines, beaching his vessel without loss of life.

Meanwhile the *Trenton,* which was being carried along the

edge of the reef by a favorable current, drifted in with the
Vandalia, whose hull was practically submerged. Then from
the *Vandalia*, above the roaring hurricane and the crashing
waves, came the stirring strains of the *Star Spangled Banner!*
It is probable that never before has a country's national anthem been played under more unusual circumstances.

As the two American craft came together, lines were
thrown aboard each vessel, and scores of men were saved
from the *Vandalia* by those on the *Trenton*. Finally the flagship collided with the *Vandalia* and sank to the bottom, submerged to the level of her gun deck. But the *Trenton* lost
only one man, and he was crushed to death when the sea burst
open a gun port.

By 10:00 that night of the sixteenth the beach was deserted,
and the vengeful sea had accomplished its terrible task. A few
natives and white men who walked the beach found a young
ensign still alive from the *Vandalia*, and he proved to be the
last one saved.

One hundred and fifty-four persons had perished in this
mighty hurricane which had swept in on the harbor of Apia,
Upolu, Samoa, that March day of 1889. Ninety-one were
Germans, fifty-one were Americans and the two others were
from schooners. Only a third of the bodies ever came ashore.

On the day following the storm Captain Kane steamed the
Calliope back into the wreck-strewn harbor to his anchorage.* Hours before, the hurricane had gone out to sea, and
the harbor was relatively quiet. But what a scene of disaster
those aboard the British ship witnessed!

---

* Of the officers and men aboard the *Calliope* when she made her
splendid dash out to sea, the world has come to know the Hon. H. L. A.
Hood, killed at the battle of Jutland as a rear-admiral while leading his
battle cruiser squadron into action aboard the *Invincible*. Vice Admiral
John C. T. Glossop commanded the cruiser *Sydney* during her historic
fight with the German *Emden*, and Captain Cecil H. Fox commanded the
light cruiser *Amphion* when she was sunk by mines in August 1914 off the
British east coast.

The morning sun was shining on a shore littered with wreckage. A shattered schooner lay athwart the reef. The streets of Apia were crossed and recrossed with trees felled by the hurricane, and scores of roofless houses stood in the forest of fallen trees. A large fragment of the *Eber's* bow was high on the shore. Far up on the western reef lay the *Adler.** The *Olga*, still relatively unharmed, was on the eastern shoal. All that was visible of the *Vandalia* was the bow from which the brave men in the ship's band had played their national anthem. By her side was the *Trenton*, impressive in her ruined condition. And above all, from the highest point on the *Trenton's* mast, floated the Star Spangled Banner, the inspiration for the thrilling performance of the musicians aboard the *Vandalia* at the height of the gale.

---

* For months after the storm the *Adler* lay high and dry on her beam ends. When Robert Louis Stevenson viewed her he remarked that the wreck was the "largest structure of man's hand within a circuit of a thousand miles, tossed up there like a schoolboy's cap upon a shelf."

CHAPTER TWENTY-TWO

NEWBURYPORT, PLUM ISLAND
AND SALISBURY BEACH

*There are many advantages in sea-voyaging, but security
is not one of them.*

MASSACHUSETTS HAS BEEN the scene of hundreds of shipwrecks and there are many stories concerning them, but little has been written about two locations which are almost in the same longitude at opposite extremities of the state. The first is the coastal area around the mouth of the Merrimack River at the northerly border of Massachusetts; the other is the outermost island of the Elizabeths, Cuttyhunk, in Buzzards Bay to the south, dealt with in the following chapter.

Newburyport, Massachusetts, at the mouth of the Merrimack River, was for years one of the leading maritime centers of New England, and it was here that Donald McKay first built many of his beautiful clipper ships in the Bay State. Because of the nature of the dangerous sea approaches, Newburyport has been the scene of many shipwrecks.

Plum Island extends about nine and a half miles to the south of the Merrimack River off Newburyport. It is a relatively barren, sandy island with great dunes, fragments of ancient wrecks and occasional summer residences, many of which are located so near the sea that they are periodically washed away by storms. A fort was built years ago in the vicinity of Lighthouse Point at the northern end of the island, and in 1783 the Newburyport Marine Society erected two beacons there for ships entering the harbor.

There had already been serious tragedies off Newburyport and Plum Island shores. Shortly after the alleged visit of pirate Harry Main, who built a house nearby, disasters began to take place. Old wives, who didn't have radio or television then to absorb most of their spare time, made up yarns about poor Harry. They claimed that after he died, he was being punished eternally for his earthly misdeeds, none of which seems to have gotten into the local court records. For the dark and terrible crimes he had committed he was chained forever to the shifting sands off the area and doomed to shovel them back and forth. Thus it was, according to the wives, that whenever a storm hit the coast, the vengeful sea was helping Harry Main "growl at his work."

Early records of this area tell many sad tales. In 1723 Amos Morris was drowned while coming over "the bar." On March 10, 1755, Lieutenant John Boardman and Mr. John Rogers were "cast on Shore on Castle Hill Beach and Perish'd with the Cold & Snow." Daniel Ringe and Robert Spiller, in a two-masted craft, lost their lives at Plum Island in the winter of 1775-1776. On September 12, 1785, Isaac Galloway, Philip Lord, Jr. and Thomas Lord were drowned "Crossing Plumb Island River in a wherry been on a claming voige."

A great storm began December 4, 1786. The wharves of Boston were under water in the record high tide, and other fatal wrecks were reported up and down the New England coast, but the event which attracted public attention for years afterward was the strange experience in Plum Island Sound of two men who had left their homes to hunt and dig clams in the marshes.

Just before the storm Samuel Pulsifer and Samuel Elwell had gone down to Hog Island on Rowley Marsh to stay for the night. On Monday they started digging clams, but when snow began to fall they returned to the island. There they soon found that the storm was getting worse. Deciding to return to Rowley they started out, only to lose themselves completely in the swirling snow.

After wandering aimlessly through the confusing flakes, they became utterly bewildered, finally climbing into the comparative warmth of a near-by haystack to rest. The two men decided to stay there until the storm ended and they spent the night in their relatively comfortable refuge.

With morning, however, the storm was worse, and the tide surprised them by sweeping in around the hay staddle. Soon the haystack was rocking, and then to their amazement and horror it was raised completely off the supporting framework and started drifting away.

Hour after hour passed as the haystack drifted around Plum Island Sound. It eventually began to go to pieces, but just before the men would have dropped into the sea, what was left of their rude craft bumped into a larger stack. They transferred to it at once and continued their strange journey. Finally, some time later the second stack grounded at Smith's Cove, Little Neck (later known as Fish Island on the Hudgen farm property). It had been a journey of at least three miles, and the men at first did not feel equal to clambering ashore, for their bodies had become frostbitten and their clothes were already frozen stiff. Finally, grasping his trousers firmly at the knees, Pulsifer slowly and painfully lifted his feet one at a time and reached dry land. Elwell climbed on an ice cake and pushed it ashore. Both were discovered and taken to the residence of Major Charles Smith of Ipswich, with whom they stayed until they had fully recovered.

In 1802, during another great storm, a vessel from Brunswick, Maine, smashed across the bar. Everyone on board drowned. The body of Captain Joseph Melcher, 21, was found and interred in the High Street burying ground at Ipswich, on the mainland off the southern tip of Plum Island. The inscription on his grave is partially quoted below:

> Amidst the raging billows drove,
> My life to save in vain I strove,
> And soon my strength began to flee,
> I perished in the Cruel Sea.

The schooner *Dove* of Kittery, Maine, was lost with all hands on October 9, 1804. Shortly afterward another schooner from Kittery met the same fate. It is believed the remains of those who came ashore were buried on Bar Island Head.

Small houses of refuge had been erected in 1787 by the Massachusetts Humane Society at various locations along the shore, and soon after the turn of the century the Merrimack Humane Society built three more shelters.

During a severe storm in October, 1805, the sloop *Blue Bird* was driven ashore about where the lighthouse stands today. Although her cargo of books, stationery, woolen goods and hardware, valued at about a hundred thousand dollars, was practically a total loss, all persons aboard were saved.

On November 2, 1837, the schooner *Lombard*, loaded with grindstones, hit Plum Island south of the Lighthouse. Three people were lost, but the captain was saved. For years afterward the grindstones were sold in many of the local towns and cities.

Two years later came a storm in which occurred a famous Plum Island wreck. The brig *Pocahontas*, bound from Cádiz to Newburyport, was terribly battered by a great hurricane

in December, 1839. On the twenty-second she drifted by the
Isles of Shoals at night while poet Celia Laighton Thaxter was
in the tower. The keeper's family heard the signal gun, and
later Miss Thaxter wrote a poem concerning the episode, excerpts from which I quote below:

> The sails that flecked the ocean floor,
>   From east to west leaned low and fled;
> They knew what came in the distant roar
>   That filled the air with dread!
> Flung by a fitful gust, there beat
>   Against the window a dash of rain;
> Steady as tramp of marching feet
>   Strode on the hurricane.
>
> When morning dawned, above the din
>   Of gale and breaker boomed a gun!
> Another! We who sat within
>   Answered with cries each one.
> The thick storm seemed to break apart
>   To show us, staggering to her grave,
> The fated brig. We had no heart
>   To look, for naught could save.
> One glimpse of black hull heaving slow
>   Then closed the mists o'er canvas torn
> And tangled ropes swept to and fro
>   From masts that raked forlorn.

The poet had seen the ill-fated *Pocahontas* on the brig's
journey to her rendezvous with death on Plum Island. After
crashing against the sand bar, the vessel soon lost her master.
The anchors began to drag. Stern first she drove ashore nearly
half a mile east of the Plum Island Hotel.

Shortly after daylight the following morning she was discovered by Captain Brown of the hotel, who notified the
people of Newburyport. Attempts were made to launch a
dory, but the waves were tremendous surges which offered

no chance of survival. Two men had been seen on the bowsprit and another one holding on to the taffrail. A moment later the man clinging to the bowsprit was the only one visible. Just before noon the brig was pushed across the remaining part of the bar and pounded ashore on the sandy beach a short time later. One survivor who had lashed himself to the rigging of the *Pocahontas* was rescued by the townsmen. Taken ashore, he was tenderly placed above the reach of the breakers. He indicated feebly that he was anxious to speak. As the others bent down to hear his final words, he died from exhaustion, leaving his story forever a mystery. There were no other survivors.

The craft was owned in Newburyport, and Captain James G. Cook actually perished in sight of the smoke ascending from his own Newburyport chimney. Of the thirteen men aboard, seven were eventually found and buried by members of the Newburyport Bethel Society, which erected a simple marble monument, still to be seen, in the Old Hill burial ground.

In thick blustery weather on Thursday night, December 15, 1847, the brig *Falconer*, from Belfast, Maine, commanded by Captain Joseph Rolerson of that town, was carrying a cargo of 350 tons of coal from Sidney, Cape Breton Island, to Boston. Fifty-three persons made up the ship's company.

Around 10:00 that night, Captain Rolerson sighted what he believed was Scituate Light. Tacking, he stood to the northward, but when he sighted both Ipswich and Newburyport Lights, he realized that he was mistaken. Not recognizing either of the lights and realizing that there were no beacons any such distance from Cohasset, he did what any prudent sea captain would have done—he dropped anchor about three miles from shore. If he had known where he was, he could have run into Newburyport Harbor in perfect safety.

The vessel rode out the gale through Thursday night and all day Friday, but about seven o'clock Saturday morning she began to drag both anchors, eventually fetching up on a reef three-quarters of a mile from the shore, off the southerly end of Patch's Beach, two miles from the lighthouse.

After being subjected to a terrific battering from the sea, the *Falconer* bilged, and then the seas overwhelmed her. All passengers were forced to go up on deck when three feet of water filled the cabin, and those who were able to, lashed themselves in the rigging.

The keeper at Ipswich Light had been watching the brig ever since Friday noon, but when it did hit the bar he had no boat to launch. Seven men on the wreck, however, put over the jollyboat, reached the breakers and seemed about to get ashore safely. At that moment a towering wave caught them, engulfed the boat in foam and threw the crew into the sea. Four of the sailors, after fighting the great billows, struggled to safety on shore, but the other three drowned. The survivors were taken to the home of the lighthouse keeper. There was one other family living on the island in the vicinity, that of Captain Humphrey Lakeman, whose house was almost two miles from the wreck. Captain Lakeman sent news at once into Ipswich that a vessel was ashore.

Crowds soon began to gather on the beach opposite the wreck. Some of the onlookers had been thoughtful enough to bring thick clothing and hot drinks with them in case any of the sailors got ashore.

One by one the victims out on the wreck lost their grip and slipped to their death in the sea. Finally, only thirty-two of the fifty-three members of the ship's company remained stranded. The snow continued to pelt down, and the only boat available on shore was small and leaky In spite of the odds against him, William Chapman declared that he couldn't stand by and see the people drown. Watching his chances, he launched the unseaworthy craft and soon was rowing desperately for the brig. The watchers ashore expected him to be capsized, but miraculously he eluded breaker after breaker. Arriving at the *Falconer*, he scrambled aboard just in time to watch his boat fill with water and go down.

But Chapman's gesture was not in vain. Not only were the survivors encouraged by the fact that he had reached them, but several local fishermen, shamed into action by the man from Ipswich, followed his example and brought boats from as far as two miles distance to a position opposite the wreck. Soon there were four craft making their perilous way out to the brig. One by one the fishermen came in under the lee of the *Falconer*, loaded as many passengers as possible, and started ashore until all were rescued. Not a boat capsized on the trip back and everyone landed safely. Thus, of the fifty-three aboard, thirty-six were saved. Taken up to Captain Lakeman's home, they were cared for and brought back to life and vigor. But Captain Rolerson survived only half an hour after reaching land, and his wife and son Charles also were lost. Most of those who had perished, died of exposure. One poor soul had been washed overboard in full view of all the others, and his body was never found.

A mass funeral was given the victims in the town hall of Ipswich on December 20 with impressive services. A long procession then formed which followed the remains to the High Street burial ground where all were interred except the captain and his family.

As Captain Rolerson had been a member of the Odd Fellows, the Ipswich Lodge took charge of the three bodies and placed them in a special tomb where they stayed until they were sent to Belfast, Maine. There, five orphaned Rolerson children were awaiting the bodies of their mother, father and brother.

Many years afterward a slate stone, still to be seen by present-day visitors, was placed over the remains of those *Falconer* victims interred at Ipswich.

An unusual episode of this disaster was the action of one of the men who was saved. He had thrown into the boat a large bag of Spanish pieces of eight. When the boat hit the beach it smashed in two and the coins were lost in the surf. As the years went by the incident was forgotten. In 1887 several young men went hunting. They were hiking along the shore after a strong northeast gale when suddenly one of the hunters stopped. Reaching down, he picked up a Spanish piece of eight, then another and another.

The incident, of course, created great excitement, and in the afternoon of the same day no less than thirty boys of Ipswich, armed with rakes, hoes and shovels, went down on the beach and worked diligently, much harder than they would have worked at home, attempting to find more coins, but they were unsuccessful.

On December 3, 1849, the Wiscasset, Maine, schooner *Nancy*, loaded with bricks, hit near the southern end of Plum Island. All five persons drowned. In December of the following year the schooner *Argus* from Frankfort, Maine, was wrecked near Emerson's Rocks. While the captain, Allard Crockett, survived, the other seven men aboard perished. Two of the sailors successfully reached shore, but they wandered into a thicket and died of exposure.

In the Minot's Light Storm * of April 16, 1851, the brig *Primrose* was driven ashore at Plum Island, but all hands were saved. The vessel freed herself from the sand the following summer after her cargo of coal had been removed. Several schooners at Newburyport and Ipswich broke away from their moorings in the hurricane, and the Merrimack River was twenty-two inches higher than the mark of December,

---

* During this gale Minot's Light off Cohasset, Massachusetts, fell into the sea.

1839. In spite of the damage caused by the storm, many visitors came to Newburyport to see the high tide, thronging Water Street to witness "the ravages that the wind and waves had made." It is said that spray was thrown as high as the second story Newburyport windows all the distance to Hale's wharf. The turnpike to Plum Island was broken through, causing thousands of dollars in damage. In Ipswich the schooners *Ornament, Teazer* and *Votary* went adrift, but except for one of them which hit a warehouse owned by William Pulsifer, the damage was relatively slight.

On January 8, 1858, the schooner *Sunbeam* from York, Maine, struck the north breakwater, and her captain James Toggerson was washed overboard and drowned. Two other members of the crew were saved shortly afterward by boats from the Salisbury shore, north of Newburyport and Plum Island.

In the diary of John E. Lord, a copy of which is now at the Newburyport Library, we read that on January 3, 1873, the steamer *Sir Francis* was lost in a fog and hit off Salisbury Beach. The wreck was one of the two outstanding disasters at Salisbury during the last part of the nineteenth century.

Captain John Whiting had sailed the 1500-ton steamer *Sir Francis* out of Liverpool on November 12, 1872, with a general cargo consigned to Warren & Co., Boston. After a few days at sea the seven-month-old steamer hit such heavy weather that she had to return to Queenstown for repairs.

Again leaving for America on December 9, she ran into a bad storm, but continued across the Atlantic. From then on the captain had no chance to take a sight. His first contact with America was Breaking Rock Ledge, a cruel series of boulders lying off Salisbury Beach. Around 2:00 in the afternoon of January 3, 1873, the *Sir Francis* crashed heavily on the ledge.

Captain Whiting had made no less than forty voyages

across the Atlantic, eighteen of them as captain, with no trouble at all until the January 3, 1873, disaster. His luck had now ended, however, for the *Sir Francis* was doomed. Built in England at Hull and insured there, she was worth the equivalent of $190,000, while her cargo was estimated at $600,000.

When the ship struck, her second mate took the single passenger and started to row ashore, but after attempting to land at Salisbury Beach, they went across to Plum Island near the lighthouse, where keeper Henry Hunt was waiting for them and helped them to safety. Hunt brought the two men inside his home, where they stayed until two o'clock Saturday afternoon at which time the British consular agent took them to Boston.

Mate John Smith had also been taken to Plum Island Light because while out at sea he had suffered a terribly lacerated leg when shifting machinery on board the steamer caught his body. Although it was unfortunate that he was hurt, he would have gone overboard to his death if the machinery had not held him. Immediately after his arrival at the lighthouse he was placed under a doctor's care, and eventually he fully recovered.

On Sunday wreckmaster Tower arrived from Boston Harbor with the steam tug *C. M. Winch* and two lighters, while the tug *Mattie Sargent* was made ready to go out from Newburyport. Captain Robinson towed the schooner *Romeo* out beyond the breakwater from where she sailed to the steamer with thirty men, in charge of George W. Jackman, Jr., to handle the freight.

A short time before they had noticed a Portsmouth wrecking craft leaving the scene headed for Rockport with a load of salvaged goods. They had two fishing schooners with lighters in tow all heavily ladened with bales of wool, hoisting machinery and other material. The *Mattie Sargent* with customs officer Little aboard was put in chase. On their arrival at Rockport Little took charge of the situation and arranged for the Rockport customs officer to superintend the unloading there. Just how the salvage was divided is not known.

Great progress was made at the *Sir Francis* that day, with a large proportion of movable cargo transferred. As news of a coming storm had been received, everyone worked at top speed. Toward evening the wind went into the northeast, and a heavy rain soon began to fall. When the men left the wreck, they agreed that further salvage was useless, for the ship then lay with her back broken and two-thirds of her length across the reef, her bow facing shore.

In spite of these circumstances, a $5,000 pump was sent out to the *Sir Francis* during the next calm spell, and substantial removals were made after the water had been pumped out of several holds.

The cargo consisted of coils of wire rope, hoisting machinery, bleaching powder, soda, glassware, flax, earthenware, bales of wool, rollers, yellow berries, boiler flues, sheet iron, a large shipment of iron rails consigned to Kidder, Peabody in Boston, and a supply of mixed spices for Stickney and Poor in Charlestown.

A second gale rose suddenly on January 18, bringing such a high surf that the workmen were forced to abandon the $5,000 pump, which was lost in the storm with the remainder of the cargo when the steamer slid off the rocks into deep water. On the day of the final disappearance of the steamer hundreds of persons flocked down on the Salisbury shore, most of them in time to watch the ship slide under the waves forever.

Wreckage of all sorts then began coming ashore along the beach. Whole spars and planks washed up, together with other fragments of the ship ground into kindling wood.

Although there were many discussions about how to salvage the pump as well as some of the remaining cargo, nothing of value was ever recovered from the sea bottom there. The wreck is still out off the Salisbury shore awaiting some venturesome skin diver or deep sea diver who wants to find out how the cargo has survived the more than eighty-three years which have elapsed since that disastrous day in 1873.

Possibly because of the wreck of the *Sir Francis*, a lifesaving station was erected in 1874 on Plum Island at Sandy Beach. The first keeper was Robert Floyd, and he had six patrolmen under his command. The station was moved to a position near the lighthouse in 1881.

On Saturday morning, May 26, 1883, at 3:30, the side-wheeler *City Point*, in command of Captain O. Ludlow, struck on Emerson's Rocks during a thick fog. Bound from Annapolis, Nova Scotia, to Boston, she had sixty-five persons aboard. One boat upset while it was being rowed ashore, but no one was lost. The rescue steamer *Carlotta* arrived by 10 A.M., but the *City Point* was already breaking up as the rising surf hit her, and her cargo of eggs, halibut and potatoes was soon scattered along the shores. Long after the hull had disappeared, the walking beam remained in sight. Today one of the few relics from this wreck is a stateroom door which can still be seen in Ipswich at the home of Ida Elvira Small.

On May 4, 1893, the schooner *Brave* from Deer Isle, Maine, was driven on the shore near Knobb's Beach and all four on board perished.

Possibly the wreck which is best remembered by the past generation is that of the *Jennie M. Carter.** As no one ever came ashore alive from her, the details of just what happened

---

* The official number of the *Jennie M. Carter* was 75700 and her call letters were J. Q. N. V. A three-masted schooner, her length was 130 feet, her breadth 35 feet and depth 10 feet and her gross tonnage 296.22. She was built at Newton, Maryland, in 1874, and her home port was Providence, Rhode Island.

will always be in doubt, but a fairly reliable series of events concerning this vessel can be deduced.

At five o'clock on the morning of Friday, April 13, 1894, the three-masted schooner was seen drifting along Salisbury Beach opposite the end of the plank road by a Mr. Fowler, a resident of Hampton. Evidently, even then, there was not a soul aboard.

An hour later the lifesavers at Plum Island Point sighted her just as she went aground. Although the crew at the station was at that moment sitting down to breakfast, they all sprang up, donned oilskins and rubber coats and launched their lifeboat. Crossing the harbor, the surfboat proceeded up Black Rocks Creek and thus reached the scene of the wreck.

Meanwhile, Fowler and a companion had followed the *Carter* along the beach, and when she grounded they had waited a short time and then climbed up into her chains and reached her deck. They were unable to find a single person on the schooner and soon left the vessel.

About an hour later the lifesavers boarded the wreck and removed the compass, the quadrant, the papers and a clock which was still going. Its hands pointed at 10:25 as it was tossed ashore. By this time the schooner's back was broken by the heavy cargo of paving blocks and there was no hope of salvaging her.

Judging by reports, the *Carter* was carried directly over the Breaking Rocks Ledge where the *Sir Francis* hit in 1873, then drifted ashore opposite the present site of the old Ocean Echo, now the Frolics.

On April 10 at 10:00 A.M. the *Carter* had been sighted by the schooner *Smuggler* off Highland Light, her rudder missing and the jibboom, bowsprit and fore topmast gone as well. The *Smuggler* lay by for two hours, but at that time Captain Wesley T. Ober of the *Carter* was confident that he could reach land without assistance and so the *Smuggler* sailed away.

Later the new yawl of the *Carter* was discovered by Patrolman C. M. Noyes of the Plum Island Station near Sandy Beach. The handle of a grip sack was found tied to the gunwhale of the boat indicating that someone had put his belongings in the yawl as an effort was made to reach shore. However, Keeper Elliot of the Plum Island Lifesaving Station did not concur in this theory, believing instead that all the crew were gathered at the anchor attempting to lower away when a great wave came over the side and took every man into eternity with it. Nevertheless, the fact that the yawl washed ashore with the grip sack handle and other material would indicate to most people that the ship's company had at least attempted to leave by the yawl. Other articles were found near by.

For some time on the morning of the disaster it was reported that every man in the crew had reached shore safely and had been taken up to the Hampton Beach Hotel where they were safe and sound. But a visit by interested people disclosed that no one from the wreck had been seen in Hampton, or anywhere else, for that matter.

Another point of dispute was the alleged presence of a woman on board. When the lifesavers reached the wreck they discovered several lady's garments in the cabin. Later Captain A. L. Crowley of East Boston, brother of the *Carter's* steward, stated that the captain's niece had made the trip. Still later it was discovered that the captain's niece had not made the trip after all. Quite often the captain's wife went with him on the sea journeys from port to port, but apparently she did not go on this trip. It is now believed that there were no women on board during the fatal voyage. There had been seven men aboard, the captain, the mate, the cook and four seamen, not one of whom was ever seen again alive.

By Friday afternoon the seas were washing off the deck houses. The mizzenmast fell and the other masts went during that night. A large crowd, many of them disorderly, gathered on the beach to watch the craft break up.

The first body to come ashore was that of Sven Sigfred Petersson of Sweden, a twenty-five-year-old seaman who had been in America only a few years. The captain's body washed ashore near Knobb's Station, Plum Island, on April 19, and the remains were sent to Sedgwick, Maine, there to be interred with those of his father.

A coat belonging to the mate, J. W. Preble, came ashore on April 23. A letter in it from West Harrington, Maine, was dated December 18, 1893.

The great cargo of paving stones was sold at auction on April 23 at 10 o'clock in the morning. Crowds continued to go down to Salisbury Beach to view the remains of the wreck, which even today, in 1956, shows a few blackened fragments of her keel when there is an unusually low tide during times of full or new moon. The loss of the *Carter* was one of the epic shipwrecks of the area.

The strange fate which befell a homemade motorboat is the last major disaster of the vicinity.

Sunday morning, May 10, 1908, was cloudy, and a moderate northwest breeze was blowing. A heavy easterly sea hit the coast, the result of a strong northeasterly gale two days before, and the high surf on the bar was made worse by a freshet in the river. It was about two-thirds ebb tide at the time that George E. Bailey, owner and captain of a motor launch, attempted to go out to sea. Aboard besides the captain were his son, William Bailey, and also Thomas Keenan, Frank Teague, Berado Parisso, Pietro Milone, Rocco Schina, Joseph Colombo and Tamaro Bernardino. The last five men could not swim.

Mr. Bailey employed the others in his Newburyport shoe

factory. He was particularly anxious to go out in his craft that morning. Some time before he had purchased a "knock-down" launch frame and had partly built the boat in his yard. When the task proved too difficult for him, a local builder worked on it, finishing the vessel on the evening of Saturday, the ninth. As soon as it was ready Bailey had his men come over and help launch the craft, after which he invited them all to go for a ride the next morning about 10 o'clock.

Everyone appeared on time, and the launch cruised around the river until 11:20 and then headed downstream. Across at the Newburyport Lifesaving Station, Keeper Thomas J. Maddock noticed the crowded boat near the north jetty, but at the moment he was concerned about another craft which had anchored in a dangerous position. He had remarked to his patrolman that "there is going to be trouble!", but the vessel in question finally hauled anchor and proceeded in toward the harbor.

Meanwhile Bailey started for the ocean. Although the seas were rough, they didn't break in the channel. After crossing the bar Bailey steered northward, presumably aiming for the fishing grounds. Maddock heaved a sigh of relief, exclaiming as he did so, "They're all right now. Let's have dinner."

Not three minutes after Maddock had descended from the tower, leaving his son and the lookout, there was a shout and the lookout came bounding down the stairs.

"She's gone over!"

Everyone rushed for the boathouse and launched the surf-boat. Keeper Maddock realized that Bailey, instead of continuing to the fishing grounds, had come across toward the bar three hundred yards above the channel at the shallowest part. With four hours' ebb and a heavy sea running, Bailey hadn't a chance and the boat capsized.

As the launch went over three of the Italians disappeared at once in the ocean. Another grabbed Keenan and, panic-stricken, began choking him in his efforts to keep from drowning. Bailey helped Teague who could not swim.

The younger Bailey clung to the launch. When the first great wave hit the overturned craft another Italian was swept away, and the man who had been choking Keenan also lost his grip and perished in the sea.

Two fishing boats were on their way to the rescue, one in charge of Leslie Wood and the other operated by Andrew Gynam. Gynam reached the scene first and picked up Teague who was all ready to let go, after which the rescuer threw a lobster pot line to Keenan, who was too weak to grasp it. Fortunately, Walter Bradley, from the other boat, grabbed Keenan just as he was going down. The two Baileys were then saved by both rescue boats. The lifesavers, rowing hard, reached the scene at this moment. Not one of the five Italians was seen again.

The capsized launch all this time was being swept by the strong ebb tide toward the sea and was now a quarter mile from the place where she had overturned.

The survivors were hurried to the lifesaving station and given first aid. On advice of a physician, Mr. Keenan was told not to attempt leaving the station until the next day.

On May 31 two bodies were found, those of Parisso and Schina. That of Bernardino was discovered at sea June 16. An unusual aftermath of the affair was the finding on the body of Parisso $558, while $318.45 was removed from Bernardino's pockets.

CHAPTER TWENTY-THREE

THE *Aquatic* AT CUTTYHUNK

Toll for the brave—
The brave! that are no more.

EVERY ONCE IN A WHILE when I dip into New England's rich and mysterious past, I realize how comparatively little we know of the spectacular history of the heroic men who have lived along the coast and on the many islands off New England. The story of the *Aquatic* is one of courage seldom equaled.

Beginning on the twentieth of February, 1893, a great storm swept New England, driving vessels of all types and sizes ashore at Vineyard Haven, Cape Cod and other locations on Massachusetts Bay.

The brig *Aquatic*, owned by George Tufts at Saint John, New Brunswick, was only seven years old. On February 12 the 361-ton craft had sailed from Sagua, Cuba, with 3933 bags of sugar worth $40,000 and consigned to G. P. Welch of Boston.

On the night of February 24, when the gale seemed to be going down rapidly, the *Aquatic* was off the Cuttyhunk Islands near the Sow and Pig Rocks, and although battered by the gale, she had evaded the worst dangers of the great storm. Her captain and his crew were already exchanging congratulations on having escaped the sea's vengeance in this particular gale. Near by the great four-masted schooner *Douglas Dearborn* had crashed ashore at Cuttyhunk just three days before, but they were not aware of it. They entertained no fears of shipwreck that night as the long storm had practically subsided, but fifty-three-year-old Captain Lawrence A. Halcrow had been bred to the sea and should have known well the need for constant vigilance. Nevertheless, for some reason he must have momentarily relaxed his attention, possibly feeling that with the ending of the storm the danger was over.

The trip up the coast from Cuba had been remarkably fast all the way to Cape Hatteras. Once the "stormy Cape" was on the *Aquatic's* quarter, gale after gale had smashed into the brig, and every man aboard was worn out from the constant ordeal.

And so it was that at dusk, Friday night, February 24, the *Aquatic* was approaching the Elizabeth Islands in a brisk northwest wind. The topsails, three staysails, two jibs and the mainsail were all set; Amerston, the Norwegian, was at the wheel; and Captain Halcrow was forward on the watch.

Shortly after 8:00 Halcrow ordered a reef taken out of the staysails. There was nothing at the time to indicate trouble ahead.

Suddenly, a moment later, the captain's keen ears detected the fearsome sound of breakers on a lee shore just off the starboard bow. Alert at once, he swung into action, barking out his orders:

"All hands on deck! Brace the yards! Put your helm hard aport!"

But it was already too late, for in less than ten seconds the *Aquatic* struck heavily, pulled free for a moment, struck heavily again, and then bore up on a hard, rocky ledge. She seemed in no immediate danger, but the crew lighted flares to notify those ashore of the wreck.

Cuttyhunk Light was located just to the northeast of the wreck, and why Captain Halcrow had not noticed the strong gleam of the beacon on a clear night is a question he never properly answered.

Across on the Cuttyhunk beach the lighthouse keeper's son, Willie Eisener, had been looking out at the shadowy outline of the great four-masted schooner wrecked near by when he suddenly saw the lighted torches. Willie had been some distance down on the shore when the *Aquatic* hit, but he rushed back toward his father's home and breathlessly told of the flares he had seen. Keeper Albert G. Eisener quickly dispatched his assistant, Will Black, to warn the villagers, and went down on the beach himself.

The entire island population was already exhausted from having saved the crew of the *Douglas Dearborn* by breeches buoy. Many of the lifesavers had their hands and feet badly frostbitten from that experience. And now there was another vessel in trouble while the four-master was still going to pieces offshore. Unfortunately, this new wreck, in the dead of night, could not be reached by breeches buoy.

There was a certain amount of rivalry at Cuttyhunk Island between the men who operated the government station on the extreme eastern end of the island and those who were connected with the Massachusetts Humane Society's station * on the west side. Josiah Tilton was the first to reach the Humane Society's lifeboat, and the other members of the crew were quick to arrive. The Humane Society station was just across from the wreck of the *Aquatic*.

Fred and Tim Akin reached the boathouse five minutes

---

* The boathouse was listed in the records of the Humane Society as Boathouse Number 43.

after Josiah Tilton, and they were followed by Eugene Brightman, Hiram Jackson and Isaiah Tilton. By this time lighthouse keeper Eisener * had arrived at the Humane House.

Because of the darkness of the night and the tumultuous breakers Eisener was anxious that the men should wait until morning.

"There's a terrible sea running," he admonished, "and you'll never make it!"

"But the government lads'll soon try, anyway, and we can't let them beat us," came the answer, and to this Eisener had no reply. A moment later the six Humane Society men launched their craft into the raging sea.

It was then nine o'clock, and as the boat hit the first wave and nearly capsized, Eisener heard a voice behind him. It was that of the Akin boys' father, old Captain Akin.

"My God, I shall never see my boys again."

A veteran of a half century of storms at Cuttyhunk, Captain Akin had taken one look at the seas then running and was quick to realize that the Humane Society lifeboat would indeed be in danger, for the waves then surging between the shore and the wreck were extremely high with giant smashing crests which would easily capsize a lifeboat should they break when just in front of the craft.

Nevertheless, the men in the Humane Society lifeboat were doing very well. Again and again they reached a towering wave just as it was cresting but managed to slide down over the smooth side before the billow shattered itself into the boat.

Soon they were less than fifty yards from the *Aquatic*, and for a time it appeared that they might reach the brig and take off the crew. But the roughest water of all was dead ahead, and Hiram Jackson, one of the oarsmen, spoke up:

"Tim, do you think we're agoing to make it?"

---

* Eisener was later to serve as keeper at Boston Harbor's Lovell's Island Range Lights.

"I doubt it," came the answer.

They avoided two more terrible breakers by a narrow margin, and soon were only thirty feet away, with the current sweeping them toward the wreck. It was agreed that they would anchor at that location and pay out the line until the lifeboat was in under the lee of the *Aquatic*, and then the transfer of captain and crew could begin.

All was now ready for the attempt. A moment passed and then Fred Akin pulled in his oar to let go the anchor, but as he did so a fearsome breaker began to tower over the boat. Ten seconds later, regardless of what they tried to do to prevent it, the mighty wave smashed into the lifeboat and swamped it at once, with every man now struggling for his life in the icy, swirling current a few feet away from the shipwrecked brig.

Floating bottom up, the boat surged toward the two Akins and Hiram Jackson, and they clambered across the capsized craft as they tried to grasp the keel. Unfortunately, there had been no grip holes bored in the keel.

Both Fred Akin and Jackson battled desperately to retain some sort of hold on the boat, but first Fred slipped off to his death and, less than thirty seconds later, Jackson followed him. As far as is known Eugene Brighthame never came to the surface after the capsizing.

Tim Akin fought through the numbing water to reach a point just a few feet from the men on the *Aquatic*, for his body had bumped into the side of the wreck. Second Mate William Davis of the brig was there waiting for him and now succeeded in dropping Akin a line. Pulling the lifesaver to a point just below him, he leaned far over to help him aboard. Both men were exhausted. Davis reached down into the foaming surf, grabbed Akin's hand and hopefully began the slow pull up the icy side and over the gunwhale.

Now the mate grasped both of Akin's hands in his own.

One more pull would land the struggling Cuttyhunk Islander aboard the brig.

Another wave smashed against the side of the *Aquatic*, and under the tons of surf Davis could feel Akin's hands slip from his grasp. When the surge passed on toward shore, Akin had vanished. The second mate pulled the line back in, but there was no one clinging to it.

Suddenly, Akin's head was sighted twenty feet away! The mate hurled the line again, and Akin caught it. He swam with it toward the brig, but those aboard the *Aquatic* could see that he was fast weakening in the freezing seas. He lost his hold on the line, made a final attempt to grasp it again, failed, and sank to his death in the swirling sea before the horrified gaze of the watchers.

Another occupant of the lifeboat, Isaiah H. Tilton, the father of two children, also drowned shortly afterwards but the circumstances of his death were never known. He vanished from the other side of the capsized lifeboat shortly after Akin was lost.

Josiah H. Tilton was now the only survivor of the six men who had gone out into the surf to aid those stranded on the *Aquatic*. Unable to swim, he was just about to sink to his death when those aboard the brig sighted him floating around on the other side of the vessel, pulled there by the powerful current.

Luckily, as Tilton was approaching the stern, Captain Halcrow and two of the crew reached the taffrail. Watching their chances as the surf surged in and out, they noticed the current was taking the man closer and closer until he was just below them. All three men leaned far down. One grabbed Tilton's clothing, another dropped a line over his shoulders, and soon they had pulled him up over the rail and aboard the shipwreck just before the advent of a towering breaker which would have swept him to his death. The strange part of it was that Josiah could not swim, and yet he became the only survivor of the Humane Society's boat!

It was then 10:00 P.M. Tilton was given warm clothes by those on the *Aquatic* and became a fellow survivor. Before midnight the great waves battered in the house of the cabin, and all hands then took to the rigging, where they awaited the break of day.

The government lifesavers, after rowing around the west side of the island, wisely decided to wait for the morning light before attempting to reach the shipwreck. Neither they nor the island residents, of course, had any way of knowing the fate of the Humane Society lifesavers at that time.

Those ashore were desperately anxious concerning their loved ones in the lifeboat. In the morning their worst fears were realized when first Fred Akin's body was found and then the remains of the wrecked lifeboat were discovered.

Captain David P. Bosworth, captain of the government boat, launched the next day at dawn and rowed out until he could hail the tug *Elsie*, which was then standing by near the wreck. Bosworth put the Lyle gun aboard the *Elsie* and made plans to shoot the projectile from the gun across to the *Aquatic*.

The first shot was successful. The line was soon rigged, the breeches buoy sent across and the first survivor from the *Aquatic* swung out over the waves. When he neared the *Elsie* a shout of joy went up, for his fellow islanders recognized him as Josiah Tilton, the lifeboat's only survivor, but his sad news concerning the others soon turned their happiness to grief.

Two other sailors were pulled across the high seas, and then Captain Bosworth took his lifeboat directly over to the wreck where the remaining six survivors went down over the spring stay to the waiting boat. By this time it was three o'clock on Saturday afternoon.

The survivors were soon brought ashore at Cuttyhunk Island. There the islanders who had been stunned by the finding of Fred Akin's body and the lifeboat, learned definitely that the four other lifesavers had perished. Eventually the body of Timothy Akin came ashore on Cuttyhunk, while that of Isaiah Tilton washed up at Gay Head, the home of his childhood. The other two bodies were never found.

Stunned by the loss of five leading members of its population, Cuttyhunk Island thus suffered the greatest personal disaster in its long history. Tim Akin, whose wife had died the preceding year, had been left a widower with seven children, who were now orphans. They were Henrietta, the eldest who had been acting as a mother to the other six, Eva, Alvah, Ralph, Ruth, Orin and Cora. Hiram Jackson left a wife and three children, Samuel, Robert and Levi,* while Isaiah Tilton's wife was left alone with her two little ones, Henry and Warren. Thus there were fourteen persons in all, besides the parents of the two other single men, Eugene Brightman and Fred Akin, all dependent on those who had given their lives in a vain attempt at rescue!

Challenged by this great tragedy, the newspapers and societies of the state sprang into action. In many different ways the citizens of Massachusetts raised $26,702.52 for the support of the fourteen persons.**

The funeral for Fred Akin, whose body was the first from the disaster to come ashore, was held at the Seamen's Bethel in New Bedford after the people of Cuttyhunk had paid

---

* Levi Jackson, on January 23, 1910, at the age of 32, covered himself with glory when he saved the captain, the captain's wife and the crew of the ill-fated *Mertie B. Crowley*. I personally interviewed Ida Haskell, the captain's widow, in the year 1953.

** Nine years later, in March 17, 1902, after taking five workmen from the stranded barge *Wadena* off Monomoy, all five passengers and seven of the eight lifesavers were drowned when the hysterical workmen panicked and caused the lifeboat to capsize. This time $36,583.52 was subscribed for the families of the lifesavers thus bereft.

their respects in a brief ceremony conducted by the school-master on the island.

On the following day there were services also at the Sea-men's Bethel for his brother Timothy whose remains had been recovered shortly afterward. His body was transported back to Cuttyhunk for burial on the island.

Years later I stood by a gravestone on Cuttyhunk Island and read a simple inscription:

TIMOTHY JR.

son of

Timothy & Nina

Akin

One of the Heroes, who was
drowned at Cutty Hunk while
trying to save the lives of the
crew of the Brig Aquatic

Feb. 24 1893

Aged 36 yrs. 11ms. 11ds.

* * * * * *

Cuttyhunk Island has often been the scene of shipwrecks because of its position at the very end of the chain of Eliza-beth islands. In 1849 the brig *Spartan* piled up on the rocky ledges. There were two wrecks in 1852, the *Mary Chilton* and the *A. Dunbar*. Three years later the brig *Saint John* hit at Cuttyhunk, and in 1857 the brig *Vernon* was lost off-shore. In 1890 the *Maria Adilaid* came to grief.

On March 11, 1892 lighthouse keeper Albert Eisener and his family distinguished themselves by saving the crew of the British ship *Rob and Harry* which had been wrecked at Cuttyhunk. Dismasted three miles west of Hen and Chickens Lightship, the vessel drifted against the west end of Cutty-hunk. One man, Steward Ephraim McNeil of Richibucto,

New Brunswick, was lost. Eisener had noticed the masses of laths ashore, and after alerting the island, he called upon his wife, their daughter Edith, Frederic Akin and one other to help him. Willie Eisener, his young son, assisted in the launching of the boat but stayed behind to tend the lighthouse while the rest of his family rowed through tumultuous seas to the wreck of the *Rob and Harry*. There they managed to take off all survivors and returned safely with them to the shore. This remarkable rescue later brought a medal to keeper Eisener and rewards for each member of his family.

The schooner *Monticello* was lost at Cuttyhunk in 1902, and the next episode in the island's history was that of the last whaling ship ever to leave New Bedford Harbor, the *Wanderer*.

On August 25, 1924, the Reverend Mr. Charles S. Thurber, chaplain of the same Seamen's Bethel where the Akins' funerals were held, conducted ship services aboard the *Wanderer* before the vessel left on a whaling voyage.

Sailing from New Bedford Harbor, the bark anchored off Mishaum Point so that Captain Antone Edwards could return to finish recruiting his crew to the necessary twenty-seven members needed on the long trip ahead.

Shortly after the captain left the bark a heavy storm hit, which increased in intensity until a hurricane wind of seventy-five miles an hour was lashing the coast. Mountainous surf soon made the *Wanderer's* anchors drag, and before long the bark reached the area off the fatal Middle Ground near Cuttyhunk. Within a short time she grounded heavily.

Two whale boats were launched into the breakers as soon as possible, but they became separated from each other almost at once. First Mate José Gomes and his crew landed safely at Cuttyhunk soon afterward, but the other boat drifted many hours before rescue. With all hands rescued, the *Wanderer* itself became the center of attention. Efforts to save her

failed completely, and she remained for some time a pictur-
esque but costly wreck on Cuttyhunk Island. It was a sad
ending to an epochal event, the last sailing of a New Bedford
whaling ship.

During the famous 1944 hurricane the Vineyard Sound
lightship, located off the Sow and Pigs Ledge, was forced to
stay at its post when other ships fled to safety before the
great hurricane. The lightship went down with all eleven
of the ship's company lost, probably at the height of that
September 14th gale.

The captain of the doomed vessel, Warrant Officer J. Edgar
Sevigny, had planned to reach home on leave the day after
the hurricane hit, but the skipper of the lightship went down
with his vessel. Thus the dangerous area off Cuttyhunk had
claimed another craft, but this time more victims were lost
than in any other disaster in the island's long history of marine
tragedies.

CHAPTER TWENTY-FOUR

AMERICA'S WORST
MARINE STORM

Of all the crew and passengers,
Not one to tell the tale.

IN THE CENTURIES-OLD history of easterly gales there has never been a northeast storm which caused such devastation to shipping as the terrible hurricane of November 26, 1898, known as the Portland Gale. In fact, the damage from other great easterlies pales into insignificance when compared to the loss sustained during this mighty tempest.* Because of the peculiar marine conditions existent at that time, there can never be another storm which will equal it.

Almost six decades have elapsed since this great gale swept along the shores of Long Island and New England. Nevertheless, no one has ever compiled an authoritative list either of the vessels which were caught by the tempest or of the members of the ship's company who perished to the last soul in the storm's greatest single disaster.**

---

* Benjamin Franklin was the first to discover that northeast storms usually come from a southeasterly direction.
** In 1898 passenger lists went to sea with the ship, and if the ship foundered there was no way of recording those who were lost.

The hurricane of 1898 raged with unprecedented violence for twenty-four hours, tapering off during another ten and a half hours of diminishing winds. The storm will be remembered as that in which the side-wheeler *Portland* put out to sea with almost two hundred persons on board, not one of whom lived to tell his story. But much more than the loss of a single ship was involved. Such unbelievable devastation was created wherever the gale hit that if it struck today it would smash to pieces no less than 5,000 houses and buildings in the New England area alone!

The human race easily forgets and for those hundreds ashore who suffered property losses because of the Portland Gale in 1898, there are now thousands who have built cottages all over the same area, in many instances erecting summer residences where even the most daring builders of sixty years ago would not venture.

The reason no future easterly storm could inflict an equal amount of damage out on the ocean is that the entire system of transportation of people and freight has changed radically since the Portland Gale. The fleets of sloops, brigs, barks, brigantines, barkentines, ships and steamers then plying commercially up and down the northeastern coast have vanished forever from our coastal marine highways.

Those beautiful inspiring craft have been replaced, except for a few vessels which can be counted on the fingers of one hand, by trucks and trailers which lumber through every New England village and town; by busses, trains and airplanes which carry passengers to their respective destinations; and by the millions of automobiles which are privately owned. The days of the sailing vessels and the coastwise side-wheelers and steamers are gone forever.

Whenever a strong northeasterly gale hits the New England coast during the month of November those whose families have lived along the shore for generations remind each other of stories of the beautiful side-wheeler steamer *Port-land*,* launched at Bath, Maine, on October 11, 1889. She was 291 feet long and was considered the outstanding paddle-wheeler of the day. In November, 1898, slightly more than nine years after her launching, the *Portland* was to attract national attention.

Saturday, November 26 that year came two days after Thanksgiving, and because of the holidays there were more passengers than usual anxious to make the trip on the steamer from India Wharf, Boston, to Portland, Maine. However, since it is seemingly human nature to want to be connected with a disaster after it has happened, hundreds of others claimed that they had been planning to go aboard ** but had either changed their minds at the last minute or were delayed in reaching the pier.*** Actually the steamer had 190 persons aboard as she prepared to sail.

The background history of the weather of the Portland Gale is interesting and little known. At 8:00 in the morning of November 25, 1898, an anticyclone was present over the Ohio Valley and a slight cyclonic depression was causing snow over the Great Lakes. Another cyclone, bringing rain, lay over the Gulf of Mexico. Twelve hours later the anticyclone had reached the coast and at eight o'clock the following morning was centered over Northfield, Vermont. It was still

---

* More details of the Portland story may be found in my books, *Strange Tales from Nova Scotia to Cape Hatteras* and *New England Sea Drama*.
** See Appendix A for the list of *Portland* victims.
*** If all of them had told the truth about their plans and had been able to get aboard the *Portland*, the disaster would have occurred at India Wharf, Boston, for the side-wheeler would have gone down at her pier, terribly overloaded with the thousands of people aboard.

Likewise, the trolley car which was delayed would by necessity have become a full train of cars extending from South Station to India Wharf itself. And the bar room where so many allegedly lifted the final drink which delayed them just long enough so that the *Portland* sailed without them would have had a bar half a mile long stretching from the original location on Atlantic Avenue to some place in the vicinity of the present Federal building.

being forced northward by the cyclone in the Great Lakes then over Toledo, Ohio.

During the day of the 26th, the cyclone from the Gulf of Mexico connected itself by a long trough with the storm over Toledo, and soon the two tempests were proceeding as one, having united in almost unprecedented fury.

Although heavy snow was falling in New York, the morning in Boston had been fair with a light breeze and during the afternoon the clouds became heavier. But by the time the *Portland* was about to sail, the weather was still free of snow or rain at India Wharf.

There had been considerable discussion as to what went on between Captain Hollis H. Blanchard of the side-wheeler and the various company officials both at Boston and Portland in the several hours immediately before the *Portland* sailed. The relatives of Blanchard later claimed that he was ordered to sail while the officials stated that they had ordered him not to sail.

Regardless of what the pre-sailing orders were, at precisely 7:00 that Saturday night the final departing whistle from the *Portland* split the chill night air of Atlantic Avenue and the ship sailed away from the India Wharf pier forever.

It is still commonly believed that nothing was ever heard from the *Portland* after she left the pier. Actually this belief is incorrect. Again and again as the side-wheeler sailed down the bay, she was sighted and recognized. This did not happen just once or twice but at least a dozen times.

Hardly had she left her India Wharf pier when Superintendent Sullivan at the Narrow Gauge railroad terminal in East Boston looked across the harbor and noticed her lights. He watched them as the steamer sailed down the bay, for the visibility was excellent. Another observer was Captain Albert Nielson, later in command of the Narrow Gauge ferry boat *Newtown*. He was on Rowe's Wharf and saw the *Port-*

land sail by him at exactly 7:05 that evening, on time, remaining in sight down the bay for the next fifteen minutes. Nielson later "saw her lights pass Long Island." "It was not snowing," he observed.

Off Long Island the *Portland* approached and passed the *Kennebec*, the Bath steamer often mistakenly called the Kennebec boat. After the *Kennebec* had sailed, her captain had decided to return and anchored in the harbor. The two vessels exchanged whistles as the *Portland* proceeded to sea.

Meanwhile, passing Deer Island Light, Captain Joseph I. Kemp, later Boston's best-known sailing master, was aboard the tug *Elsie* approaching the inner harbor. "Around 7:15 P.M. the *Portland* came down the harbor and passed fairly close to us near Deer Island Light," Captain Kemp recorded.

The *Portland* reached the outer harbor and soon was abeam of Nahant. Charles T. Martell of Medford, mate aboard the tugboat *Channing*, was then at the wheel steering in a southerly direction to reach Boston Harbor. As Mr. Martell's remarks to me on November 24, 1948, have never been accurately recorded before, I give them below:

"The weather began to spit snow about 8:00 that night, and when the lights of the *Portland* came into view I steered up close. The weather was not bad at the time, but I knew a serious storm was coming.

"There were ten or twelve young men gathered on the topside just forward and aft of the paddle wheel box. When one of the young bloods on the *Portland* shouted across at me to get my old scow out of the way I shouted back at him, 'You'd better stop that hollering, because I don't think you'll be this smart tomorrow morning.'

"By this time I was less than twenty feet from the *Portland*, and could easily make out the features of the young men sailing to their death. I gave three blasts of the *Channing's* whistle, and Captain Blanchard, whom I could easily recognize in the wheel house, answered them promptly. Thus I was the last person to speak to anyone aboard the *Portland*, and even after fifty years it makes me feel queer whenever I think of it."

Captain William A. Roix aboard the *Mount Desert* passed the *Portland* in the vicinity of Graves Ledge, while the master of the *Sylph No. 8*, in the general vicinity of the Boston Lightship, saw the *Portland* on her way toward Thacher's Island.

As the great side-wheeler approached Thacher's Island Lights on her course up the coast, visibility was still satisfactory. At about 9:20 P.M. Captain William Thomas of the fishing vessel *Maud S* saw the lights of the *Portland* when he was less than four miles southwest of Thacher's Island, two miles away.

At exactly 9:30 the *Portland* steamed close to Thacher's Island, less than 500 feet from shore, passing between Thacher's and Londoner Ledge. She was observed from the island by Lynes B. Hathaway of Brockton as she continued, on schedule, up the coast.

Thus it is evident that Captain Blanchard was keeping well ahead of the storm, as he had done on many previous occasions when sailing from Boston to Portland during northeasterlies. But what Captain Blanchard did not know and would not find out until it was too late was that this gale on reaching the Massachusetts coast would develop into a terrible hurricane because of the union of the two storms.

Ashore at Rockport, Massachusetts, at the time, Captain William D. Knowlton said that the "glass in the early evening did not indicate a storm. There was nothing up to 9:00 to prevent a prudent captain from going to sea." He stated that "the storm arose with the most suddenness of any storm I have ever seen!"

Even at 9:30 light keeper W. W. Williams on Boon Island said that there was no indication of a bad storm, while up to midnight there was nothing to trouble the *Portland* in any way at Boon Island.

All evidence indicates that a series of cyclone-like fingers of hurricane snow and winds, actually tiny tornadoes, apparently reached out ahead of the storm for miles. At the very moment when the *Portland* sailed with visibility more than five miles at 7:00 that night one of the storm fingers had brought spitting snow within three miles of India Wharf, Boston, while two hours and a half later, as Captain Hathaway was watching in good visibility from Thacher's Island a few miles away, across at Rockport another finger of the storm was beginning to ravage the mainland.

Thus it is reasonably certain that these advance squalls of snow and wind then at Rockport * soon moved out over the water. All known facts point to the probability that one of the storm fingers reached down and disabled the *Portland*. The storm, moving slowly northward, hit the entire area around Thacher's Island about 10:00.

Freight clerk James F. Hunt, who did not sail on the fatal trip, later told the writer that whenever the *Portland* rolled, pulling one paddle wheel out of water, there was a terrific strain and vibration.

Evidence from other vessels limits the distance north which the *Portland* actually reached. We know that she was afloat and in good order near Thacher's Island at 9:30 P.M., keeping ahead of the snowstorm with great success. Less than ninety minutes later she was sighted twelve miles southeast of Thacher's Island Lights. Therefore in that ninety-minute period the storm must have caught up with her somewhere less than five

---

* Captain Frank Scripture stated that the advance fingers of the storm struck with such force that for years afterward their evidence was still present in the forests because of the rows of trees which the tornado-like wind in the storm fingers knocked down.

miles to the north of Thacher's between there and the Isles of Shoals in order to allow the *Portland* to be in a position twelve miles south by east of the lights of Thacher's Island at 11:00.

It was Captain Reuben Cameron * aboard the schooner *Grayling* who sighted the *Portland* at 11:00 P.M. The snowstorm had hit suddenly and hard shortly after 9:30, battering everything in its path and creating an indescribable pandemonium of wind and sea.

As he sailed near the *Portland* Captain Cameron noticed that the side-wheeler was already rolling and pitching badly apparently attempting to head out to sea. Evidently even then, Captain Blanchard, overwhelmed by the intensity of the gale, realized that he could not bring his craft into Gloucester or any other harbor. It is probable that his port paddle wheel was already causing him trouble and that he decided to attempt staying out on the open sea until the storm ended.

Captain Cameron, seeing the *Portland* bearing down on him, burned a Coston flare warning Blanchard away. At that time the superstructure of the *Portland* was intact.

Fifteen minutes later Captain Frank Stream of the *Florence E. Stream* passed the *Portland*, and at 11:45 P.M. Captain D. J. Pellier of the *Edgar Randall* narrowly escaped a collision with the side-wheeler. At the time Pellier believed that the superstructure of the *Portland* had been damaged.

Meanwhile, all along the coast those craft which could do so were scurrying for shelter. Vessel after vessel, failing to reach a snug harbor, was tossed ashore somewhere on the eastern seaboard, and every coastal area in the path of the double hurricane was seriously damaged. Giant breakers swept right through many main thoroughfares, and the tide

---

* Captain Cameron and I had a long interview in 1945 concerning this point.

rose even higher than during the storm which destroyed
Minot's Light in 1851.

The *Portland* was unreported from 11:45 P.M. until 5:45
the following morning, but Captain Blanchard must have
continued his efforts to stay out on the open sea, for the next
known position of the *Portland* was off the shores of Cape
Cod. Evidently the force of the storm had pushed him steadily southward, and Blanchard's relatively feeble efforts to
keep offshore resulted in a postion at 5:45 A.M. just off Race
Point.

At that time keeper A. C. Fisher of the Race Point Lifesaving Station heard four blasts from a steamer's whistle. His
statement follows:

"At 3:00 A.M. the storm was the worst I have ever seen.
At 5:45 I heard four short blasts—a distress signal from a
steamer whistle—I rang the gong to summon my crew and
then telephoned to the station at Peaked Hill Bar that there
must be a steamer ashore. Conditions were the worst I have
ever known!"

The eye of the hurricane passed across Cape Cod between
9:00 and 10:30. I quote now from a letter in my possession,
written by Captain Benjamin C. Sparrow, superintendent of
the Cape Cod lifesaving stations:

"Between 9:00 and 10:30 A.M. on Sunday Nov. 27 there
was a partial breaking up of the gale, the wind became moderate, the sun shone for a short time, and the atmosphere cleared
to an extent which disclosed two coastwise steamers, also a
fishing schooner lying to under short sail. About 11:00 A.M.
the gale again increased and vision was obscured from the off-
ing until after daylight on Monday morning. During the
interval above named, wreckage could have been easily discovered had it been upon the beach."

The last part of the statement answers misinformed people
who believed that wreckage from the *Portland* came ashore

on Sunday morning, but no debris from the side-wheeler was on the beach at that time.

Later it was determined that the two steamers reported by Captain Sparrow were the *Portland* and the *Pentagoet*, for no others were in the vicnity, while the fishing schooner must have been the *Ruth M. Martin* whose master, Captain Michael F. Hogan, had appealed to those on the *Portland* for help by hoisting a distress flag. Hogan eventually was able to double the Cape unaided and bring his battered craft to Provincetown, but both the *Portland* and the *Pentagoet* went down with all hands. The *Pentagoet*, a small screw steamer, was commanded by Captain Orris R. Ingraham of Rockland, Maine, and carried a great load of Christmas toys and gifts for Maine communities.

At sunset that Sunday night the Cape Cod shore presented a weird, desolate appearance to the faithful lifesavers then making their way against the bitter wind along the outer beach and bank. By this time the tide was coming in rapidly. High, white-tipped lines of breakers crashed heavily on the freezing sands, sending their foam-laden advance guards of surf far up on the beach, the spindrift whipping off in the gale to fly hundreds of feet through the air, already heavy with wet snow and biting sand.

Clothed in heavy oilskins and boots, Patrolman John J. Johnson of the Race Point Lifesaving Station fought his way through the storm along the bank. Every so often he stopped to get his breath and looked out to sea. He wondered about the poor unfortunate mariners offshore in the blizzard-like tempest and what their thoughts were at that very moment.

After a short rest, he would start out on his lonely vigil again, the feeble light of a small lantern his only help in detecting driftwood or wreckage coming ashore. Ever alert, his glance swept up and down the beach every few seconds.

Suddenly he came to a complete stop. There below him,

being swept in and out of the breakers, was a small white object, the discovery of which excited him strangely. A wave, greater than the others, caught the thing in its grasp, pushed it high on the beach and then retreated seaward.

Down the slope Johnson plunged, realizing his danger but knowing that he must retrieve the object. He reached the level of the sloping shore, ran a few steps and snatched it up. Just before the roaring surge of another breaker caught him, Johnson gained higher ground and then clambered over the edge of the bank to safety.

Lighting a Coston flare, he examined his find. It was a life preserver,* and on it he read the words STR PORTLAND. Turning his back to the wind, he pulled out his watch and noted that the time was 7:20.

However, the discovery of the life-jacket did not necessarily mean that the *Portland* had gone down. A single preserver might have blown off the upper deck or been thrown to someone who fell overboard. Even if the *Portland* was going to pieces a life-jacket could come ashore long before the side-wheeler sank.

From that moment on other articles from the steamer came ashore from time to time. But shortly before 11:00 that night masses of debris pushed up on the Cape Cod beach in fearful piles ten to twelve feet high. It was then high tide. Not until later were bodies washed ashore, however. When bodies of the victims did start to come in upon the beach, most of the watches found on them had stopped between 9:15 and 9:20, indicating that the actual sinking of the *Portland* took place at about that time Sunday night.

Evidence now before me indicates that the two-masted granite schooner *Addie E. Snow*, not in sight when Captain Sparrow made his morning report, crashed into the *Portland*

---

* That identical life jacket is now in my possession.

shortly after 8:00 that tempestuous night. Following the collision, both vessels must have gone to the bottom within an hour or so, but no bodies from the *Snow* ever came ashore.*

The Portland Gale raged all night long, but after dawn Monday morning the wind backed into the north. Later that day the gale diminished and ended a few hours afterward.

No word that the *Portland* was even in trouble reached either Boston or Portland until Tuesday, as all regular systems of communication were out of order because of the storm. Hundreds of telephone poles were down, while great drifts prevented trains from running or roads from being used, and transportation of any kind was practically impossible.

Finally, however, on Monday afternoon, Charles F. Ward, Chatham correspondent of the *Boston Herald* started from Hyannis on a work train that ran as far as East Sandwich where a washout prevented further progress. Ward struggled through the great drifts to reach Sandwich at 11:00 Monday night. Hiring a horse, he rode until he came to Buzzards Bay where the tracks were cleared all the way to Boston, and he arrived at Boston by train early Tuesday morning with word that the *Portland* had gone down. Thus the first news of the disaster was revealed to the world.

Meanwhile, wreckage and bodies washed ashore at Cape Cod. Thirty-six victims eventually were taken from the surf and the beach in the next few days, every one from the *Portland*.** The rest of the bodies from the ill-fated side-wheeler, well over a hundred in number, never were recovered. No man, woman or child escaped to tell the story of the sinking.

Because of the tragedy scores of relatives and friends of the

---

* The *Addie E. Snow* lies on the bottom relatively close to the *Portland*, which in 1945 lay on her side, still showing evidence of the collision. Wreckage from the *Addie E. Snow* and the *Portland* came ashore together, but material from the *Pentagoet* was found some distance down the beach.

** Although the beach was searched for weeks afterward, not a single body ever came ashore from the *Pentagoet* or the *Addie E. Snow*.

victims of the storm attempted to reach the outer beach at Provincetown and Truro hoping to find some sign of their loved ones amidst the great mass of wreckage, but the storm had made traveling almost impossible in certain areas of the outer Cape. Adding to the confusion of identifying bodies and taking care of off-Cape visitors, another great snowstorm hit late Tuesday night and caused further delays. Finally, on December 6, the last body from the steamer *Portland* washed up on the beach, and although for weeks afterward a careful watch was kept along the shore, no further victims were ever found. Wreckage, however, continued to break off the sunken hull of the side-wheeler, and washed ashore for the next six months.

One by one those looking for family and friends left the Cape and sorrowfully returned to their homes. By spring Cape Cod was left in relative isolation.

Many relics were salvaged from the wreck of the *Portland*. There is hardly a cottage or residence along the back side of Cape Cod that doesn't have its *Portland* mementos. The late Cy Young had a great collection of empty coffins, state-room numbers and doors, cabin posts, bunks and life pre-servers in his antique shop up to the time of his death. It is still possible for visitors to purchase many authentic souvenirs of the Bath-built side-wheeler, but the residents of the Cape cling tenaciously to the more valuable relics and hand them down in their own families from generation to generation.

There is one mistaken legend about the wreck which has been fostered through the years; that the huge main beam of the vessel, with the tonnage mark *2283*, actually washed ashore and was seen. This is incorrect, for although the sea evidently ripped off much of the upper works before the *Portland* took her final plunge, the main beam stayed with the side-wheeler.

Those whose relatives or friends had gone down with the steamer seemed to feel a common bond and they began to get together annually on the anniversary of the disaster to pay their respects to the victims. Eventually they formed a society known as the Portland Associates. The last president of this organization was the late John A. Thornquist. The society was disbanded in 1948. A new group, Sons and Daughters of the Portland Associates, was formed in 1951 with the leader at this moment Miss Helen J. McClintock of Melrose.

Years after the *Portland* sank Captain Charles G. Carver of Rockland, Maine, brought up material from the ship. On July 1, 1945, acting for and with funds provided by the writer, Diver Al George descended into the waters off Cape Cod at the location given by Captain Carver and thus became the only person of this century to reach the *Portland* and stand aboard her.

It is now possible to take underwater television pictures. A well-known Massachusetts diver plans to make pictures if the steamer is still visible off the Cape Cod shores after eleven additional years at the bottom of the sea. But there is a new threat to the success of eventual photography of the *Portland*. Sea worms have invaded this area and are in action as far north as Brant Rock, Massachusetts, so possibly even by this time all wooden material on the *Portland* has been consumed, making her discovery at best unlikely.

There is a fine five-foot replica of the famous side-wheeler now on exhibition in Boston. John H. Dodge of Kenyon, Rhode Island, labored for many hundreds of hours to make an authentic model of the beautiful steamer, and it is on permanent display at the Old State House Marine Museum in Boston.

Because of the many relatives and friends of those who

went down on the steamer, the unusual conditions preceding her sailing and the mystery which still surrounds her sinking, the story of the *Portland* will always remain New England's greatest saga of the vengeful sea.*

* See Appendix B for the list of vessels lost or damaged in the Portland Gale.

CHAPTER TWENTY-FIVE

THE *Vestris*

Their winding sheet the cold dark wave,
Their gallant ship her liegemen's grave.

AT 3:30 on the afternoon of Saturday, November 10, 1928, the veteran British steamer *Vestris* left New York, bound for South America on what was expected to be her last voyage and what proved to be one she never finished. Her master, Captain William J. Carey, was looking forward with anticipation to the completion of the trip, for the *Vestris* was then to be retired from the sea, while he was to take command of Lamport and Holt's flagship, the *Voltaire*, as commodore of the fleet. Captain Carey had an enviable forty-year record, his only loss at sea being the *Titian*, torpedoed by a U-boat.

Just before her sailing, the United States steamboat inspectors had gone aboard the *Vestris* and the huge cargo, which included massive crates of machinery and equipment, together with scores of automobiles, had apparently been loaded in shipshape fashion by the stevedores.

However, it would be a mistake to say that the *Vestris* was being sent out to sea in proper condition. At the last moment a substantial load of cargo had arrived at the pier with company orders that it must go aboard, although when these last two hundred tons were stowed away, the cargo line of safety as instituted by Samuel Plimsoll was under water.

Listing slightly to port, the overloaded ship proceeded down the bay and out beyond Sandy Hook Light. Besides the United States mail for West Indian ports and South America and the heavy cargo, there were 128 passengers aboard.

Unfortunately, the *Vestris* was soon encountering a bad sea, driven by a northwesterly wind. As the storm increased in intensity, she changed her list from port to starboard, and the quartering sea made her wake of extreme concern to the experienced sailors aboard.

A short time later the captain learned that his vessel was taking water, and an inspection by the mate revealed that the ash ejector and a starboard port were leaking. Temporary sealing was placed to stop the leaks but they soon started again in another location, believed to be under the bunkers.

By early afternoon it was impossible to keep the *Vestris* on her course even at half speed, and the captain decided to heave to. As though he was not in enough trouble, the wind increased to a gale which began to hit at almost seventy miles an hour, causing gigantic breakers to smash over the now helpless steamer.

Dinner that night was only for the hardy souls, but as they were halfway through their meal, a disheartening crash overturned several tables, plates of food hit the deck and the ship heeled over to the starboard. Another mighty sea caught the *Vestris*, and her list went from ten to twelve degrees. As the seas continued to smash into her it reached eighteen and then twenty degrees! Finally the vessel recovered slowly and worked her way back to ten degrees, only to return to a fifteen-degree list where she held. Below deck the automobiles had shifted to crash through into the forecastle, knocking two lifeboats from their positions.

According to later testimony, Captain Carey now made his first mistake by ordering the number two tank pumped out. As the pump worked, the list increased rather than diminished. When the tank was empty the *Vestris* heeled over at twenty degrees!

The sea now began to subside, giving Carey false courage, and he decided against sending out a signal of distress. This might have caused his firm to frown on future promotions!

Several of the old-time sailors were wondering why the captain hadn't tried to wear ship * but of course none dared to bring the subject to his attention.

Up on the bridge Carey now received a terrifying report from below to the effect that the *Vestris* was listing thirty degrees and making water steadily. He dared to wait no longer and ordered Mr. Bolger to have a C Q message sent out over the wireless asking other vessels to stand by.

When the distress signal finally flashed out, the operator at the naval radio station at Bethany Beach, Delaware, plotted the location as best he could. On Monday morning the station obtained a new fix and in a conversation with the wireless operator aboard the *Vestris* learned that they were anxious to know where the nearest coast guard station was. Meyers, the chief operator at the Delaware Naval Station told them that Cape May was the closest. As a precaution he also notified the Cape May Coast Guard headquarters of the trouble, and they dispatched a cutter at once.

Finally, Captain Carey ordered an S O S sent out. It was then almost 10:00 in the morning and the ship was listing at thirty-two degrees!

The 800-foot Tuckerman transmitter at Hickory Island,

---

* The opposite to tacking.

New Jersey, received the S O S call. Within a short time more than fifty-five ships responded with their positions, and every craft within striking distance of the stricken vessel started under forced draft for the general area, hoping to get a clearer position as they neared the scene. Unfortunately, there was considerable confusion regarding her exact longitude and latitude, which did not clear as the hours went by.

The wireless operator aboard the *Vestris*, R. O. O'Loughlin, followed his first message of distress with another S O S half an hour later, and at 11:00 that morning, released the following poignant appeal:

VESTRIS ALL SHIPS OH PLEASE COME AT ONCE.

Seven minutes later still another appeal:

VESTRIS RUSH ALL HELP NOW SHIP SINKING SLOWLY.

At 12:30:

VESTRIS S O S S O S WILL SOON HAVE TO ABANDON NOW.

At 1:17:

VESTRIS CAN'T WAIT ANY LONGER GOING TO ABANDON.

Eight minutes later came the final message ever sent from the doomed liner:

VESTRIS ABANDONING SHIP TAKING TO LIFEBOATS S K.

At the moment that the final sign-off letters S K went out through the air waves a small American freighter was plowing through the seas about thirty-four miles away. With no wireless aboard, she was unable to know of the tragedy then being enacted just out of sight, and probably missed seeing the *Vestris* by only a few miles.

It had been difficult enough to attempt getting a fix on the *Vestris* before she went off the air, but now it was impossible. Given a wrong position at first, the coast guard cutter *Manning* was still rushing toward the new fix, but she had lost valuable time.

Back aboard the sinking liner, women and children had been ordered into the smoking room at 7:00 that Monday morning.

The ship gradually heeled over on her starboard side and panic overcame those who were attempting to load the lifeboats. It was now almost impossible to get the lifeboats away, for the ship had such a list that the ones on the starboard side were hanging so far out over the water it was hard to get into them in many cases, while those on the port side were being slid down the iron sides of the ship.

There had been no lifeboat drill since the *Vestris* had left New York and few passengers knew what to do in case of emergency. If the captain had allowed the lifeboats to be lowered and they had gotten away from the ship before the list became so pronounced, many more would have been saved.

Finally the motorboat was launched, but it was found to be without an engineer. Eventually, in spite of everything, there were eight lifeboats in the water. By now men, women and children were leaping into the ocean to reach craft which in several cases were half empty, only to fail in their efforts and drown when no attempts were made by those in the boats to help them.

Then came the final struggle of the liner to avoid her death plunge. Six lifeboats were still in their davits, and the steamer vibrated tremendously as she settled lower in the water. Her port side was almost flush with the ocean as she began to take her final dive into the depths of the sea.

Captain Carey walked downward into the water at the last minute, and there are those who say his final words were, "My God, I am not to blame for this!"

Unfortunately, he was to blame for it. He had committed blunder after blunder, and his delay in sending the actual S O S was possibly his worst error. Unquestionably, at least two vessels could have reached him and taken off every person long before the ship was to sink. And for that he can never be pardoned.

Those same vessels which would have arrived on the scene in plenty of time were even then churning the waters to reach the *Vestris* before it was too late.

The *American Shipper*, whose master was Captain Schuyler Cummings, a man who had already participated in two rescues, was nearing the location of the tragedy. The French tanker *Myriam* was also almost at the scene, with the North German Lloyd liner *Berlin* close behind, while the *U. S. S. Wyoming* was rapidly approaching the last known position of the *Vestris*. And a host of others, the *U. S. S. Modoc*, the *U. S. S. Mascoutin*, the Coast Guard cutter *Manning*, the *Santa Barbara* and the *Voltaire*, which Captain Carey had been promised on his next voyage, all were on the way.

But it was too late, for the *Vestris* had gone down.

Of the 326 persons aboard her when she sailed from New York, many were still alive in lifeboats and others, in the water, would be saved. The hours went by, however, and not a rescue ship came in sight. Midnight passed, and then 3:00. Suddenly, at almost half past three in the morning, those in the first lifeboat could see the faint beam of a searchlight far in the distance. They lighted their Coston flares at once.

Miles away, high on the bridge of the *American Shipper*,

Captain Schuyler Cummings had just been told by Second Officer Ohman that Coston flares had been sighted. Half an hour later the great ship drew alongside the tiny lifeboat and began the actual rescue work. Soon all survivors from the first boat were aboard and being cared for. Chief Officer Johnson of the *Vestris* was closeted with Captain Cummings, giving him the details of the sinking and the possible position of the other seven lifeboats.

Now that one boat had been picked up and the fix was known, the position of the *American Shipper* was radioed to all the other rescue craft, and the message was relayed from both the Tuckerton, New Jersey, and Chatham, Massachusetts, stations.

Less than half an hour after the last survivor from the first lifeboat had clambered aboard the *American Shipper*, the French tanker *Myriam* picked up the second lifeboat from the lost liner, and by 5:00 that morning the *American Shipper* was approaching three more lifeboats, and had all the passengers aboard by a quarter of six. The number saved by the *American Shipper* at that time was ninety crew members and thirty-two passengers.

Then came word that the *U. S. S. Wyoming* had taken five living persons from a mass of wreckage. No further reports were received for several hours, but shortly before 10:00 Captain Cummings' craft rescued a man and a woman, Paul A. Dana and Mrs. Clara Ball. The *Berlin* took one man from the sea shortly after 11:00 to make a total of twenty-three she had saved. The *Wyoming* had rescued nine in all. But not one of the twelve children aboard was ever found!

Two hundred and nine persons survived the sinking of the *Vestris* but the other one hundred and seventeen had been claimed by the sea.

CHAPTER TWENTY-SIX

HURRICANES AND FLOODS

> *God, what was that, like a human shriek,*
> *From the winding valley? Will nobody speak?*
> *Will nobody answer those women who cry*
> *As the awful warnings thunder by?*

ON OCCASIONS ALL too numerous the vengeful sea challenges the mighty continents, wreaking havoc on the shore, and at times striking far inland to overwhelm, temporarily at least, entire villages and townships, causing damage running up into millions of dollars. The sea has also summoned aid from its strong ally, the West Indian *HURACÁN*, which although extremly powerful and violent over the ocean, almost always weakens in intensity when proceeding over land to any extent.

In this country the storms best remembered during each century of recorded history were those of August 15, 1635; February 22, 1723; September 23, 1815; and September 21, 1938.* Other great storms or hurricanes which attracted considerable attention at the time they occurred, took place

---

* This disastrous hurricane caused more than 682 deaths and property damage of half a billion dollars.

in 1676, 1717, 1786, 1804, 1821, 1841, 1851, 1869, 1888, 1898, 1909, 1931, 1938, 1944, 1954 and 1955.

Because the two years 1954 and 1955 were so decidedly unusual weatherwise in matters pertaining to floods, hurricanes, heat and cold, they shall be included in this chapter.

Unfortunately, the sea and the *HURACÁN* combined have a final terrible weapon in the form of devastating floods, as has been demonstrated remarkably in recent times.

In spite of the great inundations of the last few years, the reader would be wrong in assuming that floods of this type are a new phenomenon of nature, and I do not have to go back to Noah and the Ark to prove my point. In every century of recorded history this country has suffered disastrous floods, although those which have struck the United States through the years have been more or less ignored by weather historians.

The northeastern part of the United States, with a longer recorded history than elsewhere in the country, has had a surprising number of outstanding floods and violent freshets.*

New England shores were flooded in 1635 and 1723. A mighty freshet occurred along the Connecticut River in 1755, but details are lacking. The first inland flood which is recorded in any way took place on January 8, 1770. The Connecticut River, the Androscoggin River and the Kennebec River overflowed their banks, and at Bowdoinham, Maine, the water rose fifty feet higher than normal.

On October 20, 1785, after a record nine-inch rainfall, many New England mills and bridges were carried away. During the flood the graves of a substantial number of Pilgrim fathers washed into the sea from the Cole's Hill Burial Ground at Plymouth.

---

* Freshets are floods. The term was used almost exclusively by local historians up to 1890 to denote a flood, but few people today, even weather experts, are familiar with the full significance of its meaning.

Another flood of unusual proportions hit New England on March 21, 1801, causing tremendous damage in Vermont, Massachusetts and Connecticut. It was followed six years later by the February, 1807, freshet, called by many the first great flood of the nineteenth century. This washed away bridges at Lawrence, Haverhill, Portsmouth, Pawtucket and East Chelsea, Connecticut, and did untold damage to farm lands in the area.

On May 13, 1814, rain fell in torrents "more than had ever fallen before in Maine history," and the Mousam, Saco and Androscoggin rivers overflowed.

Other floods of importance include the spring freshets of 1823, 1826 and 1827, as well as the Great Freshet of 1830, during which fourteen persons were drowned at West Mills, Vermont.

On March 26, 1846, a remarkable flood inundated the Penobscot region of Maine, carrying no less than forty-four saw mills to destruction and piling up ice in the streets of Bangor to a depth of twenty-five feet!

On Sunday, November 13, 1853, a great rainstorm brought such dark clouds and gloom that in many of the unlighted Boston churches the congregations could not see their preachers. Up in Vermont the rain brought floods which swept away the Dummerston bridge, while another bridge which collapsed at Ansonia, Connecticut, caused the death of several persons.

On May 16, 1874, at 7:00 in the morning, gate tender George Cheney noticed that the entire bottom section of the great Williamsburg Dam was about to collapse. He told as many as he could reach of the impending disaster, and others set out to warn the surrounding country side. Young Collins Graves galloped his horse everywhere he could in the brief time and asked other people to pass the word along, but when the dam collapsed the flood carried all before it and 136 people perished.

In the year 1839 on May 31, a mighty freshet inundated the region around Johnstown, Pennsylvania. Before the waters had gone down, no less than 2,200 persons had perished in what has been called the worst of all floods ever to hit America.

Because man builds nearer and nearer to the banks of rivers, every substantially heavy snow or rain offers potential danger to increasing numbers of people who either work or live in riparian areas. Although man has made great progress in dam construction in certain sections of the country, there is still a staggering amount of building to be done before floods can be controlled with any degree of success.

The worst Vermont flood of the twentieth century occurred on November 2, 1927, when 120 persons met their death in the raging waters which hit whole sections of towns and villages in the Green Mountain state. The government has built several dams since that time in strategic locations, and it is hoped that never again will the state suffer such loss.

Hurricanes and floods of yesteryear, however, from a financial point of view, must take second place in importance to the disasters of recent times.

The Year 1954

At the close of the year 1954 it was the opinion of weather observers that this country had experienced the most erratic weather on record. That year gave the United States its lowest temperature. The truck gardeners in Florida watched their crops freeze, and the east experienced its coldest spring. Dust storms formed in the southwestern plains and were followed by cloudbursts which flooded the Rio Grande area. Chicago experienced twelve inches of snow in one single day.

Hurricanes visited the eastern seaboard and caused untold suffering and damage.

In the beginning of 1954, Montana offered something in the way of weather never equaled before. On January 20 of that year the temperature at Helena was 36 degrees below zero, but a warm chinook wind descended on the Montana capital that day and within fifty-three and a half hours brought the temperature up to 54 degrees, or a record rise of 90 degrees.

Up on the Continental Divide the same day, however, at Rogers Pass, Montana, there was a temperature reading of 68 degrees below zero, which the weather bureau later announced meant a probable reading, with corrections, of 69.7 degrees below zero.

Returning to the east, New England had heavy rains in May, Boston enduring two days with a total of 5.74 inches and a record 13.38 inches for the month.

Early in August Hurricane Alice moved in over Texas, with the subsequent flood the worst in Rio Grande history. Over 153 were listed as dead or missing.

During August Hurricane Carol swept up the coast from the tropics to smash into Long Island and New England. On the 28th Carol was off the Bahamas. By August 29 it was reported near the Carolinas, passing by Cape Hatteras, where it was apparently losing strength, for it was loafing along at about fifteen knots and seemed about to veer out to sea.

Nevertheless, the weather bureau issued a danger warning that a storm of gale force, slightly less than a hurricane, was on the way toward Long Island and New England. The early forecast issued at 5:00 in the morning of August 31, 1954, predicted high tides and gales along the shore from Long Island to Nantucket.

When Carol hit, however, it was no gale at all, but a full-fledged hurricane with winds reaching 105 miles an hour at

Providence, 100 miles an hour at Boston and as high as 80 miles an hour at Portland, Maine.

Hurricane Carol assaulted the Rhode Island coast with terrific intensity, causing millions of dollars in damage. Misquamicut Beach, in Westerly, Rhode Island, was devastated again, having been almost wiped away in the 1938 hurricane and suffering severely in the 1944 blow. A swath three-quarters of a mile wide was cut right through the pleasure resort, but unlike the 1938 disaster, not a life was lost there. At the height of the storm a blazing cottage, lifted from its foundations by the flood, drifted into another house setting fire to it so that the inhabitants were forced to flee in waist-deep water.

Providence and the areas immediately adjoining were inundated with rising tides which put many locations in downtown Providence under several feet of water.

Pawtucket was overwhelmed. The Edgewood Yacht Club was shattered, while the Rhode Island Yacht Club was battered into a shambles.

Thousands of persons in Rhode Island and Massachusetts were marooned in the fast-moving storm, with trees crashing down around them, fragments of buildings collapsing, telephone wires and poles smashing down about their cars, and tall chimneys falling into the streets. Utter chaos reigned.

Every town or community had its tale of hardship and terror, and the coastal towns and cities had the added problem of yachts and boats ashore, streets inundated by the ocean, and giant waves sweeping all before them. Block Island was hard hit, as were the fishing communities across the sea at Point Judith, Galilee, and Matunuck, all in Rhode Island.

Sweeping along unchecked, Carol struck deep into Massachusetts, tearing down trees, smashing beach cottages into piles of debris, pulling boats from their moorings and crunching them into kindling wood. The rising water soon floated

off scores of Cape Cod residences, one of which drifted across
to smash into a shapeless pile of timbers against the railroad
causeway at the Buzzards Bay entrance to the Cape Cod
Canal, the tracks of which were rendered useless because of
a washout.

Cutting along up the coast, Hurricane Carol battered into
Plymouth, Duxbury, Marshfield, Scituate, Cohasset and Hull,
sinking and crippling scores of beautiful yachts and cabin
cruisers.

Lurching into Boston Bay, Carol swept across Boston dashing the steeple of the Old North Church to the ground thus
duplicating a similar occurrence on October 9, 1804.* Carol
battered the harbor severely, sinking further scores of craft
of all types, and then started up the coast ravaging relentlessly
the North Shore. The cities of Newburyport and Portsmouth,
New Hampshire,** were next in line, but by the time the hurricane hit Portland, Maine, it was almost spent, and shortly
afterward its intensity subsided.

Overwhelming destruction had visited New England again
with damage approaching half a billion dollars, and more than
seventy-two persons lost their lives.

The sea and its ally, the *HURACAN* had not finished. On
September 9 a new hurricane, Edna, raced toward New England, but when the weather bureau's warning alerted both
Rhode Island and Massachusetts, the storm veered out into
the Atlantic to hit the Maine coast with great impact, where
nine persons were killed. In Nova Scotia a record apple crop
was ruined.

---

* At that time the steeple crashed into an adjoining house.
** Hurricane Carol caught the forty foot cutter *Pendragon*, owned by
Allen T. Klots and under charter to William Mathers, at the Isle of Shoals,
New Hampshire. Cast adrift, she put to sea with her crew of four. While
riding out the gale in the Atlantic, Mrs. Mathers was swept overboard,
but a following wave washed her back so that she could be rescued from
certain drowning.

At Rockland, Maine, many craft were wrecked, the famous Samoset Hotel was forced to operate with candles and lanterns, and damage to homes and trees in the city itself was extremely heavy. In Rockland Harbor the power cruiser *Nessa* was battered to pieces against the public landing seawall, while many other craft in the area were sunk.

At Camden several fine yachts felt the brunt of the hurricane with the cutter *Andiamo* and the yawl *Firebird* being extensively damaged against the rocky ledges of the harbor.

While attempting to sail from Seal Harbor, Whitehead, to Tenant's Harbor, the sloop *Truant* was caught in the hurricane and Mr. and Mrs. Bancroft Beatley, Jr., of Cohasset, Massachusetts, made an effort to save their craft, but he was swept into the sea to his death and she was barely able to reach shore at Marshall Point.

Fishermen in the lobster industry suffered $1,000,000 damage to their gear including traps, pot warps, toggles and buoys.

All the cruise schooners out in the hurricane were reported safe, although several had narrow escapes in the one-hundred-mile-an-hour gusts which were then sweeping Penobscot Bay. The *Alice Wentworth* unloaded her passengers at Castine as a precautionary measure, the *Adventure* was taken in tow by the coast guard cutter *Laurel*, the *Enterprise* and the *Mercantile* were both safe in Buck Harbor, while the three-masted *Victory Chimes* came through the blow with minor damage. All who were out in the gale agreed that for Maine Edna was the worst hurricane since the 1938 blow.

But 1954 was not finished. A new disturbance, Hazel, beginning in the West Indies on October 13, and sweeping up through the United States did relatively little damage to New England, but struck hard at George Washington's estate at Mount Vernon and then took a heavy toll in Canada.

Highways in Ontario crumbled because of the hurricane,

and many people died when they drove into the storm-made excavations. Hundreds of families in the Humber River Area were driven from their homes, particularly in the Mount Dennis section. One father arrived from the flooded area carrying his four-year-old daughter clinging to his neck, his wearing apparel in his overcoat pockets and two heavy suitcases tied around his shoulders, an object of great determination to all who saw him.

Hurricane Hazel, which took about fifty lives, was the worst storm ever to hit the area.

THE YEAR *1955*

Hardly had the inhabitants of this North American continent stopped talking about the unusual weather of 1954 when the new year took over with terrifying force. When 1955 ended it was easy to see that it was another record-breaking twelve-month period, with the vengeful sea, the *HURACÁN*, and great floods combining to make it even more terrible than 1954 had been.

Again nature hit humanity with some of the most fearsome weather on record. Mighty winds, staggering floods and continuous droughts in the west during the opening months of the year cost the nation scores of millions of dollars. The March dust storms took soil from Texas, Kansas, New Mexico, Colorado and Oklahoma and dropped it over the Mississippi valley. Then 11.28 inches of rain fell during May in New Mexico.

The Ohio River floods of March, 1955, left thousands homeless and caused over $12,000,000 damage. On May 25 the worst Kansas tornado in history practically wiped out Udall, with 15 tornados hitting between Oklahoma City and Wichita in the same period.

Heat waves were everywhere. In August New York endured seven consecutive days with the temperature higher than 90 degrees. Out in Los Angeles the people suffered in 110-degree temperatures on September 2 while the following six days they experienced 100-degree weather.

The season of hot weather usually breeds hurricanes, but again 1955 was unusual. The first hurricane of the year was hardly noticed by the millions of Americans who have come to fear the great storms. It started on January 2, 1955, and was labeled Alice, a young lady who passed harmlessly out to sea from the French West Indies.

The second hurricane of the season, Brenda, came in more seasonable weather, beginning on July 20 and bringing high seas and heavy rains to the coasts of Louisiana and Mississippi.

The third hurricane was known as Connie and gained notice on August 8. Roaring in from the West Indies in typical *HURACÁN* fashion with winds of 135 miles per hour as she struck the Carolina coast on August 12, 1955, Connie lost much of her strength when she passed over the land. On her way this storm capsized a sailing schooner near North Beach, Maryland, with fourteen persons aboard meeting their death. The total loss of life from Hurricane Connie was forty-three.

In New England after frightening tens of thousands of summer residents from Cape Cod, a location to which they did not return that year, Hurricane Connie dissolved her strength and never amounted to anything more than a severe summer storm. Resort owners and excursion boat companies apparently were indignant at the loss in patronage they had suffered because of the weather bureau's alarm, but the bureau continued with a firm policy of warning about possible danger.

Hurricane Diane, officially listed as number four on the 1955 roster, lost much of her force by the time she reached the northeastern states. Unhappily, although Diane officially changed from a hurricane to a tremendous rainstorm, she was to cause damage more terrible and to be the reason for the death of far more people than any similar disturbance of the year.

Having hit the Carolina coast on August 17, the storm swept across the land to lose much of her force. This brought a general feeling that the worst was over.

Damage as far as the ocean and the hurricane which had come from it were concerned was finished, but a new menace was about to hit in the form of heavy rains which would bring floods.

The citizens of Pennsylvania and Connecticut were not educated in the manner of floods and what havoc they could create. The very old inhabitants could remember vague references to other floods in the northeastern states which had caused much trouble, but almost no one was ready for this deluge.

And so it was that on August 18, few people worried very much when the rains came. During the afternoon it almost seemed that the rain was ended, and it did stop briefly, only to commence again with renewed energy Thursday night. While hundreds of thousands slept, a disaster was in the making. The Pennsylvania countryside, deluged by this time with no less than fourteen inches of rain in the period of thirty-six hours, resembled a giant saturated sponge, and the land could absorb no more water. The rain soon formed tiny brooks, then streams, then mighty rivers where no rivers had flowed before, sweeping almost everything away in their path. Where the new rivers joined old, devastation resulted.

Without question, the worst single calamity of the flood was the disaster which struck the religious retreat at Camp Davis, near Stroudsburg, Pennsylvania. I visited there a few days after the storm and was told that the relatively calm Brodhead Creek with its source in the Pocono Mountains had become a raging torrent. Rising thirty-one feet in a terrible quarter-hour span, the gyrating mass of furious water and wreckage smashed into the camp.

Mrs. Jennie Johnson was one of about forty women at the camp. I quote her words:

"We had a bungalow at the camp. Suddenly, without warning, a regular wall of water hit our house and began to rip it to pieces. I ran with my children to higher ground, where another house stood, and there with about thirty-five others we watched the water get higher and higher.

"First we went to the second floor, then the attic, but it was no use, for the water kept getting higher and higher. When it reached the attic the house gave a convulsive shudder and simply collapsed. It fell apart all around us and we went tumbling out into the torrent, screaming and terrified.

"Drowning must be awful. I went down and down and down, but I kept fighting back. I don't know what happened then, but something must have struck my head and I became unconscious. When I awakened I was alone with a small girl on a pile of debris. I didn't know what had happened to my children. I later discovered my daughter alive, but my two sons have gone. I shall never forget that wall of water!"

In addition to Mrs. Johnson's boys thirty other campers met their death, and twenty more people in the region lost their lives.

Dozens of helicopters were rushed into service to save those who were marooned by the flood, and in Pennsylvania an entire fleet rescued 235 passengers from a stranded Lackawanna Railroad train in the Pocono Mountains. An air force helicopter saved a man and a woman from a second-story window in Scranton, Pennsylvania.

Hurricane Diane struck with great force in Connecticut. As early as 11:00 the night before, the Mad River at Winsted had been overflowing its banks, and those who realized the immediate peril organized squadrons to alert residents along the river. A building was halved down through the center, exposing a two-story wall, with sink and set tubs one above the other on each floor, and a sink still full of unwashed dishes exposed on the lower floor.

Winsted was isolated for two days by the great flood, which turned Main Street into an unbelievable gully with the force of the torrent. There was no water to drink after the flood, no telephone service, no electricity or gas. People had to revert to conditions which their grandparents had forgotten, boiling water over campfires, communicating on foot, hiking extra miles around washed-out bridges, and in all this time no news of any type came from the outside world!

New England helicopters were put into service early in the storm and saved scores of people. Mr. and Mrs. Robert Lambert were ferried across the sky to Hartford from Unionville where they had lost their home. Another helicopter rescue at Unionville was that of Maurice Hurley, who clung precariously for some time to the helicopter hook after being saved from a rooftop.

Relatively tiny Connecticut streams and rivers now assumed demoniacal proportions that terrible night. Small streams such as the Scantic, the Hockanum, the Quinebaug and the Blackberry became torrents of death in a few hours.

Shortly after 1:00 on the morning of August 19, the telephone rang for Governor Abraham A. Ribicoff. It was a call from Torrington's mayor, William T. Carroll, who stated that his town was simply being overwhelmed by the flooded Naugatuck River. Governor Ribicoff ordered the national guard to proceed there at once.

At Putnam, the most spectacular disaster was the burning of a magnesium plant, which caused scores of terrible fires as the flaming barrels floated along the streets, sending streams of white-hot metal hundreds of feet into the air.

After the fire the huge magnesium mill was merely a ghost structure, its walls standing as mute evidence of the disaster which had occurred there. The Metal Sellars Corporation was also completely ruined.

Hartford's multimillion dollar dike stood firm, reaching the floor crest of the Connecticut River at 30.6 feet, the third highest on record.

Many policemen figured in heroic rescue activities. Policeman Charles Yodkins saved a tiny baby from death in the Farmington, Connecticut, area and then went out on another mission of mercy from which he never returned.

State Policeman Robert Dee, in Station F's tiny outboard motorboat, rescued many residents, at one time carrying the entire family of Clifford Dubois to safety.

In Unionville, John Daniels lost everything in his home, but his family of four, his wife and daughters Janet, Diane and Margaret, together with the dog Shrimp were all saved.

Animals were as bewildered as humans, and a frightened dog was seen for some time on a Farmington highway, unable to escape the torrential flood. Along the submerged road a determined farmer finally guided his three cows to safety.

In Simsbury, tobacco sheds were inundated, with water lapping at the overhead netting, and the crop was entirely lost.

The famous arch, on the dividing line between Unionville and Farmington, became a hopeless mass of debris. Steel rails and wooden ties were smashed into a jumble of wreckage.

A great hole was torn into the foundation of the Stafford Printers Building at the time that the Rhode Island Worsted Mill in Stafford gave way. Hollow Dam at Stafford spilled over the side of the dam to cut a new course.

Even after the first stages of the rains had ended, new hazards were created when weakened dams finally gave way to send terrifying crests down into the areas below. Giant mills collapsed into crumbled debris and tons of river bed sand infiltrated factory windows to bury expensive machinery.

Thousands of plate glass windows gave way under the water pressure, while scores of fine new automobiles were reduced to debris, battered into shapeless caricatures of their former beauty.

On Saturday morning the sun greeted the stunned Connecticut survivors. The rivers went down as fast as they had risen, and tons of excess rainfall reached Long Island Sound. Connecticut residents gradually returned to their centers of industry and were shocked as they looked with unbelieving eyes at what they viewed. Entire sections of the towns and cities that they loved were damaged irreparably, and in certain areas the surroundings had been so altered by the flood that they were not recognizable.

Many Massachusetts areas suffered heavily; in fact, Massachusetts was the second hardest hit of all the states. Southbridge, Otis, Worcester, Belchertown, Springfield, Chicopee and scores of other communities were ravaged, with damage in many cities going into the millions. At West Springfield the Bear Hole Reservoir gave way, but residents had already been removed to safety. Hundreds of families were evacuated at Southbridge, Otis, New Boston, Russell and Sheffield.

The Blue Hills Observatory in Milton, Massachusetts, reported that all records for rainfall over a seventy-year period had fallen before the rainfall of 13.76 inches for a twenty-four hour period beginning on August 18, while the month as a whole had a record of 18.78 inches.

The Defense Service Administration tabulated the damage done during Hurricane Diane. There were 179 deaths, 6,992 seriously injured, 813 homes completely destroyed, and total damage sustained of $457,674,044 divided roughly as follows:

Connecticut	$215,245,004.00
Massachusetts	110,412,808.00
Pennsylvania	70,206,700.00
New Jersey	27,525,532.00
Rhode Island	18,000,000.00

Of course the financial loss was stupendous, but we must add to the staggering amount totaled above the loss of thousands of objects of sentimental value which can never be replaced. Nor can the homes which were destroyed or the ravaged communities be restored to their original state.

In addition, the industries which were ruined represented a great loss, but the pay checks which were stopped and the ending of a means of livelihood for thousands of workmen must also be considered.

However, during and immediately after every great disaster there is a common feeling of comradeship in despair which speaks highly for human nature. The appearance of the Red Cross and other agencies creates a spirit of helpfulness which is reflected wherever there has been death and suffering.

Hurricanes Edith on August 24 and Flora on September 3 passed harmlessly out to sea, but on September 5 Gladys rushed across the Gulf of Mexico to smash into Mexico City causing great damage. She was followed on September 12 by Hilda, a hurricane which brought disaster to Tampico.

Hurricane Ione,* officially listed as number nine of the season, gathered force slowly. Skipping out to sea to avoid Florida altogether, she smashed ashore in North Carolina and did considerable damage. For once all professionally concerned with the weather decided to do things right. Radio and television broadcasters began interrupting their regularly

---

* The last Ione to attract the reading public's attention was Bulwer-Lytton's heroine in the *Last Days of Pompeii*. Strangely enough, she was driven out to sea when Vesuvius erupted.

scheduled programs to announce the definite approach of
Hurricane Ione, while weather bureaus in general predicted
a bad time ahead for the northeastern states.

Airlines grounded flights, New York City called in extra
policemen, Civil defense everywhere girded for the attack.
The coast guard sent out emergency bulletins and America's
greatest city called a special meeting of its planning and oper-
ration board to cope with the expected gale.

Then, just as the great hurricane was about to batter its
way into communities which for once were especially prepared, Ione hesitated. In spite of continued warnings which
were still being announced, the storm proceeded to dissolve
into unimportant gusts of wind accompanied by moderate
rain.

Public reaction was interesting. Instead of uttering prayers
of thanks at not being subjected to the fury of a hurricane,
most of the reprieved potential victims felt that they had been
made fools of, and protested vehemently the Weather Bureau's alleged perfidy. But the Weather Bureau had a good
answer and explained to the uninitiated that an extremely high
altitude wind suddenly came down to the earth unexpectedly
at Virginia, stopping completely Ione's progress toward Cape
Cod. This explanation did not end the public's grumbling,
however.

On September 28 Hurricane Janet roared through the West
Indies eventually bringing great loss of life and property to
Tampico.

After everyone in the northeast believed that the hurricane
season was over, on October 14 Hurricane Katie came along
with moderate winds but heavy rain, which provoked another
series of floods in regions of the states which already had suffered severely in August. Connecticut was especially hard
hit. The October floods seemed almost too much to endure

for those who had gone through the terror of the August disaster.

Indeed, the year 1955 overwhelmed the northeast. Let us hope that never again, at least in our lifetimes, will we be faced with such extraordinary weather conditions as the two consecutive years, 1954 and 1955, brought to the inhabitants of the United States.

I attended the conference of the American Geophysical Union at Wood's Hole during the summer of 1955. As a member of that group I am affiliated with the sections interested in Meteorology, Oceanography and Hydrology. At the conference I listened to the talk by Vincent J. Schaeffer,* the first man to change the weather by dropping ice from an airplane. Mr. Schaeffer said that he would be "very much surprised if man may not eventually control hurricanes in part."

In keeping with this hopeful attitude the government itself is planning campaigns for extensive hurricane study. Twenty-seven stations from Trinidad to Florida will launch weather balloons and study the weather reports which the balloons relay to the listeners. The air force will have actual flying laboratories inside each hurricane as it roars along, with B-50 bombers allotted to the area between one thousand and twenty-five thousand feet and B-47 jet bombers in the altitudes between thirty thousand and fifty thousand feet.

Appropriately named, Wallops Island, Virginia, will be the center of a hurricane reception group of the navy, standing by with two-stage rockets, capable of soaring one hundred miles above the hurricane and photographing it as they soar along. The recording gear inside the rockets will parachute

---

* On March 6, 1947, he sprayed a layer of stratus cloud with a moderate amount of dry ice to produce a substantial area of clearing. I interviewed him in detail on this.

itself into the sea, after which a signal will automatically locate it by radio, and navy rescue crews will be able to pick it up.

The Weather Bureau plans to drop a balloon inside the eye of the hurricane whenever it appears. The balloon is so built that it will float with the storm, reporting its own position, thus allowing the weather experts to track the center.

Sweeping northward, the hurricane will be measured by experts on *Texas Towers,* hydrographic officials on land and trained observers from the Coast and Geodetic Survey.

Dr. Schaeffer's belief that it is possible to prevent a hurricane from forming by careful seeding of dry ice or silver iodide particles evidently is shared by other scientists, for it is now becoming apparent in the minds of some that if the rate of energy in one section of a hurricane can be increased or decreased, the dreaded *HURACÁN* may change its direction and miss a particularly vital part of our coast line.

But it is possibly too early to proclaim that the hurricane will eventually be conquered. According to Dr. Roger R. Revelle, director of the Scripps Institution of Oceanography in California, automobiles and other inventions of modern man are releasing tremendous quantities of carbon dioxide into the air, and he believes this may have caused a remarkable change in the climate. "The increase in the number of hurricanes on the east coast is certainly tied in one way or the other with the general northward movement of the warm air," was Dr. Revelle's conclusion.

Dr. Charles F. Brooks of the Blue Hills Observatory does not believe that man will ever control a hurricane. His statement follows:

"To affect the formation of a hurricane in the first place one must be on the spot at the crucial moment when a hurricane is deciding, you might say, whether to start or not, and it seems a remote possibility to find the spot even if the plan would work when the exact spot is found. Hurricanes are too monstrous things to control. The amount of energy involved is so enormous in human terms. I cannot see how humans can ever control hurricanes."

CHAPTER TWENTY-SEVEN

THE QUINTUPLET SNOWSTORMS
OF 1956

If Winter comes, can Spring be far behind?

SHORTLY AFTER NOON on Wednesday, March 14, our daughter
Dorothy Caroline was inspecting the shrubbery in front of
our residence. Suddenly she called excitedly, "Mommy,
Daddy, come look!" There before our unbelieving eyes were
crocuses in full bloom.

The winter of 1955-1956 had not been unusually severe,
and now with the blossoming of the crocuses we believed
that we were to enter a delightful period of springtime and
then summer.

Less than forty-eight hours later began the first of five
great blizzards and snowstorms which would leave the northeastern states and especially New England with stories to rival
those that grandfathers and grandmothers had been telling
their incredulous offspring for years.

Even the blizzard men of '88 and those less hardy souls
who went through New York's great snowstorm of Decem-

ber 26, 1947, would have to look to their laurels. Some believed that to find a comparable period of overwhelming snow we might have to go back to the winter of 1717.

When the first of the 1956 blizzards swept into the northeast it began in modest fashion in a wide area from Virginia to Canada but soon showed its true colors and caused devastation of major proportions.

At the height of the blizzard there were many ships in distress. The most sensational disaster took place in Scituate, Massachusetts, when the 441-foot, 7000-ton Italian freighter, *Etrusco*,* smashed aground at Cedar Point in that town.

The lights of the freighter were first seen by Charles P. Howland from his residence a short distance from the old Scituate lighthouse. Both he and his wife were startled by the appearance of the craft and amazed at its size, for according to Mrs. Howland "the ship seemed as big as the *Queen Mary*." She called up the Scituate Coast Guard and reported the fact that a vessel was ashore, and that James Turner of Scituate Lighthouse could verify her story.

Scituate's veteran Coast Guardsman William A. Hersey had already been notified from the Coast Guard Radio Station at Marshfield that there was a ship ashore, apparently at Plymouth. With Mrs. Howland's call telling of the large vessel near the beach in the Cedar Point, Scituate, area, it was deduced that probably the ship reported off Plymouth had actually pounded ashore at Scituate. Hersey notified his skipper, Boatswain Miller, who alerted the station.

The headquarters of the Coast Guard Search and Rescue Department in the Boston Custom House was now given the new location of the wreck, but because of language difficul-

---

* Built in British Columbia in 1940 as a Canadian Liberty ship, she burned coal, but her fuel was later changed to oil. The *Etrusco* sailed from Emden, Germany, in ballast. After stopping at the Azores to leave a sick seaman, she arrived off the Massachusetts coast just as the storm broke.

ties ninety minutes were to elapse before all confusion about its position was ended. Rescue apparatus in charge of Boatswain William E. Miller was now dispatched to Cedar Point. Meanwhile, William A. Rich, Bms, AN, in charge of the Point Allerton Coast Guard Station, set out for the wreck with ten men and more apparatus, while other groups of Coast Guardsmen were ordered to their assistance.

Arriving at the scene, Boatswain Miller soon realized the potential danger of the situation. At its height, the blizzard was hitting the area with an 83-mile-an-hour wind, and the snow drifts in the vicinity were piling up nine feet high. Heavy seas were then smashing all along the Massachusetts Shore, causing hundreds of thousands of dollars damage in low-lying beach areas. Actually the tide rose to heights approaching those of the Portland Gale and the Minot's Light Storm, with the highest tide reading at the Boston Base 13.7 feet.*

The wind that night had the ominous high velocity shriek of a great hurricane heard rarely in a lifetime, and those out in the gale realized its terrible force. The pelting sand and driving snow was then hitting almost horizontally. The Coast Guardsmen with rescue equipment forced their way through the blinding blizzard, fighting drifts and splashing through flooded areas until they reached the scene of the wreck. There they attempted to shoot lines out over the *Etrusco*. By this time the ship had bumped, thudded and scraped its way over the treacherous, gigantic boulders in front of the lighthouse, and the vessel was finally pushed by wind and waves from its first reported location of 900 feet offshore to a position just short of the average high tide mark.

Boatswain Miller, terribly concerned with the fate of the thirty Italian crewmen on the *Etrusco*, conferred with his

---

* The height of 13.7 feet was registered on March 17, 1956 at 1:42 A.M.

men in the parlor of former Selectman and Mrs. James Turner, in charge of the old Scituate Point Lighthouse. As the ship was in very shallow water, and the darkness, high surf and strong, snow-laden winds made rescue by breeches buoy extremely hazardous, it was deemed advisable to wait until daylight for a rescue attempt. The great bulk of the vessel offered more security at the time than the breeches buoy, providing it did not begin to break up under the merciless waves, and no power on earth could have made it possible for a lifeboat to reach the *Etrusco*.

At dawn Coast Guardsman Ralph J. Keller of Point Allerton fired the shoulder gun that sent the shot line aboard the ill-fated freighter. The difficult breeches-buoy rescue was then carried off very smoothly with no casualties.*

The *Etrusco*, the largest vessel ever wrecked in the vicinity of Scituate, became without any question the most publicized New England marine disaster of the century. Tens of thousands of autoists marooned in their cars and hundreds of thousands of others imprisoned in their homes and unable to continue their normal activities listened with anxiety to the frequent news bulletins on their radio and television sets as the story of the wreck of the *Etrusco* was unfolded. In sub-

---

* The *Etrusco* came ashore at exactly the same location as the ship *Elizabeth*, a famous wreck. Cedar Point, also known as Lighthouse Point, has an interesting history. In September, 1814, two daughters of Lighthouse Keeper Reuben Bates fooled the British Redcoats attempting a Scituate landing by beating a drum and playing a fife. The British, hearing the martial music, thought the American troops were about to attack them and fled from the harbor.

Scores of shipwrecks have occurred in the vicinity. The *Delaware* in 1840; the *Elizabeth* in 1859; the *Elsie Fay* in 1885 were three outstanding marine casualties in that period. The *Edward H. Norton* was lost in 1888 under spectacular circumstances with fifteen drowned and one saved. Ten years later the Pilot Boat *Columbia* was wrecked with all five aboard perishing. Two relatively recent disasters were the schooner *Nantasket*, lost on December 26, 1909, with all saved, and the four-masted schooner *Kenwood*, wrecked in a great snowstorm with no loss of life on February 4, 1926.

sequent weeks thousand upon thousands of motorists came to
see the wrecked freighter towering above Scituate Lighthouse.
Traffic jams extended for miles along the feeder-roads leading
to the scene of the disaster. Without question the *Etrusco*
attracted far more motorists than had ever viewed a New
England shipwreck before.*

All over the northeast people suffered because of the blizzard. One of the more heart-rending incidents was the death
of three sailors from the destroyer *Preston* in the Newport
area. They had perished from exposure in an open launch
which finally washed ashore with their bodies on the estate
of Barclay Douglas.

In the same area six vessels of a destroyer fleet broke from
their moorings in Coddington Cove. They were the *M. C.
Fox*, the *Fiske*, the destroyer-escort *Colbaugh*, all of which
were refloated at high tide the next day, and the *Willis A.
Lee*, the *Hickox* and the *Perry*, which were later pulled into
deep water.

At the height of the storm the Tanker *Sylvia* lost her rudder four miles off Long Island. The ship was eventually
saved and towed into port by the Coast Guard cutter *Owasco*.

At Norfolk, Virginia, the Italian merchant ship *Laura
Lauro* smashed into two destroyers tied up at the Naval Base.

All around Boston Harbor damage approached that of the
1909 Christmas storm. At Boston Light, according to Keeper
Jack Horner, forty oil drums were lost at the height of the
gale. Smashing across the tiny reservation the ocean cut the
island in two, ripping shingles from the homes and leaving
sea wreckage knee deep in the valley between the two residences.

Deer Island Light was mercilessly battered, the Coast

---

* Mrs. Lena Russo, who was able to speak to the crew of the *Etrusco*
in their native tongue, opened her home to the stranded Italian sailors, and
for this voluntary service was later awarded a plaque by the Coast Guard.

Guardsmen there losing their skiff. In Winthrop serious damage to the shore area was sustained.

At the height of the storm the Coast Guard 83-foot craft *83-448* started out to reach the scene of the *Etrusco* disaster. Seriously damaged by the waves, the *83-448* was forced to turn back because of the terrible conditions of the blizzard. Much of her deck gear was lost while one side of the hull was beaten in.

On the South Shore two buildings were blown down at Nantasket Beach, a washout cut off Weymouth Lower Neck, and a building floated across near the mouth of the North River to land at Damon's Point, Marshfield.

Humarock Beach, Massachusetts, was subjected to serious surf and water damage with many families having their residences flooded to such an extent that their refrigerators and freezers were completely underwater.

Motorists who were unable to reach home in the storm were numbered by the thousands. Entire sections of arterial thoroughfares were snowbound with innumerable cars abandoned on the highways and in the cities. Between Sturbridge and Auburn, Massachusetts, more than 700 persons were marooned in their cars overnight.

The mid-century auto age now experienced its greatest challenge. Because of the relative mildness of the average winters, millions of motorists had become careless toward the possibility of great snowstorms, and now suffered in consequence. Many died either in their cars from monoxide gas or after exertion from attempting to push their vehicles. Those who survived the storm seemed to resent the fact that nature had overwhelmed them. In Massachusetts there was discussion of possible legislation to make it compulsory for winter drivers to have snow tires or chains for their cars. Many radio and television commentators, anxious to blame someone for their own inconveniences, intimated that unless the weather bureau could do better, there would be trouble.

Hardly had the snow from the first storm finished falling when another blizzard rushed across the northeastern coastal states. This time New York City was paralyzed with a 13.5 inch snowfall, the worst since 1947. In Massachusetts, Connecticut and Rhode Island high winds, great drifts, and below-freezing weather closed most of the schools and caused rail and air travel to be almost completely at a standstill. This time all Boston records for March in the history of the government weather bureau were broken with a 13.3 new snowfall. Nevertheless, New Englanders had been forewarned by the previous blizzard, and transportation was not paralyzed to a similar extent.

The third storm hit New England March 24th leaving up to a foot of snow. A fourth March gale, that of the twenty-ninth, brought ten inches of snow. The Blue Hills Observatory reported a total snowfall for March of 48¼ inches making it the snowiest March in the history of the Observatory and indeed "a month to remember."

After several warm spring days during Easter week a northeast gale which began late on the night of April 7th deposited from 10 to 20 inches of snow on New England, but the discouraged residents slogged through. The storm was an unusual combination of snow, sleet, rain, thunder, lightning and wind. While the other four storms did not cripple telephone and electric wires to a noticeable extent, the soggy snow which hit New England in this fifth major storm in twenty-four days did more damage to power lines than the other four gales combined. Melrose, Massachusetts, lost 95% of its power, while there were hundreds of line breaks in Malden, Revere, Medford, Everett and Winthrop. Although the warming temperatures of Monday softened the hardship it was still necessary to close many schools.

No less than 1,115,000 New England homes were without heat, lights, refrigeration and cooking, with those lucky enough to have fireplaces or old-fashioned stoves gratefully using them.

Nevertheless, the facts are against those ambitious souls who would like to rank the 1956 stormy season with that of 1717. On Sunday, February 24, 1717, thirty-foot snowdrifts prevented the holding of a single church service in all New England. On the level the snow was ten feet deep in Boston and twelve to fifteen feet deep in the surrounding suburbs at that time.

But for at least the next sixty years those who witnessed the five great snowstorms of 1956 will be able to tell their children and grandchildren about them, even as their own grandparents recounted the famous storms of their day.

*   *   *

While man has apparently become venturesome in his plans to attack the sea's great ally, the hurricane, the sea itself seems secure for years to come against invasion from presumptuous humanity. Although sea walls, jetties and other marine barriers have been built to protect the land from the ocean, all definite efforts to harness or control storms at sea, with one exception,* have failed.

Joseph Conrad tells us that the sea has no generosity. "No display of manly qualities," Conrad goes on to say, "hardihood, endurance, faithfulness—has ever been known to touch its irresponsible consciousness of power. He . . . has remained the irreconcilable enemy of ships and men ever since ships and men had the unheard-of audacity to go afloat together in the face of his frown. From that day he has gone on swallowing up fleets and men without his resentment being glutted

---

* Casting oil on troubled waters works at sea.

by the number of victims—by so many wrecked ships and wrecked lives."

There is nothing to indicate, even today, that the sea is not just as eager and ready as always to engulf the optimistic sailor abroad on the ocean. The vengeful sea is always alert to drown and to wreck. Perhaps the most remarkable part of the sea is its impersonal cruelty, which seems unfathomable and meaningless.

In spite of everything, however, the sea will always be a source of inspiration for man because of its power and its mystery.

APPENDIX A

KNOWN PORTLAND *VICTIMS*

Allen, H. G.
Allen, Mrs. Theodore
Allen, Miss
Arrington, J. P.
Ash, Mrs.
Baker, Mrs. E. L.
Barron, Matthew
Beardsworth, William
Bemis, Walter L.
Berry, Mrs. Margaret
Billings, Mr.
Blanchard, Captain Hollis H.
Blake, R.
Bonney, George A.
Bruce, D.
Buckminster, Joseph
Bunker, Mr.
Carroll, Mrs. J. A.
Carter, Allen
Cash, W. H.
Chase, William L.
Chase, Phillip
Chickering, Mrs. G. O.
Clark, Albert
Clark, Edna
Cobb, Miss E. L.
Cohen, Solomon
Cole, George
Cole, Miss
Collins, Elizabeth M. A.
Conley, Mr.
Cropley, George

Daly, Jerry
Daly, John H.
Davidson, James or Joseph
Delaney, G. W.
Dennett, Wm.
Dennis, Mrs. E.
Denton, William
Dillion, J. Albert
Doherty, Barney or John
Dotheney or Dauphinie, E.
Doughty, William J.
Dukeshire, Mrs.
Dunbar, Burke
Dunn, Wm.
Dwyer, W. Y.
Dyer, Ansel
Dyer, N. J.
Edmonds, Mrs. J. G.
Edwards, Lawrence
Flowers, James W.
Foreman, Lee
Freeman, Hon. E. D.
Frye, Isaiah
Frye, Ruth
Foden, Mrs. John
Foden, Robert
Galley, John G.
Gatchell, D. Osborne
Gately, J. Richard
Gately, Ellen Driscoll
Gotter, A.
Graham, George

Silverstaine
Silverstaine child
Small, M. L.
Smith, F.
Smith, Harry
Schmidt, Anton
Schmidt, Jessen
Schmidt, Mrs. Jessen
Schmidt, Jorgen
Stevens, Fred
Stucker or Tucker, Alice
Sullivan, Mrs. John
Swift, Alice
Sykes, Maude
Tetrow, Annie
Thompson, Charles H.
Thompson, Mrs. Charles H.
Thompson child
Thompson, G. A.
Tibbetts, Charles A.

Timmins, Mrs. Elmira
Totten, Eva
Twombly, Mrs.
Tucker, Alice
Turner, A. R.
Turner, Mrs. A. R.
Underwood, Louis F.
Van Guysling, C. E.
Verrill, Charles V.
Walton, John T.
Watson, George, or John Jones
Welch, Mrs. Mary
Wells, Fred
Wheeler, Mrs. Augustus
White, Horace
Whitten, J. C.
Williams, John
Wilson, C. F.
Wilson, Frank
Young, Harry de M.

APPENDIX B

VESSELS LOST OR DAMAGED IN THE PORTLAND GALE

A. B. Nickerson (schooner)
Cape Cod
A. B. Nickerson (steamer)
Cape Cod
Abel E. Babcock
Boston Bay
Abby K. Bentley
Vineyard Sound
Addie E. Snow
Cape Cod
Addie Sawyer
Vineyard Sound
Adelaide T.
Hither Plain, N. Y.
Africa
Portland, Me.
Agnes
Cape Cod
Agnes May
Cape Ann
Agnes Smith
Pt. Judith, R. I.
Albert H. Harding
Boston Bay
Albert L. Butler
Cape Cod
Alida
Islesboro, Me.
Aloha
Block Island, R. I.

Anna Pitcher
Block Island, R. I.
Anna W. Barker
Southern Island, Me.
Annie Lee
Cape Ann
Arabell
Block Island, R. I.
B. R. Woodside
Boston Bay
Barge (Unknown)
Boston Bay
Barge (Unknown)
Boston Bay
Barge (Unknown)
Boston Bay
Barge (Unknown)
Boston Bay
Barge (Unknown)
Boston Bay
Barge (Unknown)
Cape Ann
Barge (Unknown)
Cape Ann
Barge No. 4
Boston Bay
Beaver
Vineyard Sound
Bertha A. Gross
Cape Ann

Bertha E. Glover
 Vineyard Sound
Brunhilde
 Point of Woods, N. Y.
Byssus
 Vineyard Sound
C. A. White
 Boston Bay
C. B. Kennard
 Boston Bay
Calvin F. Baker
 Boston Bay
Canaria
 Vineyard Sound
Carita
 Vineyard Sound
Carrie C. Miles
 Portland, Me.
Cassina
 Block Island, R. I.
Catboat (Unknown)
 Short Beach, N. Y.
Cathie C. Berry
 Vineyard Sound
Champion
 Cape Cod
Charles E. Raymond
 Vineyard Sound
Charles E. Schmidt
 Cape Ann
Charles J. Willard
 Quoddy Head, Me.
Chillion
 Cape Ann
Chiswick
 Boston Bay
Clara Sayward
 Cape Cod
Clara P. Sewall
 Boston Bay
Columbia
 Boston Bay
Consolidated Barge No. 1
 Boston Bay

D. T. Pachin
 Cape Ann
Daniel Boone
 Cape Cod
Daniel I. Tenney
 Boston Bay
David Faust
 Nantucket
Delaware
 Boston Bay
E. G. Willard
 Vineyard Sound
E. J. Hamilton
 Vineyard Sound
Earl, Edith
 Cuttyhunk
Edgar J. Foster
 Boston Bay
Edith McIntire
 Vineyard Sound
Edna & Etta
 Great Egg, N. J.
Edward H. Smeed
 Block Island, R. I.
Ella F. Crowell
 Boston Bay
Ella Frances
 Cape Cod
Ellen Jones
 Cape Cod
Ellis P. Rogers
 Cape Ann
Elmer Randall
 Boston Bay
Emma (wreckage)
 Boston Bay
Ethel F. Merriam
 Cape Cod
Evelyn
 Cape Ann
F. H. Smith
 Cape Cod
F. R. Walker
 Cape Cod

Fairfax
Cuttyhunk
Fairfax
Vineyard Sound
Falcon
Vineyard Sound
Fannie Hall
Portsmouth, N. H.
Fannie May
Rockland, Me.
Flying Cloud
Cape Ann
Forest Maid
Portsmouth, N. H.
Fred A. Emerson
Boston Bay
Friend
Cuttyhunk
Fritz Oaks
Boston Bay
G. M. Hopkins
Boston Bay
G. W. Danielson
Block Island, R. I.
Gatherer
Cape Ann
George A. Chaffee
Cape Ann
George H. Miles
Vineyard Sound
Georgietta
Spruce Head, Me.
Grace
Cape Cod
Gracie
Cape Cod
Hattie A. Butler
Vineyard Sound
Henry R. Tilton
Boston Bay
Hume
Boston Bay
Hurricane
Rockland, Me.

Ida
Boston Bay
Ida G. Broere
Lone Hill, N. Y.
Idella Small
Davis Neck, Mass.
Inez Hatch
Cape Cod
Institution launch
Boston Bay
Ira and Abbie
Block Island, R. I.
Ira Kilburn
Portsmouth, N. H.
Isaac Collins (schooner)
Cape Cod
Isaac Colline (schooner)
Cape Cod
Island City
Vineyard Sound
Ivy Bell
Jerry's Point, N. H.
J. C. Mahoney
Cape Ann
J. M. Eaton
Cape Ann
James A. Brown
Vineyard Sound
James Ponder
Vineyard Sound
James Webster
Boston Bay
John Harvey
Point Judith, R. I.
John J. Hill
Boston Bay
John S. Ames
Boston Bay
Jordan L. Mott
Cape Cod
Juanita
Boston Bay
King Phillip
Cape Cod

Knott V. Martin
Cape Ann
Leander V. Beebe
Boston Bay
Leora M. Thurlow
Vineyard Sound
Lester A. Lewis
Cape Cod
Lexington
Block Island, R. I.
Lillian
Portland, Me.
Lizzie Dyas
Boston Bay
Lucy A. Nichols
Boston Bay
Lucy Bell
Boston Bay
Lucy Hammond
Vineyard Sound
Luther Eldridge
Nantucket
M. E. Eldridge
Vineyard Sound
Marion Draper
Vineyard Sound
Mary Cabral
Cape Cod
Mary Emerson
Boston Bay
Mascot
Cuttyhunk
Mertis H. Perry
Boston Bay
Michael Henry
Cape Cod
Mildred and Blanche
Cape Cod
Milo
Boston Bay
Multnoman
Portsmouth, N. H.
Nautilus
Cape Cod

Nellie B.
Block Island, R. I.
Nellie Doe
Vineyard Sound
Nellie M. Slade
Vineyard Sound
Neptune
Portland, Me.
Neverbudge
Cuttyhunk
Newburg
Vineyard Sound
Newell B. Hawes
Plum Island, Mass.
Ohio
Boston Bay
Papetta
Vineyard Sound
Pentagoet
Cape Cod
Percy
Block Island, R. I.
Phantom
Boston Bay
Philomena Manta
Cape Cod
Pluscullombonum
Boston Bay
Portland
Off Cape Cod
Powder vessel (unknown)
Boston Bay
Queen of the West
Fletcher's Neck, Me.
Quesay
Vineyard Sound
Rebecca W. Huddell
Vineyard Sound
Reliance
Point of Woods, N. Y.
Rendo
Portland, Me.
Rienzi
Cape Ann

Ringleader
  Portsmouth, N. H.
Robert A. Kenner
  Boston Bay
Rose Brothers
  Block Island, R. I.
Rosie Cobral
  Boston Bay
S. F. Mayer
  Rockland, Me.
Sadie Wilcutt
  Vineyard Sound
Sarah
  Cape Ann
School Girl
  Cape Cod
Schooner (unknown)
  Boston Bay
Schooner (unknown)
  Boston Bay
Schooner (unknown)
  Boston Bay
Schooner (unknown)
  Boston Bay
Schooner (unknown)
  Cape Cod
Schooner (unknown)
  Cape Cod
Secret
  Cuttyhunk
Seraphine
  Boston Bay
Silver Spray
  Portland, Me.
Sloop (unknown)
  Boston Bay
Sloop (unknown)
  Boston Bay
Sloop (unknown)
  White Head, Me.
Sport
  Cuttyhunk
Startle
  Boston Bay

Stone Sloop (unknown)
  Boston Bay
Stone Sloop (unknown)
  Boston Bay
Stranger
  Block Island, R. I.
Sylvester Whalen
  Cape Cod
T. W. Cooper
  Portsmouth, N. H.
Tamaqua
  Boston Bay
Thomas B. Reed
  Cape Cod
Two Sisters
  Portsmouth, N. H.
Two-Forty
  Boston Bay
Union
  Boston Bay
Unique
  Cape Cod
Unknown vessel
  Boston Bay
Valetta
  Vineyard Sound
Valkyrie
  Block Island, R. I.
Verona (wreckage)
  Boston Bay
Vigilant
  Cape Cod
Virgin Rocks
  Boston Bay
Virginia
  Boston Bay
W. H. DeWitt
  Cape Ann
W. H. Y. Hackett
  Portsmouth, N. H.
Watchman
  Boston Bay
Wild Rose
  Cranberry Isles, Me.

William Leggett
  Cape Ann
William M. Wilson
  Washapreague, Va.
William Todd
  Vineyard Sound

Wilson and Willard
  Cape Ann
Winnie Lawry
  Vineyard Sound
Woodruff
  Northport, Me.

INDEX